Technology for Justice

How Information Technology Can Support Judicial Reform

Dory Reiling

Leiden University Press

Law, Governance, and Development

The Leiden University Press series on Law, Governance, and Development brings together an interdisciplinary body of work about the formation and functioning of legal systems in developing countries, and about interventions to strengthen them. The series aims to engage academics, policy makers and practitioners at the national and international level, thus attempting to stimulate legal reform for good governance and development.

This book has been made possible by a grant from the Netherlands Organisation for Scientific Research (NWO MAGW SaRO).

Cover design: Studio Jan de Boer, Amsterdam
Layout: The DocWorkers, Almere

VRIJE UNIVERSITEIT

Technology for Justice

How Information Technology Can Support Judicial Reform

ACADEMISCH PROEFSCHRIFT
ter verkrijging van de graad Doctor aan
de Vrije Universiteit Amsterdam,
op gezag van de rector magnificus
prof.dr. L.M. Bouter,
in het openbaar te verdedigen
ten overstaan van de promotiecommissie
van de faculteit der Rechtsgeleerdheid
op vrijdag 11 december 2009 om 13.45 uur
in de aula van de universiteit,
De Boelelaan 1105

door

Abeline Dorothea Reiling

geboren te Ooststellingswerf

promotor: prof.mr. A. Oskamp
copromotor: prof. A.J. Harding

van dit proefschrift verschijnt een handelseditie onder
ISBN 978 908 728 071 0

Acknowledgements

Getting a PhD is not always fun, but having a PhD is fun all the time, my coach Marijke Spanjersberg wrote to me a while ago. The latter I have yet to find out, but the former is only very partly true. The work on this dissertation has, on the whole, been a great joy. In this place, I want to express my gratitude to the many people who made it so: those who put up with my preoccupation with the book, who commented on early drafts, who pointed me in new directions, everyone who generously gave their time to my project for free. Most of them will have to remain nameless, because, due to the fact that the process that went into this book was so lengthy, there are so many of them. If you recognize your own contribution in this book, please feel included in these acknowledgements.

The first person I should acknowledge is Toon Peters, my professor of sociolegal studies with whom I did my master's degree. He taught his students to always write and reflect on their work practices. He knew that was no easy task, as it requires balancing involvement and critical distance. My subsequent writing has attempted to match this standard.

In 1993, the Automation Platform of the Netherlands judiciary was convened. With similar IT enthusiasts, I was on it from the start. It later became the Advisory Council for IT of the Judiciary. All those involved helped bring along some of the understanding that has gone into this book. Those who stand out from this period are: Guus Harten, whose practical sense is a wonderful complement to the visionary wishful thinking of many IT enthusiasts; Charlotte Keizer, then in charge of the Court Improvement Program, who helped me understand more about reforming courts, about projects and programs, and about the science behind them; Rocus Brasz who managed the IT program for the courts at the Ministry of Justice and taught me about policy making and about the importance of cooperation.

Marijke Spanjersberg, my coach during the transition time towards the Council for the Judiciary, made me realize how much I enjoy research. Marco Fabri and his team at IRSIG provided me with a platform for comparing IT across Europe. Andrew Cannon, Gregory Reinhardt, Anne Wallace and the Australian Institute for Judicial Administration repeatedly served as a forum for discussing court IT in an experienced and supportive setting.

Maria Dakolias brought me to the World Bank's Judicial Reform Practice Group. My colleagues at the World Bank shared their professionalism and their passion for justice and development. I have learned a lot of what has gone into this book from Linn Hammergren when we wrote the Justice Sector Assessments Handbook.

Of the many people I met during my international years, I will highlight Beth Wiggins at the Federal Judicial Center, specially for inviting me to the Federal Judges IT Round Table, my colleague Nan Shuker at the Washington, DC Superior Court, my colleague Mary Wagner and everybody at the County Court at Kenosha, Wisconsin who showed me great court IT, and Justice G.C. Bharuka who shared his experiences in developing IT for the courts in Bangalore and throughout India.

When I returned after my years at the World Bank my colleagues at the Netherlands Council for the Judiciary provided an intellectually stimulating environment that helped me get started on the book itself.

Many people commented on early drafts of the book. I am especially grateful for Roland Eshuis' careful reading, Michael Johnston's helpful comments and for the support from David Steelman and Richard Van Duizend at the U.S. National Center for State Courts.

My colleagues at the Amsterdam Court deserve a lot of thanks for putting up with my preoccupation, but mostly for taking over my court hearings when the book needed more work. In the final phases, Diederik Radder valiantly plotted, and managed, to find me replacements for two months of full time court work at very short notice.

Frans van Dijk, head of the Policy and Research department at the Council for the Judiciary, supported the idea of a dissertation from its inception. Without his support, this dissertation would not have materialized. He provided the funding to free up enough of my time to make the idea into reality. I thank the Council for the Judiciary in the Netherlands for the opportunity to share my knowledge and experience. It is my hope that it will serve to improve the administration of justice.

Anja Oskamp made me realize doing a PhD might be fun. She became my professor only much later. Our monthly discussions were a great source of inspiration. Her experience was indispensible for me, an outsider to the academic world. Andrew Harding came into the process when it was near the half-way mark. Although this limited his scope to influence the end result, his thoughtful reading of my manuscript brought about many essential changes.

Adriaan Bedner may not realize it, but his contributions have been significant. He pointed me towards the VSR, the society of sociolegal scholars, and he helped me find first a second professor, and then a publisher.

In my family, getting academic credentials, and particularly a PhD, was always a big thing. My father got his, in theology, just after his fiftieth birthday. I remember that wasn't always fun, either. He was nearly eighty years old when I told him I might get an opportunity to do a PhD of my own. He was overjoyed, and decided to stick around long enough to see it. Unfortunately, because I took so long, and the condition of his heart did not allow it, he had to let go in early 2005. My mother, when I told her my PhD was nearly finished late in 2008, immediately started planning the party in her brain, by then damaged by hemorrhages. She passed away as the final editing was being done. I am sad they did not live to see the book published and the thesis defended. It would have given them great joy.

To Wim, I am grateful for many things that will stay between the two of us. He also built the computer I wrote the dissertation on, read all the drafts, kept me focused and helped me out of many writer's blocks. Most of all, he inspired me to reach for what seemed unrealistic and impossible. This book is proof that he was right.

Haarlem, October 2009 Dory Reiling

Table of Contents

Table of Figures

Acronyms

ABA	American Bar Association
ADR	Alternative Dispute Resolution
AML	Anti-Money-Laundering
ARIZ	Adviesraad Informatievoorziening Zittende Magistratuur (Advisory Council for Information Services of the Judiciary)
AUSTLII	Australasian Legal Information Institute
BAILII	British and Irish Legal Information Institute
BPI	Bribe Payers Index
CAB	Citizens' Advice Bureau
CCJ	Conference of Chief Justices
CEO	Chief Executive Officer
CEPEJ	Commission Européenne pour l'efficacité de la Justice, European Commission for the Efficiency of Justice
CIA	Central Intelligence Agency
CIO	Chief Information Officer
CM/EFS	Case Management/Electronic Filing System
COE	Council of Europe
COO	Chief Operational Officer
COSCA	Conference of State Court Administrators
CPC	Claims Production Centre
CPI	Corruption Perception Index
CTC	Court Technology Conference
DB	Doing Business
E+W	England and Wales
EAP	Enforceable Payment Agreement
ECHR	European Convention on Human Rights/European Court on Human Rights
ERV	Elektronischer Rechtsverkehr (Electronic Legal Communication)
EU	European Union
FJC	Federal Judicial Center
GCB	Global Corruption Barometer
GCR	Global Corruption Report
GRECO	Group of States against Corruption
HBS	Hoger Beroep Systeem Strafrecht (Criminal Justice Appeal System)
HDI	Human Development Index
HMCS	Her Majesty's Court Service
IBA	International Bar Association

ICCPR	International Covenant on Civil and Political Rights
ICT	Information and Communication Technology
IRSIG	Istituto di Ricerca sui Sistemi Giudiziari
IT	Information Technology
JIG	Judicial Integrity Group
JSC	Judicial Services Commission
LTTE	Liberation Tigers of Tamil Eelam (Sri Lanka)
MCOL	Money Claim On Line
NATO	North Atlantic Treaty Organization
NCSC	National Center for State Courts
NGO	Non-governmental Organization
NJB	Nederlands Juristenblad (Netherlands Legal Weekly)
NVVR	Nederlandse Vereniging voor Rechtspraak (Netherlands Association of Magistrates)
OECD	Organisation for Economic Cooperation and Development
OS	One-Shotter
PARC	Performance Assessment Resource Center
PCOL	Possession Claim On Line
PDF	Portable Document Format
RP	Repeat Player
TCPS	Trial Court Performance Standards
TI	Transparency International
UNCAC	United Nations Convention against Corruption
UNDP	United Nations Development Program
UNODC	United Nations Organization for Drugs and Crime
USAID	United States Agency for International Development
WDR	World Development Report
WGI	World Governance Indicators

Part 1 Introduction

Chapter 1.1 Introduction

In 1994, the Netherlands judiciary set up its first platform for discussing information technology for its courts. The initiative for the platform was taken by the Dutch Association of Magistrates NVVR. The platform served as a discussion partner for the Ministry of Justice, which was in charge of providing the courts with information technology (IT). It was the beginning of my involvement with IT for courts. The involvement went from this simple talking platform through the first IT policy for the Dutch judiciary into the international arena of advisory work for World Bank-supported judicial reform projects. Understanding what IT can do for what judiciaries and courts do has, in all those contexts, been the thorniest question around. This difficulty is not something only judiciaries have. Understanding IT implications for business has been identified as the most important problem all organizations and businesses face when dealing with IT. As we shall see, this understanding is critical for judiciaries who want to use IT to improve their performance. That is the starting point for this study.

Judicial reform

Changing, adapting and improving judiciaries, courts and their processes are all included in the broad term judicial reform. In this study, the term judicial reform includes all those activities. There are many impulses for judicial reform.

Around the world, judiciaries are faced with new problems. In North America, the demand for court decisions has increased considerably. In Western Europe, demand for judicial decisions has grown as well, and the jurisprudence of the European Court of Human Rights has led to reforms in procedures and governance structures. In Eastern Europe, courts experience the same influences, but they also have to meet new demands as their countries develop into free market economies and aspire to join the European Union. In Latin America, the rise of democratic government has also increased the demand for judicial decisions. In Asia, the picture is mixed as some countries have quickly developed into fast-growing market economies, while others stay behind in terms of economic development. In all developing countries, the influence of globalization is felt. A properly working judiciary is a condition for joining the World Trade Organization. For some, there is also the struggle with a legal system inherited from a colonial past. Information technology is popular as a possible means to resolve some of those problems. In practice, IT does not solve any of them quite so easily. Judicial organizations and justice authorities struggle with IT in the courts. Understanding how judiciaries can solve some of their major problems with IT should be helpful.

Information technology

IT is the most striking factor in changing the world in our era. It has profoundly changed the way large parts of humanity interact and communicate. IT has increased accuracy. It has made information infinitely more available. It has facilitated communication across the globe. It is attractive because it implies the promise of things becoming better and easier. Moreover, IT is a constant source of change as computing power increases, new applications are marketed and new usages develop. Administering justice is an activity that is made up of having information available, communicating about it, and producing new information. It seems IT will affect the way the administration of justice works. Understanding such effects, and how they can be used to improve the administration of justice, should be useful.

Concept for a thesis

Improving the understanding of how information technology can support improving the administration of justice and resolving the major problems judiciaries face is, therefore, a deserving undertaking. In some judiciaries with which I am familiar, the feeling generally is that the most pressing problem related to IT is that the technology is not understood. However, to my mind, a better understanding of technology is not the right starting point for researching this topic. The first thing that needs to be understood is at the other end of the spectrum: it is in understanding court processes and the role of information in them. Second, improving the processes requires an understanding of what the problems are. Therefore, my first question is to inquire about the most pressing problems. The second question will be to examine the role of information in the context of those problems.

In order to find out what the most pressing problems are, I have chosen to draw on the experiences and opinions of users of the courts. The reason for this is that judiciaries, with their decision making monopoly and their institutional independence, risk not being in touch with those who use their services. Over the centuries and all over the world, three major complaints have been heard that can still be heard today: court processes take too long, courts are difficult to access, and judges are corrupt.

In my view, delay, access and corruption are three crucial issues any judicial organization or court faces. They are the three most common complaints of court users around the world. The empirical foundation for this statement can be found in the opening sections of this thesis in Part 3 (delay), Part 4 (access) and Part 5 (integrity). The issues also relate to three of the standards laid down in the international human rights conventions' provisions on courts, discussed in Chapter 1.2. And in organizational terms, they are also the issues organizations face when doing business: internal processes, interaction with clients and the integrity of the organization. Finally, there are claims that each of them can be resolved with information technology. Consequently, I will examine the role of information in court processes using these three complaints as starting points. This will serve to produce some understanding of the role of information in those processes, and how they can be improved with IT. This understanding should uncover ways to reduce the complaints from the users.

Problem and research question

The main research question, therefore, is how IT can support improving the problems of delay, access and integrity in courts and judiciaries. For this main research question, it is difficult to find specific research. There is almost no organized expertise regarding judicial reform and information technology. Technology and the work of judicial organizations are, apparently, worlds apart. The most common sources of information on the subject each have specific perspectives and specific problems. Consultancy, external expertise hired for help with solving specific problems, brings a corresponding problem-solving perspective. For this reason, it tends to be technocratic in the sense that it treats its subject from a perspective of technical process improvement, or from the perspective of technology itself. Academic research can provide some badly needed conceptual clarity. Its limitation is that it usually lacks practical knowledge of how courts work in actual practice. Another problem is that there is, by now, a whole body of practical experience with information technology in the courts, but that it is not easily accessible because it is so dispersed.

In isolation, all these sources can provide some interesting insights. However, it is when they are judiciously combined and confronted that we can really improve our understanding with new insights.

This poses some interesting methodological challenges. The main challenges are in the use of empirical material and in using, and drawing conclusions from, sources of such wide diversity. The next section will discuss methodology, including these challenges.

Methodology

This section provides a general discussion of the methodology used in this study. More detailed methodological considerations are presented in each of the relevant chapters.

General approach

The three issues— delay, access, and integrity – are each examined separately using the following general approach.

First, in each case, existing literature and theoretical approaches of the issue at hand are explored and analyzed to provide a conceptual framework for the next step.

Then, using the conceptual framework, sources of empirical research into the issue are examined. This approach draws on a great variety of sources: primary sources, such as court case statistics and other quantitative sources; and secondary sources, like socio-legal studies and reports on judicial reform projects. The purpose is to gain an understanding of practical reality regarding the issue in question.

Next, the findings are analyzed to identify informational aspects of the issue. This should result in potential remedies for the issue involved.

Finally, conclusions are drawn on the role information technology can play in resolving or at least reducing the problem in question. The technology should be proven technology, which has demonstrated it has the potential to help a judicial organization to realize values to a larger extent than before it was introduced.

Within this general approach, each issue raises its own questions. To answer those, each issue is given its own approach. This is done, because of the nature of the issue involved. Second, empirical sources differ, which sets limitations on the approach and on the scope of the examination of the issue. These differences are accounted for in the treatment of each issue.

Studying judiciaries and courts in an international perspective poses particular challenges. Legal systems have evolved over time, mostly in their own national political context. They each have their own practices and conceptual frameworks. Their processes and cultures are influenced by their environment and by the issues they have confronted. The specific conceptual clarity that is required to meet this challenge is discussed later in this chapter, in a section that deals with the concepts of courts and related matters. At the same time, courts the world over have some things in common: their role in the legal system and their activity in deciding individual disputes.

The most important challenge, however, has to do with empirical material. Practical experience of court processes is often lacking. I consider this a key ingredient in the analysis of court processes. Without an empirical foundation, a foundation grounded in practice, the value of research on courts and judiciaries is limited at best. My first source of practical experience is my own professional history as a judge since 1986. My next source is a collection of materials that has formed over the years. I have collected many sources and empirical materials. Some of them are from my research for the World Bank in 2003-2007. That research is the subject of Chapter 1.3. The others are common sources that judicial reform experts at the World Bank and elsewhere use for their work in supporting judicial reform projects. There is a more detailed discussion of those sources in Chapter 1.3 as well. Nearly all of my sources are publicly available on the Internet. The URLs are included in the list of references. The empirical material I use generally serves to illustrate an argument and make it understandable for the audience. It usually does not serve to test a hypothesis, or to prove that IT supports judicial reform.

Another challenge is in the use of sources that are different in their concepts and approaches. This variety poses the question of how concepts can be translated from one approach to another. Part of the solution is to strive for conceptual clarity: this is addressed later in this chapter with some general definitions. Apart from that, trying to answer this question in general is not very useful. Therefore, my translations will, in each case, be accounted for in the context in which they are made.

Limitations on the scope of the study

This study's scope is IT support for courts and judiciaries in the light of delay, access and integrity. I have limited the scope on some important points that need clarification.

The first limitation is the decision not to examine court management. Court management is also a highly relevant area that has undergone much change under the influence of IT. However, I am a judge without any court management experience. My expertise is in judicial processes, not in managing courts. My expertise does not justify making statements about court management. Hence, I limit myself to the judicial processes. All those highly competent court managers out there are invited to take up their pens and write about court management and IT.

The second limitation is in the case studies. They deal with civil law only. The first reason for this limitation is that the case studies, particularly the ones on case delay, build on earlier work in the same field. Another reason is again my lack of expertise, in this case in administrative law. Moreover, in my experience, discussing administrative law in an international perspective is very difficult because the institutional arrangements for it are so fundamentally different that they are difficult to compare and study apart from their context. As for criminal law: Criminal justice operates in its own information chain with the police, the prosecution, defense lawyers, probation services, victims' support agencies and others. This information chain has its own dynamic. The field deserves more attention than I could have given it in this study.

Finally, the study will not discuss matters relating to cost. Cost is a highly relevant perspective for the issues of delay and access. IT was claimed as a way to reduce costs. IT was going to make processing cases cheaper. I have not found evidence supporting this claim. Whether cost can be reduced, thereby increasing access to justice, is an interesting and relevant research question. It emerged several times during my research. Costs come in different categories: cost for justice seekers, cost of courts, and cost of individual procedures. Studying whether each of them is affected by the introduction of different forms of IT would require comparing them individually over time. Operationalizing the different kinds of costs for the purpose of examining the impact of IT support turned out to be not feasible, at least not within an approach that necessarily encompasses so many other perspectives. As it would also have detracted from the other topics, I decided to exclude it.

Positioning this study

This study examines the complex phenomenon of information technology in courts and judiciaries. Hence, it is of necessity interdisciplinary in nature. In its approach, it uses a variety of methodologies and sources. They methodologies and sources are drawn from information science, political and organization sciences and socio-legal studies. The sources also draw on empirical information from more generally available sources such as statistics and opinion polls. The study intends to show how approaches from all those disciplines are required, and need to be integrated, in order to understand the complex phenomenon of IT in courts.

Guidance for the reader

This study was written with several audiences in mind:
- Those in charge of policy and decision making in judiciaries all over the world
- Those specifically charged with IT policy in and for courts
- Those involved in judicial reform in developing countries
- Those involved in researching IT and courts and the law in general.

Different parts of the study may be of interest to different groups of experts in the respective fields.

The study is organized into 6 parts and 22 chapters.

Part 1 provides the framework and the information needed to understand the other parts. It begins with this chapter introducing the research. Chapters 1.2 to 1.4 present materials needed to understand the rest of the study.

Part 2 presents an overview of the information technology available in courts, and an analysis of the most frequent problems with implementing it.

Next come three parts dedicated to the three issues identified as the starting point for the research:
- Case delay (Part 3)
- Access to justice (Part 4)
- Integrity and corruption (Part 5).

Each of these parts is generally organized the same way. First, there is a discussion of basic theoretical knowledge about each issue, and how it can be diagnosed. Then, the issue is examined from an empirical point of view, followed by an analysis of the information aspects of the issue. Finally, conclusions are drawn on how using information technology can help with the issue in question.

Part 3 focuses on case delay. Chapter 3.1 discusses case delay as a problem. Chapter 3.2 examines case handling as a process of information management. Chapter 3.3 analyzes judicial roles in detail.

Part 4 examines access to justice. Chapter 4.1 examines the concept of access to justice and its impediments. Chapter 4.2 analyzes access to justice as access to information. Chapter 4.3 looks at access to justice from the perspective of access to courts.

Part 5 analyzes corruption. Chapter 5.1 develops a theoretical framework for judicial impartiality, integrity and corruption. Chapter 5.2 examines empirical evidence of corruption in judiciaries and courts. Chapter 5.3 analyzes corruption as a problem of information.

Part 6 concludes the study. Chapter 6.1 summarizes the findings of this study with regard to the role of information and information technology in judicial reform. Chapter 6.2 explores what research can contribute to developing new knowledge for judiciaries and courts regarding the implementation and use of IT.

Research for this study was concluded on July 1, 2009.

Chapter 1.2 Conceptual Framework and Terminology

This section will introduce the definitions and terms used as well as the normative framework for courts, judiciaries and judicial reform.

Court

The word "court", in the legal sense, can be used with very different meanings. The *Oxford Dictionary* defines a court as a body of people before whom judicial cases are heard, and also as the place where such a body meets. *Wikipedia*, the online encyclopedia, defines a court as an official, public forum established by lawful authority to adjudicate disputes, and to dispense civil, labor, administrative and criminal justice under the law. *Black's Law Dictionary* defines a court as a governmental body consisting of one or more judges who sit to adjudicate disputes and administer justice, as well as the judge or judges who sit on such a governmental body.

The term court, meaning a court of law, is used for a single judge or a multi judge chamber, as in: the court finds the defendant not guilty. Such a court may be adjudicating one specific dispute or certain categories of disputes. The word court is also used for the organization of these judges and chambers and their staff in a building, as in: the New York Midtown Court.

Unless indicated otherwise, the term "court" is used here primarily as *the organization encompassing individual judges, panels and juries, their legal staff and their logistical support staff*. This use of the term court includes all bodies producing decisions: courts, judges and juries. This use of the term courts does not include other forms of dispute resolution, traditional conflict resolution or traditional justice.

Judiciary

Another concept in this context is that of the judiciary. There are systems where this term is reserved for making the distinction between the state power exercising the judicial function, and the executive and legislative branches of government. In some contexts, the term "judiciary" is also used to identify the national organization of the courts. As this study focuses on reform in the sense of changing the organization as well as its processes, the term judiciary will be used to mean *the judicial branch of government, including the national organization of all the courts.*

Normative framework

This section discusses the normative framework for courts as laid down in the international human rights instruments. These instruments serve other purposes besides offering a framework for courts. However, because national institutions and legislation with regard to the administration of justice vary, the international human rights instruments serve as a single standard that applies to all of them.

The Universal Declaration of Human Rights of 1948[1] states that everyone is entitled in full equality to a fair and public hearing by an independent and impartial tribunal, in the determination of his rights and obligations and of any criminal charge against him.

> The International Covenant on Civil and Political Rights (ICCPR), Article 14, affirms this statement by stating that everyone is entitled to a fair and public hearing by a competent, independent and impartial tribunal established by law. So do the regional human rights conventions. All these conventions award everyone the right to impartial judges and courts. The ICCPR states that in the case of criminal charges, cases must be disposed by courts without undue delay.

The African Charter on Human and People's Rights, Article 7, states that every individual shall have the right to have his cause heard, comprising the right to be tried within a reasonable time.

The American Convention on Human Rights, Article 8, states that every person has the right to a hearing with due guarantees and within a reasonable time.

The European Convention on Human Rights (ECHR), Article 6, accords everyone in the member states of the Council of Europe the right to a fair and public hearing by an independent, impartial tribunal, within a reasonable time. The Court of Justice of the other European organization of states, the European Union, has recognized the ECHR as an important source of law and takes Article 6 into account when considering issues that have to do with reasonable time. Article 6 is also echoed in Article 47 of the Charter of Fundamental Rights of the European Union, according everyone the right to a fair and public hearing within a reasonable time by an independent and impartial tribunal previously established by law.[2]

Within this framework, procedural rules or codes prescribe the way in which a hearing (this includes all case processing that courts do) should reasonably ensure compliance with the values in the Declaration and in the Conventions. Since the vast majority of countries are party to one or more of the instruments mentioned above, the normative framework as described binds the judiciaries and courts of those countries directly or indirectly.

Two concepts deserve special attention: independence and impartiality. It is common to regard independence as a first value of a judiciary. However, that is not how this study approaches the concept. From the perspective of a court user, impartiality is the primary value for judiciaries. In order to safeguard impartiality, judiciaries need to be institutionally independent. Independence, therefore, is an institutional arrangement underpinning the value of impartiality. Thus, judiciaries need independence in order to process cases impartially, on the basis of facts and in accordance with the law. For the discussion of impartiality in Part 5, the distinction between de facto and de jure independence is relevant. De iure (legal, constitutional) judicial independence can be derived from looking at the formal legal arrangement. De facto (actual, practical) independence is the independence factually enjoyed by judges as a result of, for instance, the degree to which their judgments have an impact on government behavior (Feld p. 3).

Box 1 Human Rights Instruments

Universal Declaration of Human Rights
December 10, 1948, General Assembly Resolution no. 217A(III), U. N. Doc. A/3
Article 10
Everyone is entitled in full equality to a fair and public hearing by an independent and impartial tribunal, in the determination of his rights and obligations and of any criminal charge against him.

International Covenant on Civil and Political Rights (ICCPR)
December 16, 1966, General Assembly Resolution no. 2200A (XXI), U.N. Doc. A/6316
Article 14
1. All persons shall be equal before the courts and tribunals. In the determination of any criminal charge against him, or of his rights and obligations in a suit at law, everyone shall be entitled to a fair and public hearing by a competent, independent and impartial tribunal established by law. The press and the public may be excluded from all or part of a trial for reasons of morals, public or-

der (ordre public) or national security in a democratic society, or when the interest of the private lives of the parties so requires, or to the extent strictly necessary in the opinion of the court in special circumstances where publicity would prejudice the interests of justice; but any judgment rendered in a criminal case or in a suit at law shall be made public except where the interest of juvenile persons otherwise requires or the proceedings concern matrimonial disputes or the guardianship of children.

African Charter on Human and Peoples' Rights
June 27 1981, OAU Doc. CAB/LEG/67/3 21 I.L.M. 58 (1982)
Article 7
Every individual shall have the right to have his cause heard. This comprises:
- The right to an appeal to competent national organs against acts of violating his fundamental rights as recognized and guaranteed by conventions, laws, regulations and customs in force;
- The right to be presumed innocent until proved guilty by a competent court or tribunal;
- The right to defence, including the right to be defended by counsel of his choice;
- The right to be tried within a reasonable time by an impartial court or tribunal.

American Convention on Human Rights
Adopted at the Inter-American Specialized Conference on Human Rights, San José, Costa Rica, November 22, 1969
Article 8
Right to a Fair Trial
1. Every person has the right to a hearing, with due guarantees and within a reasonable time, by a competent, independent, and impartial tribunal, previously established by law, in the substantiation of any accusation of a criminal nature made against him or for the determination of his rights and obligations of a civil, labor, fiscal, or any other nature.

European Convention on Human Rights (ECHR)
Rome, 4.XI.1950
Article 6
Right to fair trial
1. In the determination of his civil rights and obligations or of any criminal charge against him, everyone is entitled to a fair and public hearing within a reasonable time by an independent and impartial tribunal established by law. Judgment shall be pro-

nounced publicly but the press and public may be excluded from all or part of the trial in the interests of morals, public order or national security in a democratic society, where the interests of juveniles or the protection of the private life of the parties so require, or to the extent strictly necessary in the opinion of the court in special circumstances where publicity would prejudice the interests of justice.

European Union Charter of Fundamental Rights
2000/C 364/01
Article 47
Right to an effective remedy and to a fair trial Everyone whose rights and freedoms guaranteed by the law of the Union are violated has the right to an effective remedy before a tribunal in compliance with the conditions laid down in this Article.
Everyone is entitled to a fair and public hearing within a reasonable time by an independent and impartial tribunal previously established by law.
Everyone shall have the possibility of being advised, defended and represented.
Legal aid shall be made available to those who lack sufficient resources in so far as such aid is necessary to ensure effective access to justice.

Judicial reform

Reform means to make changes in (something) in order to improve (*Oxford English Dictionary*). Reform can consist of resolving problems, improving performance and realizing values. Problems signify shortcomings in the realization of values. Improving performance constitutes a fuller realization of values. The values judiciaries are expected to create can be found in the human rights conventions: fairness, timeliness, impartiality and independence. Case delay is a problem because it contravenes the norm, and does not realize the value of timeliness. Reducing case delay implies fuller realization of the value of timeliness. Corruption is a problem because it is an infraction on the norms of fairness and impartiality. The values of fairness and impartiality are realized more fully when corruption is reduced. Access is only partly covered in the conventions, making it a conceptually more complex issue. In the conventions, access is awarded to courts. Access to justice is a broader concept that involves more than just court access. This brings some particular problems with it, which are discussed in the chapters on access in Part 4 of this study. All the activities described here constitute some form of judicial reform.

Improvement and innovation

Within the area of reform, the term improvement is reserved for remedying existing processes. Innovation is the term reserved for developing new processes and services not in existence before. Thus, introducing early hearings is an improvement, but online dispute resolution will, for most judiciaries, be an innovation.

Efficiency

Sometimes, judicial reform is understood as increasing court efficiency. Efficiency, to be precise, is the relation between input (resources, such as judges, financing) and output (mostly decisions): how much money, judges, etc. are needed to process and decide a given number of cases. Processing more cases with the same number of judges or the same amount of funding would then constitute increasing efficiency. Because cost is not included in its scope, as explained above, efficiency will not be a major focus of this study.

Western reform

The normative framework raises another problem that begs to be discussed.

This discussion starts with the question, whether reference to the international human rights conventions constitutes a solely Western perspective on courts and judiciaries, followed by the question whether this study promotes a uniquely Western concept of judicial reform. These are questions that emerged more than once in my advisory work for judiciaries in developing countries. The answer comes in two parts. The first answer is that the international human rights conventions apply to all states that are signatories to them. Only very few countries are not. The other half of the answer is that this study aims to provide lines of reasoning that may be helpful in realizing the values embodied in those conventions, for those legal systems, judiciaries and courts who choose to orient themselves on the international human rights conventions.

System and structure

Court systems have developed over centuries, each in its own political, economic and social context. The resulting court systems vary considerably. This study uses a very general idea of a court system, recognizing that the systems may, in practice, be very different. In the ideal type of court used in this study, court systems have a three-tier structure. The first tier or first instance courts decide cases on the facts and on the law. The second-tier or appeal courts review cases decided by the first tier courts on the law, and on the facts unless legislation prohibits it. Third-tier, or final instance courts decide cases reviewed by the appeal courts on the law. Their purpose is to guard legal unity.

Court systems are always the result of complex political and historical processes. Therefore, they never fully resemble the picture above. Not all systems have a second tier. In some systems, the second tier consists of only one appeal court. Some systems have a fourth tier in the form of a constitutional court. Some third-tier courts hear specific types of cases, such as violations of human rights or cases against high-ranking public officials, as a first-tier court.

Role

The role of judiciaries and courts also needs to be defined at the outset of this study. A role is a person's or thing's function in a particular situation, according to the *Oxford Dictionary*. There is not one single role courts and judiciaries fulfill. Which role is prevalent depends on the situation or, in the case of a study, on the perspective of the discussion. There are many different perspectives on the role of the judiciary.

Court users have different views depending on their particular perspective. Court users can be regarded as those for whom courts produce value. From the perspective of the court user, the judiciary's role can be seen as that of offering concrete legal protection to the individual, ensuring that the individual will not be jeopardized beyond the limits of the law. In the United Kingdom., 73 percent of respondents to the Paths to Justice survey agreed or strongly agreed with the statement that courts are an important way for ordinary people to enforce their rights (Genn p. 227). In the Netherlands, 68.8 percent of respondents in the Dispute Resolution Delta survey agreed or strongly agreed with the same statement (Van Velthoven 2004, p. 173).

Judges differ in how they view their role. Here is an example to illustrate this point. Judges in the Netherlands were surveyed by the Nederlands Juristenblad (Netherlands Legal Weekly) in 2001 (NJB 2001, p. 1930). When asked to rank six tasks of the courts and judges in order of importance, they largely replied that helping litigants comes first, with deciding legal disputes and resolving conflicts closely following in second and third place. Only members of the Supreme Court regarded actively contributing to legal development their most important task. First instance judges regard resolving disputes as their role. The role of safeguarding the unity of the legal system emerges in the perspective of the final court. How judges view their role will also be related to their culture.

From the *legal point of view*, under the rule of law, the role of the court is what the law says it is. In some countries, courts perform roles that would not be considered judicial tasks in other countries. In the United States, courts not only end marriages, they can also conclude them. In the United States, justices of the peace perform this role. In some countries in Central Europe, courts maintain the registers of real, immovable property, and/or those of enterprises. This role would not be considered the core role of the judiciary in most systems' thinking. However, where it was by law determined to be part of the role of the judiciary to maintain these registers, it is legally part of its role.

Legal sociologists have debated the nature of the role of the judiciary in society throughout the existence of their profession. As in any discipline, there are schools of thought with different approaches and convictions. At this point, those schools of thought are not very relevant for this study. In the sociological perspective, most writers on courts see dispute processing as the central focus of the judicial process (Cotterrell p. 212). Court judgments are, in most sociologists' perspective, both a resolution to a dispute as well an assertion of normative order. When deciding individual disputes, courts also contribute to confirmation of the normative order in a more general sense. For example: criminal courts process cases punishing transgressions, but their more general role is to assert the norms in order to prevent transgressions from happening. I would add that transgressions can be twofold: infractions of the substantive criminal law, but also attempts to punish those infractions by others than the justice system. This is a form of concrete legal protection for those who are alleged to have broken the law. In a sociological perspective, concrete legal protection is effected as well through the manner in which parties are afforded fair hearing. If one of the parties has to accept negative consequences from a judicial decision, it is important that they have had 'their day in court": an opportunity to influence the decision. Fair hearing in its turn legitimizes the enforceability of the decisions.

From the point of view of *society*, the general effects of the courts' role in asserting the norms on conflict-free interaction and on resolving disputes by individuals themselves are much more important than the specific effects in cases of disputes resolved by the courts (Galanter 1983a, p. 125; Griffiths p. 129). Therefore, these general effects are also a product of the courts. This general role is what distinguishes courts from bicycle factories, according to Griffiths. A more general term to describe this role is abstract legal protection. It is produced by the mere fact that the judiciary exists, and by the fact that it can be accessed in case of need. Effective and efficient concrete legal protection strengthens abstract legal protection. Abstract legal protection is also referred to as "the shadow function of the law" (Galanter 1983a, p. 122).

The courts' primary business process is processing filed cases. It involves everything a court does to process cases through the court system, from the filing of a case to archiving decisions and ensuring their enforcement. Case *management* ensures that in filed cases, justice is done promptly. It deals with individual cases and also with groups of cases. Case management implies attention to timeliness.

This study includes all the roles discussed above.

Chapter 1.3 Sources

Empirical study of social phenomena builds on the empirical material that is available. The sources of empirical material specific to each of the issues here will be introduced in the respective chapters. This chapter discusses indicators and indexes used throughout the study for comparing countries. It also presents my own empirical material: the studies I conducted examining judicial systems in developing countries.

Indicators and databases

This section introduces the concept of indicators and the main indexes this study uses for comparing countries and their systems.

Indicators

Various organizations use different definitions of indicators depending on their activities and purposes. The Vera Institute of Justice has produced a guide for constructing performance indicators. It lists a number of definitions (Vera 2003 p. 2):

An indicator is something that can be seen, experienced, or recorded. It is a sign that something exists, or has happened, or has changed. This somewhat stark definition is used by the Performance Assessment Resource Center (PARC), based in Birmingham, England.

An indicator is a direct and valid statistical measure that monitors levels and changes over time in a fundamental social concern. This definition comes from the Organization for Economic Co-operation and Development (OECD 1976).

An indicator is a piece of information with significance for the objective to be achieved. This definition comes from the Handbook of Democracy and Governance Program Indicators (Washington, DC: U.S. Agency for International Development 1998).

The World Bank does not have one single definition of indicators. Below is the one from the World Bank's Judicial Sector Indicators:

An indicator is information [that] can be used...to assess performance and assist in planning for the future.

Indicators can be constructed to reflect a state or an event and to measure change, for instance progress toward an objective. The objective can be intermediate, for example increasing the number of cases processed, or an overarching purpose, such as assuring equal access to justice. Indicators are also used in indexes listing or comparing specific aspects of countries or systems.

Indexes

The main indexes I use as sources for quantitative comparisons between countries and their systems are listed in this section. It will list the indexes, and for each of them it will discuss:

- What data they collect
- How they collect them
- What the data can tell us
- What the limitations for each of them are.

The indexes all serve to provide overviews and country comparisons. They are used by experts for all of those purposes, and for research purposes as well. They are not suitable, in themselves, to provide a diagnosis of a system that will serve as a basis for a reform program.

World Governance Indicators (WGI)

The WGI is the most comprehensive database on public governance in the world. It was developed by the World Bank Institute and the World Bank's DEC group. The WGI is published annually. It aggregates data from numerous other sources. The data are grouped into six categories, all expressing an important aspect of a country's political system: voice and accountability, political stability and absence of violence, government effectiveness, regulatory quality, rule of law, and control of corruption. The category that is most relevant for studying judges and courts is the Rule of Law indicator. The Rule of Law data measure perceived quality of contract enforcement, quality of police and courts, and the likelihood of crime and violence. The indicator aggregates data on contract enforcement, quality of police and courts and incidence of crime and violence from 24 sources (World Bank 2007b). It produces a percentile ranking for more than 200 countries. The rankings are not actionable. That means that it is not evident from them what a country can do to improve its performance and influence its ranking. The WGI database is the most hotly debated collection of data in the world. Even its critics qualify it as the most carefully constructed (set of) governance indicators (Arndt p. 49). The main criticism focuses on the methodology: lack of transparency resulting from the fact that the indicators are based on data that are aggregated from other data sources, and therefore the results are difficult to check for correctness (Arndt p. 66). This difficulty, critics say, is compounded by the fact that some of the sources are also aggregates, and one of the sources they aggregate is the WGI indicators themselves. Thus, circular aggregation leads to uncontrollable results. The makers of the WGI recognize there are limitations to what can be achieved with this kind of cross-country, highly-aggregated data (Kaufmann 2007 p. 2). They maintain that WGI can serve the purpose of providing individual countries with a set of monitorable indicators of governance they can use to benchmark themselves against other countries and over time. But in view of the limitations, this type of data cannot substitute for in-depth, country-specific governance diagnostics as a basis for policy advice to improve governance in a particular country, but should rather be viewed as a complementary tool.

In this study, WGI is used in the chapters on integrity and corruption to compare governance and levels of institutional development.

The Doing Business (DB) database

The DB database gathers information about the business climate in an annually increasing number of countries around the world, from informants who report each year on a number of topics. It is a product of the staff of the World Bank's International Finance Corporation. The *Doing Business* methodology (World Bank 2008a) is a tool for gathering and comparing data and information on the business climate in most countries in the world. Doing Business has a network of informants in all its participating countries. In 2008, 180 countries participated in the data gathering. The Doing Business process works as follows: Every year, it asks its informants in all its participating countries to provide information on the performance of a number of institutions relevant to doing business, such as the tax office, customs, and also the justice system. Its approach is criticized for not aiming to capture the benefits of regulation, but merely measuring its burden (World Bank 2008b p. 6). The other major criticism is lack of transparency about its informants and their sources (World Bank 2008b, p. 54). My own main objection regards its representativeness. DB looks at one specific way of enforcing contracts: with an adversarial court procedure involving a witness hearing. As we shall see in Part 3, this procedure is used in only a very small fraction of contract enforcement situations. Therefore, it is not necessarily relevant for businesses looking for an advantageous climate for their business.

The topic most relevant for studying the courts is that of Enforcing Contracts. It lists the number of steps needed, the time involved, and the cost of enforcing a contract. With regard to contract enforcement, lawyers in all the participating countries are asked to provide their estimates on the pursuit of a commercial contract enforcement case: the disposition time, the cost and the number of steps that need to be taken. An objection to the methodology of using informants is that accuracy of the data is difficult to check where other data are unavailable. For instance, the data on the Netherlands can be checked with actual court statistics. Where such statistics do not exist or are not available, this check is not feasible. Whether or not that is a problem depends the purpose for which the data are used. Establishing whether a given disposition time complies with a standard is one way of using DB results. If the average estimated disposition time from DB falls well within a given standard, it is probably good enough for this purpose. For other purposes, it may not be accurate enough.

As with the WGI, DB provides an approach for comparing performance with other countries. In contrast to WGI, its results are highly actionable because they focus on well defined aspects of performance relevant to the business climate. It should be kept in mind that, because the data do not capture country nuances, it is not an adequate tool for designing specific policy reforms. A reform program requires more information from other sources.

In this study, DB is used extensively in Part 3, on case processing, when discussing comparison as an approach to developing standards. Chapter 3.1 has a more in-depth discussion of the methodology.

The Human Development Index (HDI)

The HDI, like the WGI, is a summary composite index. It was developed for the United Nations Development Program (UNDP). It measures a country's average achievements in three basic aspects of human development: health, knowledge, and a decent standard of living. Health is measured by life expectancy at birth. Knowledge is measured by a combination of the adult literacy rate and the combined primary, secondary and tertiary gross enrollment ratio. The standard of living is measured by gross domestic product (GDP) per capita.

In this study, HDI is used in Part 5, on integrity and corruption, to compare development levels.

The Transparency International (TI) Corruption Perception Index (CPI)

The TI CPI is the most influential corruption perception survey in the world. It ranks countries in terms of the degree to which corruption is perceived to exist among public officials and politicians. It is a composite index, making use of surveys and scores provided by experts. The index was first released in 1995. The 2008 index ranks 180 countries by their perceived level of corruption. It draws on 13 sources originating from 11 independent institutions, using data compiled in 2007 and 2008. It gives each country a score, an absolute figure between 0 and 10, where 10 is the maximum score. Moreover, it produces a ranking, a list in which countries are arranged according to their score (Transparency International 2008).

In this study, the TI CPI is used in Part 5 on integrity and corruption.

The Transparency Global Corruption Barometer (GCB)

The GCB is a public opinion survey that assesses the general public's perception and experience of corruption in more than 60 countries around the world. Experience surveys ask about the *actual occurrence* of a phenomenon in a given situation. Perception surveys ask what respondents *think* about a certain phenomenon. Both experience and perception are relevant for the purpose of gaining a better understanding of the incidence of corruption and the levels of corruption in justice delivery, as well as the linkages between causes and possible remedies. However, they both need to be treated with caution. Experience surveys may over or under-report certain forms. Respondents may be reluctant to admit having paid a bribe. Justice officials may be reluctant to report corruption in their own profession or peer group due to a sense of loyalty to the group. That means that actual experience may not always be truthfully reported. In some surveys discussed below, this problem has been recognized by creating an opportunity to report anonymously. The perception of corrupt practices in the justice system may be caused by actual corrupt practices but also by delays or incompetence from other causes. It can also be caused by a general feeling that all public servants are corrupt. Perception of corruption may also go up when governments actually begin to tackle corruption, and the subject gets more attention in the press. A case in point is the Czech Republic; its score in the Transparency International Corruption Perception Index went down from 3.9 to 3.7 between 2001 and 2002, as the Czech Republic prepared to join the European Union (TI CPI 2001 and 2002).

The Barometer includes questions of both types: perception and beliefs about court corruption, as well as experience with actual bribe paying in court. The outcomes consist of results that do not agree. Moreover, both types of survey carry their own risks with regard to the truthfulness of the reported replies. Hence, both experience and perception surveys need to be treated with care, particularly in the context of diagnosing problems. However, they can serve to provide a sense of the incidence of corruption. This helps to identify directions for further enquiry and examination.

Commission Européenne pour l'efficacité de la Justice (CEPEJ)
The European Court of Human Rights was burdened with large numbers of complaints about undue delay in court procedures in the Council of Europe (COE) member countries, a lot of them from Italy and Russia. This was one of the reasons for setting up the Council of Europe's program for the efficiency of justice. The program is run by the European Commission for the Efficiency of Justice, called CEPEJ after its French acronym. The terms of reference for CEPEJ are:

a. To examine the results achieved by the different judicial systems in the light of the principles referred to in the preamble to this resolution by using, among other things, common statistical criteria and means of evaluation
b. To define problems and areas for possible improvements and to exchange views on the functioning of the judicial systems
c. To identify concrete ways to improve the measuring and functioning of the judicial systems of the member States, having regard to their specific needs
d. To provide assistance to one or more member States, at their request, including assistance in complying with the standards of the Council of Europe
e. To suggest, if appropriate, areas in which the relevant steering committees of the Council of Europe, in particular the European Committee on Legal Co-operation (CDCJ), may, if they consider it necessary, draft new international legal instruments or amendments to existing ones, for adoption by the Committee of Ministers
f. To improve justice systems' efficiency and functioning.[3]

The CEPEJ's data collection is not an index. It serves the wider goal of improving the functioning of justice systems of the member states of the Council of Europe. In 2002, a pilot scheme on data collection was set up. The first report was published in 2004. This study draws on the most recent report, published in October 2008. The data collection instrument collects data on courts' inputs and outputs. It is not a ranking. The instrument pays a lot of attention to the comparability of its data. It collects data on member states of COE; it has 130 questions, mostly institutional: general, justice system budget, legal aid, support for users of courts and victims, functioning and efficiency of justice, disciplinary procedures, use of IT in the court, fair trial, judicial career, lawyers, mediators, enforcement, and notaries. Questions on the use of IT in courts have been included since the 2006 report. The data are provided by a network of national correspondents, usually in the member states' ministries of justice. Because of the differences in legal and court systems, comparability of the data can be a problem. Since institutions are different across Europe, there can easily be doubts about the empirical basis of some of the data. This data collection, with those limitations taken into account, is a useful repository of information on justice systems in Europe.

Empirical material collected in World Bank work

This section introduces my own empirical material. While I was a senior judicial reform expert for the World Bank from 2003 to 2007, I worked on project advice, studies and assessments for the World Bank on judicial systems in Benin, Gambia, Nepal, Sri Lanka, Georgia, Romania, and Macedonia. The World Bank is a United Nations affiliated organization. Its purpose is to provide financing for governments for reconstruction and development of their country. The financing is provided in the form of loans or grants. The World Bank is a multilateral donor, in contrast to national governments. Judicial reform can be a component in government improvement programs, supported by loans. It can also be done in project form, supported by grants from trust funds the World Bank administers on behalf of other donors. This section describes my briefs, the work I did, my reports and their conclusions, and the most important and relevant information about the country in question for this study. Each country has evolved since I last visited it. Table 1 provides an overview of some country characteristics that are relevant for this study.

Table 1 *Country Indexes*

1 Country	*2 HDI 2005*	*3 WGI RoL 07*	*4 DB time in days 2007*	*5 TI CPI 2008*
Benin	0.437	36.2	720	3.1
Gambia	0.502	49.5	434	1.9
Georgia	0.754	42.9	285	3.9
Macedonia	0.801	41.4	385	3.6
Nepal	0.534	31.0	735	2.7
Netherlands	0.953	93.3	514	8.9
Romania	0.813	50.5	537	3.8
Sri Lanka	0.743	55.7	1318	3.2

Sources: 2 - Human Development Index, 3 - World Governance Indicators, 4 - Doing Business, and 5 - Transparency International Corruption Perception Index.

The table presents an overview of index scores for the countries I studied for the World Bank. The indexes were discussed in the previous section. Column 1 displays the country names in alphabetical order. Column 2 displays the HDI scores out of a possible 1.0, with a higher score indicating a higher level of development. Column 3 presents the WGI score, out of a possible 100, for Rule of Law. A higher score indicates a higher level of rule of law. Column 4 lists the DB number of calendar days for processing and enforcing a money claim. Column 5 lists the scores, out of a possible 10, on the TI CPI index. A higher score indicates a lower level of perceived corruption. The scores displayed were the most recent ones available when the research for this study ended.

Some observations present themselves. My work did not include countries with a development level below 0.4 in the HDI. This may be a coincidence, because the World Bank does support judicial reform in countries with such low HDI levels. On the other hand, in countries with a very low development level, institutional reform is not the first priority because the institutions are usually too weak to sustain reform. Another observation is that high or low scores for development level, rule of law and low perceived corruption generally go together, but disposition times in DB present a very mixed picture. On a more detailed level, the picture is not quite so simple. Nepal is the lowest scoring country regarding rule of law. Gambia scores lowest on corruption and human development, but higher on rule of law. In Part 5, there is a more detailed discussion of the scores.

Benin

Present-day Benin was the site of Dahomey, a prominent West African kingdom that rose in the 15th century. The territory became a French Colony in 1872 and achieved independence on August 1, 1960, as the Republic of Benin. A succession of military governments ended in 1972 with the rise to power of Mathieu Kerekou and the establishment of a government based on Marxist-Leninist principles. A move to representative government began in 1989. Two years later, free elections ushered in former Prime Minister Nicephore Soglo as president, marking the first successful transfer of power in Africa from a dictatorship to a democracy. Kerekou was returned to power by elections held in 1996 and 2001, although some irregularities were alleged. Kerekou stepped down at the end of his second term in 2006 and was succeeded by Thomas Yayi Boni, a political outsider and independent. Yayi has begun a high profile fight against corruption and has strongly promoted accelerating Benin's economic growth (CIA World Factbook).

During the month of September 2004, I was in Benin as background support for the World Bank country lawyer in the team negotiating the Poverty Reduction Strategy Credit for the next year. The Credit is a budget support loan that is based on a program agreed between the government and the World Bank. The justice sector had been added to the program as a new sector that year. Its programming, the basis for a multi-year reform program for the sector, required more than routine attention. I wrote the relevant sections in the program and in the program budget.

Gambia

The Gambia gained its independence from the United Kingdom in 1965. Geographically surrounded by Senegal, it formed a short-lived federation of Senegambia between 1982 and 1989. In 1991 the two nations signed a friendship and cooperation treaty, but tensions have flared up intermittently since then. Yahya A. J. J. Jammeh led a military coup in 1994 that overthrew the president and banned political activity. A new constitution and presidential elections in 1996, followed by parliamentary balloting in 1997, completed a nominal return to civilian rule. Jammeh has been elected president in all subsequent elections, including most recently in late 2006 (CIA World Factbook).

I visited Gambia in March 2005. Justice system reform was part of the World Bank Economic Management improvement program there. The program included a component for strengthening justice institutions. The Chief Justice of Gambia applied for funding for a court-annex mediation program. My brief was to provide ad hoc informal advice to the World Bank country economist for Gambia who was in charge of that program.

Georgia

The region of present-day Georgia contained the ancient kingdoms of Colchis and Kartli-Iberia. The area came under Roman influence in the first centuries A.D. and Christianity became the state religion in the 330s. Domination by Persians, Arabs, and Turks was followed by a Georgian golden age (11th-13th centuries) that was cut short by the Mongol invasion of 1236. Subsequently, the Ottoman and Persian empires competed for influence in the region. Georgia was absorbed into the Russian Empire in the 19th century. Independent for three years (1918-1921) following the Russian revolution, it was forcibly incorporated into the USSR until the Soviet Union dissolved in 1991. An attempt by the incumbent Georgian government to manipulate national legislative elections in November 2003 touched off widespread protests that led to the resignation of Eduard Shevardnadze, president since 1995. New elections in early 2004 swept Mikheil Saakashvili into power along with his National Movement party. Progress on market reforms and democratization has been made in the years since independence, but this progress has been complicated by Russian assistance and support to the breakaway regions of Abkhazia and South Ossetia. After a series of Russian and separatist provocations in summer 2008, Georgian military action in South Ossetia in early August led to a Russian military response that not only occupied the breakaway areas, but large portions of Georgia proper as well. Russian troops pulled back from most of the occupied Georgian territory, but in late August 2008 Russia unilaterally recognized the independence of Abkhazia and

South Ossetia. This action was strongly condemned by most of the world's nations and international organizations (CIA World Factbook).

Since the Rose revolution in 2003, Georgia has had a strong reform agenda under the leadership of its president, Mikhail Saakasvili. It is highly oriented toward the European Union. U.S. non-governmental organizations (NGOs) like the American Bar Association (ABA), are very active there in promoting what is called rule of law.

In May 2004, I visited Georgia at the invitation of a colleague at the World Bank in charge of a justice reform project financed by a grant of some few hundred thousand dollars. My brief was to interview a number of key players in the project and visit a couple of courts and report whether I thought the project should change direction.

The highest priority for nearly everyone I spoke with was to combat corruption in the judiciary. Some factors in the organization of the judiciary were put forward as facilitating corruption:

- Judges not knowing what to do with the cases for lack of training
- Lack of (professional) court management
- Lack of consistent management of resources
- Low salaries
- Integrity not being a criteria for selection of judges
- Many *rayon* (small, subdistrict) courts consisting of only one judge.

Improving court management was regarded the second-highest priority.

Macedonia

Macedonia gained its independence peacefully from Yugoslavia in 1991, but Greece's objection to the new state's use of what it considered a Hellenic name and symbols delayed international recognition, which occurred under the provisional designation of "the Former Yugoslav Republic of Macedonia." In 1995, Greece lifted a 20-month trade embargo and the two countries agreed to normalize relations. The United States began referring to Macedonia by its constitutional name, Republic of Macedonia, in 2004 and negotiations continue between Greece and Macedonia to resolve the name issue. Some ethnic Albanians, angered by perceived political and economic inequities, launched an insurgency in 2001 that eventually won the support of the majority of Macedonia's Albanian population and led to the internationally-brokered Framework Agreement, which ended the fighting by establishing a set of new laws enhancing the rights of minorities. Fully implementing the Framework Agreement and stimulating economic growth and development continue to be challenges for Macedonia, although progress has been made on both fronts over the past several years (CIA World Factbook).

In January 2005, I visited Macedonia as part of a World Bank team working on an assessment of the justice sector. Such an assessment tends to serve as preparation and foundation for a World Bank loan. My brief was to observe judges processing commercial cases in two courts: Skopje I and Štip. The judges felt they were doing too many basically administrative tasks, and my job was to find out what it was they were doing and report. Of the 23 cases I observed, not a single case was ready for a decision, mostly because documents were not handed in. Judges do not actively manage cases for timely disposal, for instance by enforcing the sanctions provided in the procedural codes. One judge said she felt timely disposal served no purpose, since everyone in the country was technically bankrupt anyway. In 2004, the disposal time for civil cases was 547 days, 25 percent over the average of the surrounding countries as reported by *Doing Business*. In 2008, the disposal time was 385 days, 10 percent below the regional average.

Nepal

In 1951, the Nepalese monarch ended the century-old system of rule by hereditary premiers and instituted a cabinet system of government. Reforms in 1990 established a multi-party democracy within the framework of a constitutional monarchy. An insurgency led by Maoist extremists broke out in 1996. The ensuing ten-year civil war between insurgents and government forces witnessed the dissolution of the cabinet and parliament and assumption of absolute power by the king. Several weeks of mass protests in April 2006 were followed by several months of peace negotiations between the Maoists and government officials, and culminated in a November 2006 peace accord and the promulgation of an interim constitution. Following a nation-wide election in April 2008, the newly formed Constituent Assembly declared Nepal a federal democratic republic and abolished the monarchy at its first meeting the following month. The Constituent Assembly elected the country's first president in July. The Maoists, who received a plurality of votes in the Constituent Assembly election, formed a coalition government in August 2008 (CIA World Factbook).

Nepal is situated in the Himalaya mountain range between India and China. Since a fatal incident in the royal family in 2001, the monarchy has been on a downward turn. It was abolished in June 2008. Nepal is now ruled by a coalition government that includes the former Maoist movement. Economically, Nepal depends heavily on India. In June 2004, I spent a month in Nepal as part of a World Bank team investigating the legal framework for the financial sector. My brief was to study those parts of the courts that serve the financial sector. I interviewed judges and court management as well as arbiters in special tribunals and representatives of other donors, for example the Asian Development Bank. The team's report was published as *Nepal, the Legal and Judicial Environment for Financial Sector Development, A Review* (World Bank 2005b). It discusses the legal framework for the banking sector, insolvency and creditor rights, capital markets and corporations, micro-finance institutions and the judiciary. A remarkable finding in my report was the judiciary's official immunity from investigation by the anti-corruption agency.

Romania

The principalities of Wallachia and Moldavia - for centuries under the suzerainty of the Turkish Ottoman Empire - secured their autonomy in 1856; they united in 1859 and a few years later adopted the new name of Romania. The country gained recognition of its independence in 1878. It joined the Allied Powers in World War I and acquired new territories - most notably Transylvania - following the conflict. In 1940, Romania allied with the Axis powers and participated in the 1941 German invasion of the USSR. Three years later, overrun by the Soviets, Romania signed an armistice. The post-war Soviet occupation led to the formation of a Communist "people's republic" in 1947 and the abdication of the king. The decades-long rule of dictator Nicolae Ceausescu, who took power in 1965, and his Securitate police state became increasingly oppressive and draconian through the 1980s. Ceausescu was overthrown and executed in late 1989. Former Communists dominated the government until 1996 when they were swept from power. Romania joined NATO in 2004 and the European Union in 2007 (CIA World Factbook).

Romania is a former member of the Soviet Union's satellite bloc in Eastern Europe. It joined the European Union on May 1, 2004.

I visited Romania on two occasions in 2005. My brief was to support the World Bank regional lawyer who was preparing a World Bank project for judicial reform. On both occasions, I visited several courts and had discussions with the judges and staff. When the project finally focused largely on reconstructing court buildings and a training program, my help was no longer needed.

Sri Lanka

Sri Lanka is an island off the coast of India. It was colonized first by the Portuguese, then by the Dutch and finally by the British. It became independent in 1948; its name was changed to Sri Lanka in 1972. Tensions between the Sinhalese majority and Tamil separatists erupted into war in 1983. Tens of thousands have died in the ethnic conflict that continues to fester. After two decades of fighting, the government and the Liberation Tigers of Tamil Eelam (LTTE) formalized a cease-fire in February 2002 with Norway brokering peace negotiations. Violence between the LTTE and government forces intensified in 2006 and the government regained control of the Eastern Province in 2007. In January 2008, the government officially withdrew from the cease-fire, and by late January 2009, the LTTE remained in control of a small and shrinking area of Mullaitivu district in the North (CIA World Fact-book).

In 2004, 2005 and 2006 I visited Sri Lanka on altogether three occasions. In the framework of supervision missions of the ongoing World Bank justice reform project, my brief was to start discussions on the content of a follow-up project. I visited a large number of courts and spoke with some influential members of the program steering committee. My observation was that their priority lay with building and rebuilding courthouses and other building projects, not with studying the judiciary's performance or how to improve it.

Summing up

These activities produced the following material:

The project advisory work in Sri Lanka, Romania and Gambia did not produce a report or document.

Nepal - an assessment of the judicial environment for the financial sector

Macedonia - a report on observations of case processing in the commercial court

Georgia - an evaluation report of the judicial reform project

Benin – draft of the reform program.

Evidently, this material does not constitute a deliberate, consistent body of research work, but it informs the rest of this study, as will become evident in the individual chapters.

Chapter 1.4 Information and Information Technology

This chapter introduces IT and the most relevant concepts concerning IT for this study. This section presents some basic concepts as well as a discussion on types of information technology, in a selection that is relevant for the topic of this study.

Information and information technology

Information technology needs to be distinguished from information. Without this distinction, the role of information does not get the attention it requires. Information technology is "the thing doing the manipulating", and information is "the thing being manipulated" (Davenport p.71). If we attempt to discuss the vehicle, information technology, right away, we miss out on what is being conveyed: the information. Processing court cases is primarily information handling. Therefore, the role of information needs to be studied in order to understand what the role of information technology can be. This study will examine informational aspects of reducing delay, improving access to justice and reducing corruption in order to identify how information technology can support those activities. Thus, before addressing information technology, the study focuses on the roles of information in those areas.

Roles of information

Information plays many roles in an organization. We can distinguish information as a focus of operational processes, production statistics supporting management, indicators supporting improvement processes, and many other roles (Davenport p. 72). This study discusses information primarily as a focus of operational processes. That means it looks at the judicial process itself as processing and managing of information. However, while doing so, the study extensively uses statistics on processes and indicators supporting their improvement. This so-called meta-information serves to provide a better understanding of judicial processes.

Basic concepts in information science

When studying information processes, it is helpful to understand the differences between data, information and knowledge: information is data given meaning, and knowledge is information coupled with experience. This discussion of the basic concepts used in information science is based on Gottschalk (p. 28):

Data are letters and numbers without meaning: independent, isolated measurements, characters, numerical characters, and symbols. For example, *2005, 3* is data. We can guess 2005 is a year, but otherwise, we have no way of understanding what this can mean.

Information is data that are included in a context that makes sense out of them. Information is data that make sense, because it can be understood correctly. People turn data into information by organizing it into some unit of analysis, for example, dollars, dates, or customers. Information is data endowed with relevance and purpose: "*in 2005, we completed 3 projects*" is something we can understand because the data have been given context and meaning. "*This is the third case in 2005*" is a different context that gives a different meaning to the data 2005, 3. The context is needed for the data to become information.

Knowledge is information combined with experience, context, interpretation, and reflection. Knowledge is a renewable resource that can be used over and over, and that accumulates in an organization through use and combination with employees' experience. Humans have knowledge; knowledge cannot exist outside the heads of individuals. Information becomes knowledge when it enters the human brain, provided the brain does the required processing. This knowledge transforms into information again when it is articulated and communicated to others. Information is an explicit representation of knowledge; it is in itself not knowledge. Knowledge is subjective: it can be both truths and lies, perspectives and concepts, judgments and expectations. Knowledge is used to receive information by analyzing, understanding, and evaluating; by combining, prioritizing, and decision making; and by planning, implementing, and controlling. The observation that *3 projects is a lot to complete in a single year* requires experience with projects to draw that conclusion. That makes it knowledge in the sense in which information science uses the term.

Differentiating information technology functionalities

Information technology comes in many forms. IT, in this study, includes *all technology capable of storing, exchanging or providing information*. This section presents a categorization of IT functionalities. This categorization helps to understand what different IT functionalities do, as well as what is involved in implementing them. It is based on the discussion in McAfee (p. 144-145). The purpose of this presentation is, in general terms, to outline:

- What the IT functionalities can do
- What their capabilities are
- The benefits they can deliver
- The organizational changes they trigger.

Understanding the functionalities, what they can do and what improvements they can bring is required for translating information needs in an organization into technological solutions. This is what Parts 3, 4 and 5 of this study will do for internal case processing, communicating with users and safeguarding the integrity of courts. The organizational changes that may be required are better-skilled workers, higher levels of teamwork, redesigning processes, and new decision rights, according to McAfee. Understanding, and subsequently making, the organizational changes the IT functionalities trigger is necessary to make implementing technologies a success. The changes triggered and required are discussed in Parts 2 and 6. The categorization will first be used in the overview of court IT in Chapter 2.1. This overview also provides illustrations of what courts do with different IT functionalities.

Function IT

This group includes technologies that assist with the execution of discrete tasks and can make the execution of stand-alone tasks more efficient. The most common examples are word processing and spreadsheets. They increase precision and enhance experimentation capacity. In text production, correction is much easier than before. Pieces of text can be reused. Spreadsheets keep data, which increases the accuracy of record keeping. Keeping electronic records facilitates not only precision, but also experimentation. These functionalities require almost no organizational innovations or changes in the way companies get work done. They do not require a network to function.

Network IT

The network group includes IT that provides a means by which people can communicate with one another. It includes e-mail, instant messaging, blogs, network technologies, wikis, and intranet web sites. These facilitate collaboration, allow expressions of judgment and foster emergence. They bring complements with them, but allow users to modify them over time. Network technologies facilitate interactions between users, but without specifying their parameters. They allow people to interact, but do not define how they should interact. This means they allow users to implement and adapt them. And it means that people can communicate and experiment with ways of communication that suit them.

Enterprise IT

The technologies in this group include work flow management systems, customer relations management systems and electronic interaction with customers. The ideal type for this group is an entirely electronic management process: customers interact electronically, their input is managed in electronic files by electronic work flow systems, both individually and according to load, outputs are sent to the customer electronically and filed in an electronic archive. In this ideal type, the management process has gone completely paperless. These functionalities restructure interactions among groups of employees or with business partners. They depend, from the outset, on new interdependencies, processes and decision rights, because they cannot work without them. This means their implementation is very much top-down. For these functionalities, business processes need to be specified in advance. The capabilities of the technologies in this group are: redesigning business processes and standardizing work flows, monitoring activities and events efficiently. This means that processes, after having been standardized for electronic work flow management, can be redesigned and standardized much more easily. Reports on events and activities are, because the entire process is electronic, much more readily available.

Concluding Part 1

This first part of the study has presented a variety of information in order to facilitate understanding the study. The central question in the study is how IT functionalities can support judicial reform: improving and innovating processes in order to realize the values in the international human rights conventions to a greater extent. The topic is very complex. It involves studying information and information technology, courts and court processes. It will draw on a large variety of source materials: comparative material, case studies, socio-legal analysis and legal texts.

The study will first inventory the IT that is available in most courts in Western Europe and the United States Next, it will explore the most frequent problems encountered in implementing IT (Part 2). Then, it will focus on three major problems courts and judiciaries face. Each problem is examined in a separate part. Each part will explore a specific issue in order to identify, for each issue, the role of information and how information technology can impact it. Part 3 examines internal processes from the starting point of case delay. Part 4 studies external interaction from the starting point of access to justice. Part 5 analyzes safeguarding integrity from the starting point of corruption. Part 6 is the final part of this study. It will sum up the findings of the study with regard to how information technology can support improving the delay, access and integrity of courts and judiciaries. The study closes by indicating some topics for further research.

Notes

1 Adopted by General Assembly Resolution 217 A (III) of 10 December 1948.
2 2000/C 364/01, signed and proclaimed by the Presidents of the European Parliament, the Council and the Commission at the European Council meeting in Nice on December 7, 2000.
3 Council of Europe Resolution Res(2002)12, Statute of the European Commission for the Efficiency of Justice (CEPEJ).

Part 2 Information Technology in Courts

This part of the study starts with a discussion of information technology in courts. Before exploring judicial reform, it is useful to have a sense of what we know about IT in courts.

This discussion comes in two chapters. The first chapter will provide an overview of the information technology courts actually use. It will look at the different functionalities courts use. The question to answer is: What IT functionalities have been implemented in the courts, and for what purposes are they used? The purpose of Chapter 2.1 is largely descriptive. It serves to identify the functionalities of court IT before we can start to discuss how those functionalities can support reforming judiciaries.

The second chapter examines a question that is, in my experience, frequently discussed in judiciaries and courts themselves: why is implementing IT so difficult? In order to find answers to that question, Chapter 2.2 analyzes what is involved in developing and implementing IT for courts and judiciaries. To that end, it will produce an overview of the most prevalent difficulties organizations in general face with IT. The risks those difficulties imply are then translated for judiciaries and courts.

Chapter 2.1 Court IT

In an early example of the use of information technology in the courtroom, the war crimes tribunals after World War II made use of film material and simultaneous translation (Radlmaier p. 67). In 1961, the court trying WWII war criminal Adolf Eichmann used simultaneous interpretation, photocopies and super8-films. Today, many different kinds of IT are used by the United Nations International Criminal Tribunals and the International Criminal Court: video and audio recording of the court sessions, simultaneous interpretation, electronic court reporting, videoconferencing for witness hearings, and electronic files. Moreover, the tribunals maintain web sites with their decisions, background information, and sounds and images from the courtroom.

What IT do the courts use?

This chapter is an inventory of information technology in courts.

It will list what IT has been implemented in the courts, and for what purposes it is used. IT for courts can be distinguished into technology for:

- The courtroom, supporting what happens in the courtroom itself
- The back office, supporting the processes that are related to case administration, document production and court management
- External communication, supporting all communication with parties and the general public outside the courts.

Finding out what technology is in use is not easy. It raises some quite complex questions: what the functionality actually accomplishes and how to establish that, what the various levels of implementation are, and how to ensure accurate comparison. The answers to those questions are hard to find. One reason is in the sources: information on computer use in courts - in Europe, the United States and some other parts of the world - is not very accessible. The sources that are available all have a different approach and they use different categorizations. That makes comparison and consolidation of results difficult. Moreover, the functionality of the information technologies surveyed is not always clear. This means, for instance, that we cannot be sure what the case management systems in the different countries actually do. These problems will be addressed on a case-by-case basis.

In this discussion, I mainly use three sources:

- CEPEJ 2008: In its collection of data about courts in the member countries of the Council of Europe, CEPEJ has included questions about information technology in the courts in its 2006 and 2008 surveys (CEPEJ 2006b, 2008). Reflecting court practice in most European countries as a paper-document-based process, CEPEJ covers back office and some communication technology. It has not included questions about the use of technology in the courtroom itself in the survey. There is a special problem with the CEPEJ data. The consolidated table on page 82 of the report and the full table on page 266 of the report do not tally. CEPEJ confirmed there are problems with the data in the full table.[1] Therefore, the data presented in this chapter come from the consolidated table on page 82 of the report. More detailed judgments on IT implementation than the consolidated table allows can, therefore, be hazardous.
- FJC 2003: The U.S. Federal Judicial Center surveyed the level of implementation of courtroom technologies. The survey did not cover back office technology. This survey, done in 2003, covered the federal district courts in the United States.

- FJC 2007: The U.S. Federal Judicial Center produced another interesting source of information on the level of implementation: a U.S. federal judges' round table on court technology in February 2007 (report, FJC 2007). The round table, convened by the federal judicial conference's IT committee, discussed a number of technology-related issues that may give us some clues about the level of implementation in U.S. courts.[2] The discussion was preceded by a survey of technology users.

My assumption at the outset of this discussion is that U.S. courts are ahead of the courts in Europe in their implementation of IT because they started implementing IT earlier than other judiciaries. In the analysis, we will be looking for commonalities as well as differences.

Approaches and categorization

Categorizing IT should facilitate answering the questions outlined above, regarding what the functionalities actually do and what the comparative levels of implementation are. The three sources each have very different approaches.

The CEPEJ survey categorizes IT functionalities by the *purpose* of the functionality:

- Direct support for judges and court staff
- Support for court management
- Support for interaction between courts and parties.

A similar categorization that looks to the purpose for which the functionality is used, rather than the functionality itself, was used in the first Netherlands judiciary policy plan (ARIZ 2000 p. 17, 19). Its categories are functionality for:

- Managing primary processes: individual cases, case load, and court calendaring,
- Managing secondary processes such as the management of buildings, reporting and budgeting.

The FJC 2003 survey of courtroom technologies did not use any kind of grouping related to purpose. The categories used in the FJC 2007 round table survey were calendaring, case management, courtroom technologies, writing and tracking opinions, and working remotely.

This chapter discusses implementing IT in courts in chronological order. Thus, it follows both the development of functionality and the history of the introduction of IT functionalities in courts as they became available.

First, it examines stand-alone functionality. This is technology that works on a computer that is not connected to a network. Next, it looks at network and communication enabling technology. Finally, it studies enterprise technology and technology enabling interaction with external partners.

Stand-alone, function information technologies

The function information technologies came first. They assist with the execution of discrete tasks and can make the execution of stand-alone tasks more efficient (McAfee p. 144). They do not require a network to function. The two major ones are word processing and database technology.

Word processing

Office automation is the most widespread form of information technology generally. It is also the most prevalent functionality used in the courts. It includes mostly word processing, but also some calendaring, and simple spreadsheets bundled in an office automation package. Word processing to produce paper documents is the most prevalent form of IT in courts (Table 2). All courts in Council of Europe member countries have word processing for most of their staff. FJC 2007 users report they are very satisfied with their word processing technology for its ease of use and suitability for the task.[3]

Databases

The functionality underlying automated registers is database technology. It is used in courts for registration and management of cases. *Case registration* systems replace the functionality of traditional court dockets. On top of the case registration systems, *court and case management* systems have additional functionality. They can provide non-judicial and judicial case management support for case tracking, case planning and document management. They can also generate information on the performance of courts. The purpose of case management systems is to ensure cases are disposed properly and promptly. Finally, there are systems supporting the financial management of the courts (CEPEJ 2008 p. 82).

Table 2 *Function Information Technology in Courts in Europe*

Facility	*100 % of courts*	*< 50 % of courts*	*< 50 % of courts*	*< 10 % of courts*	*Total no. of responses*
Word processing	42	4	0	0	46
Case registration	26	10	5	3	44
Court/case management	20	12	4	6	42
Financial management	26	8	2	6	42

Source: CEPEJ 2008 p. 86.

Table 2 shows the results of the 2008 CEPEJ survey with regard to functional IT. In the CEPEJ survey, the maximum possible number of respondent member countries is 46. In almost all member countries, all courts have word processing facilities. In a little over half of the CEPEJ countries, all courts have court case registration systems. Case registration systems have penetrated in fewer courts than word processing. Financial information systems have been implemented in about as many courts as the registration systems. Court/case management information systems have been implemented in less than half the courts.

Courtroom technologies

In common law court systems, in both civil and criminal justice, cases are ultimately decided by trial if they are not settled in an earlier phase. Very few cases actually come to trial, and trial rates vary widely across countries. Some of those trials are conducted in front of a jury.

In those trials, the principle of immediacy of evidence is very important. This means the evidence itself needs to be presented in the courtroom: witnesses making a statement, exhibits like original documents and objects. This has given rise to implementation of information technology to support conducting trials. The FJC 2003 survey results show that in 2003, a large percentage of U.S. federal district courts have access to such technology, either via a permanent installation in one or more courtrooms or equipment that is shared among courtrooms (FJC 2003). The equipment includes sound amplification; an evidence camera; monitors on the bench, the witness stands, the counsel table, outside the jury box or built into it; and monitors targeted at the audience. It also includes an interpreting system, audio and video conferencing equipment and equipment to support production of a transcript of the proceedings. These functionalities are stand-alone technology; they do not require a network to function.

Evidence cameras are used to present exhibits such as documents, photographs or objects. Another way of presenting such exhibits is through their image on a laptop computer connected to the display equipment. Monitors and digital projectors and screens are used to display the exhibits. The kill switch is a tool for the judge to control what jurors are allowed to see in accordance with evidence rules. Annotation equipment facilitates marking up images in order to point out what is significant in the display. A color video printer prints out such images for the record. Most federal district courts have an orientation program to familiarize court staff and attorneys with equipment and how it can be used. About a third of the courts have one or more full-time employees to deal with courtroom technology (FJC 2003). One user in the FJC

Table 3 *Courtroom Technology in U.S. Federal District Courts (2003)*

Functionality	*Equipment*	*Percentage of courts answering survey that confirm access to technologies*
Sound amplification	Sound reinforcement system	95
Evidence presentation	Evidence camera	94
	Wiring to connect laptop computers	93
	Kill switch and control system	92
	Monitors at the bench	89
	Monitors at the witness stand	88
	Monitors at counsel table or lectern	88
	Integrated lectern	81
	Monitors outside the jury box	77
	Monitors built into the jury box	57
	Monitors or screens targeted at the audience	77
	Digital projector and projection screen	66
Annotation	Annotation equipment	91
	Color video printer	80
Interpretation	Telephone or infrared interpreting (translation) system	92
Transcript production	Real-time software for use by court reporter	81
	Real-time transcript annotation viewer	74
Recording	Digital audio recording	66

Source: Federal Judicial Center Survey on Courtroom Technology 2003 (FJC 2003 p. 2).

2007 survey remarks: "Our equipment is old & unreliable. Monitors are on their last legs in the jury box. They take up a lot of space & are not that great for viewing written text in exhibits. The courtroom is a total mess, with wires running everywhere." The users in the FJC 2007 survey are, on the whole, satisfied with the ease of use and suitability of the courtroom technologies, provided there is help from technology staff.

Capabilities of stand-alone functional technologies

The general capabilities of these stand-alone, functional technologies are to increase precision and enhance experimentation capacity (McAfee p. 144). This, it should be kept in mind, is what they **can** do. They do not automatically produce these results without involvement and effort by the users.

Displaying actual evidence and exhibits increases precision in the courtroom. Keeping data that record events supports experimentation. For example: this study uses a lot of statistics to examine court processes, particularly in Part 3 on case delay. Those statistics are available because cases are registered using database technology. We now know so much about our processes because databases keep the data for us and make them available in ways we can use. We can study them and see where bottlenecks in case processing are. We can evaluate whether experiments to improve case processing are producing the desired results. Databases can produce correlations that we could never find otherwise. Justice G.C. Bharuka, who headed the India judiciary's IT committee, told me how he first tracked case delay in Bangalore by using a self-constructed database.[4] For the policy research needed to develop routines, databases to compare and analyze court decisions and statistics are an indispensable tool. They can be used for sentencing support and automated decisions in very simple cases.

When word processing began to be introduced, it was implemented primarily as a tool for support staff. Professionals like lawyers and judges would at first dictate to a typist, just as they had done in the age of the typewriter. Nowadays, professionals largely write their own documents. The databases for the case and court management systems, too, mostly copied the paper based registration process. They are still mostly used by support staff only.

For successful implementation, functional information technologies do not require major changes toward better-skilled workers, higher levels of teamwork, redesigned processes and new decision rights (McAfee p. 141). They do not need networks or electronic communication to do their jobs. In summary, because they do not require much organizational change, they are easy to implement, at least compared with the network and enterprise technologies discussed in the next two sections.

Network information technologies

Historically, network technology was introduced after stand-alone functional technologies had been in use for some time. Network technologies facilitate interactions between users, but without specifying their parameters. They allow people to interact, but do not define how they should interact. This means users can modify how they use them they allow users to implement and modify them over time. People can communicate and experiment with ways of communication that suit them.

Network technologies provide a means by which people can communicate with one another. In this group, I have included:
- Email
- Internet connections
- Jurisprudence databases
- Sharing documents
- Electronic files

- Groupware
- Audio and video conferencing.

Table 4 *Network Information Technologies in Courts in Europe (2008)*

Facility	*100 % of courts*	*< 50 % of courts*	*< 50 % of courts*	*< 10 % of courts*	*Total no. of responses*
Email	33	9	2	1	45
Internet connections	33	6	6	1	45
Electronic files	18	12	4	7	41
Electronic database of jurisprudence	33	7	2	1	43

Source: CEPEJ 2008 p. 86.

Email

As almost everywhere else, the killer application of networking IT in courts was email (Frissen p. 7). Email's great advantage, over more traditional communication means like the telephone, is asynchronous communication. The recipient and the sender do not need to communicate at the same moment in time, as is needed with the telephone. Email is used on a large scale in justice networks for informal communication. However, email is not used on a large scale in official communication with court users yet. According to Velicogna, this is due to requirements for official communications. For instance, legislation in Belgium, France, Greece and Italy would require both certified email and digital signature for official communications. Velicogna maintains that the absence of these technologies explains why email is not used for official communication (Velicogna 2007 p. 136). Although I agree that having those technologies in place is a condition, I do not think that is the only reason. The technologies themselves are available. However, implementing the technology also requires changes in the business processes that have apparently simply not been developed yet. I will come back to this point later in this chapter.

Jurisprudence databases

Electronic databases of jurisprudence are available in a large majority of CEPEJ countries. However, we do not know which type CEPEJ actually measured. Jurisprudence databases deserve some special attention because the functionality and capabilities behind them can be very diverse. Therefore, we need a conceptual clarification. Nowadays, jurisprudence databases can be accessed online. But there were early versions in the stand-alone functionality group. Here is a list of the chronology:

As stand-alone functionality, the first jurisprudence databases were installed in court libraries. They could be consulted on media like diskettes or CDs, or over a telephone line. They most resembled a searchable copy of the paper version of the jurisprudence collection.

As a repository of interesting or innovative decisions, they can be put into the group of network technology, discussed below. People can supply decisions on an ad hoc basis. Not every decision goes into the repository. Some infrastructure is needed, for example a framework on who decides what goes in. But that does not need to be any different from the processes that went into producing the paper version.

As a collection of all decisions in an electronic archive, it is enterprise technology. All decisions need to go in. There is a process in place that ensures they do. This type of decision database belongs in the enterprise technology group discussed below.

These are actually ideal types. The second category is very much like an electronic version of the first one.

Jurisprudence databases have had a major impact on the position of courts in the public arena from the moment they became publicly available on the Internet. For instance, reporting in the public press on court decisions has become more accurate. The databases have also enhanced the transparency of the decisions that have become available since decisions that need to go public require greater clarity. Finally, the public jurisprudence databases have strengthened the courts' role as the guardian of norms, its "shadow function."[5]

Internet connections

Where court staff and judges have access to the Internet, they use the connection mostly for email and to access information. The connection facilitates access to sources of legal research such as laws, court decisions or jurisprudence.

Electronic files

From the CEPEJ results, it looks as if electronic files have become a regular feature in a majority of courts. However, it is unclear what is meant by electronic files. If we understand an electronic file to be an electronic case file for an individual case, there are several possibilities. First, it can be a collection of documents, filed as paper and scanned in court. In this case, no electronic filing is necessary. Then, the file can be a collection of both paper documents that were scanned in court after they came in and documents that were filed electronically. Second, it can be a collection of electronically filed documents. This would require electronic filing of documents, and thereby electronic two-way external communication. The difference is such a major step in the development of business processes that electronic files of this type are not included in the networking technology group, but in the group for enterprise technology discussed below.

Other networking/communication technologies

CEPEJ 2008 has not measured the use of intranets, group sharing of documents or distance participation technology - audio and video conferencing. Strictly speaking, audio and video conferencing do not need the use of a computer network. They can both be conducted over a telephone line. But because they are so clearly communication technology, I have included them in the networking group. FJC 2003 surveyed them both. Both audio and video conferencing were common technologies in federal district courts in the United States in 2003. 93% of surveyed courts replied they had audio conferencing equipment, and 85% had video equipment. They are mostly of the moveable type. In the 2007 survey, quite a few users report technical difficulties with videoconferencing equipment.

Networking to combine databases and word processing: Standard decisions models

Although word processing and database technology do not require a network to function, their combined use over the court network gave rise to a major innovation. Office automation, merging data from the case registration system with text in the word processor has become a very common process for producing bulk decisions in small claims and debt recovery cases. It is used in many courts where the technologies were implemented. The Dutch courts use a system called JustWord that supports use of standard texts and smart merges by using Visual Basic programming. This system was developed first by users in the courts at the end of the 1990s when networks with central databases were starting to be implemented. It was re-developed when the courts were given a different word processing system, and rolled out to all the courts.

Capabilities of network technologies

The capabilities of network information technologies are:

- Facilitating collaboration
- Allowing expressions of judgment
- Fostering emergence (patterns).

Again, whether the capabilities are realized depends on the users. There is an interesting emerging process in collaboration in Dutch courts. Where judges work in panels, or where their support staff draft decisions, review of those documents is beginning to be done increasingly over the network, in the electronic document on the court network drive. Presentations at the FJC round table reported on already more developed forms of collaboration in case management and writing court decisions (FJC 2007, presentation handouts, my notes from the meeting).

With regard to implementation of network technology, some observations can be made on requirements. Users are free to experiment with ways to use the technology, as can be seen in the examples of JustWord and the document sharing. Some standards, such as a code of conduct for Internet and email use for the users and standardization of email addresses, are needed. Some of the standardization is external, but some, like the code of conduct, need to be developed inside the justice system. On the whole, network technologies do not restrict the users' freedom as much as the enterprise information technologies discussed in the next section. However, the network itself needs to be managed and maintained with standards for email addresses and for making information accessible.

Enterprise information technologies and external communication

The technologies in this group include work flow management systems, customer relations management systems and external electronic interaction with customers. This group does not include any courtroom technologies.

The ideal type for this group is an entirely electronic management process: cases are filed electronically, they are managed as electronic files by electronic work flow systems, both individually and according to load, outputs are filed in an electronic archive. In this ideal type, it is the management process that has gone completely paperless. The process of adjudication can still consist of physical court hearings.

The capabilities of the technologies in this group are: redesigning business processes and standardizing work flows, monitoring activities and events efficiently. This means that processes can be redesigned and standardized much more easily, and that reports on events and activities are much more readily available.

In order for these functionalities to work, business processes need to be specified in advance (McAfee p. 145). This means their implementation is very much top-down. They prescribe new interdependencies, processes, and decision rights. They restructure interactions among groups of employees or with business partners. In other words: from the outset, they depend on those new interdependencies, processes and decision rights, because they cannot work without them.

Workflow and case management systems

Case management includes management of single cases as well as managing case flow and managing courts. It includes managing time standards and case load, as well as analysis of court workload trends to improve planning and monitoring strategic actions (Velicogna 2007 p. 134-135). The system supporting these activities uses case data from the case administration as well as information about work processes for case processing. The more sophisticated the system, the more it requires standardizing. For instance, for planning and monitoring purposes, data need to be the same and to steer work processes, those processes need to be standardized as well. The federal district courts in the United States have a case management/electronic filing system called CM/EFS. In FJC 2007, judges in federal district courts remark how CM/EFS does not support the functionality they need. For instance, calendaring is supported for the district judges, but the magistrate judges have different case flows that cannot be calendared using CM/EFS.

The case management systems reported to CEPEJ and listed above in the functional technology category may qualify for inclusion in this group. There is not enough information in the report to determine what level of sophistication the case management systems have reached.

Interaction with external partners

Courts' external communication occurs with very different counterparts:

- With non-users and users
- With lawyers and other regular professional court users
- With non-professional court users.

Another way of looking at external communication is to look at the level of the interaction. The approach below follows the four-stage model for benchmarking e-government projects in the European Union (EU Benchmarking p. 16):

Stage 1: Information online about public services
Stage 2: Communication/interaction: downloading of forms
Stage 3: Communication/two-way interaction: processing of forms (including authentication)
Stage 4: Transaction: case handling, decision and delivery (payment).

Table 5 *Enterprise Information Technology in Courts in Europe (2008)*

Facility	*100 % of courts*	*< 50 % of courts*	*< 50 % of courts*	*< 10 % of courts*	*Total no. of responses*
Electronic web forms	11	3	5	20	39
Special web site	14	7	9	11	41
Other electronic communication facilities	15	3	6	11	34

Source: CEPEJ 2008 p. 86

Based on the CEPEJ data on electronic web forms, it appears that quite a few European courts have reached the European Union's stage

2. It is difficult to ascertain from the CEPEJ data whether any court systems have developed beyond stage 2. There is no information on what the special web sites can do. And we do not know what the other electronic communication facilities provide by way of functionality, or how any of them rate in the European Union benchmarking stages.

Conclusions for chapter 2.1

This chapter provided an overview of IT implemented in courts. From the above, some lines can be drawn regarding implementation levels and factors influencing those levels.

Across Europe, information technology implementation levels vary widely. It appears that so far, most courts have largely used IT to assist their paper based processes. They have not used technology to radically improve their processes.

With the CEPEJ results, we should be able to compare the member countries to learn about IT implementation levels in courts. CEPEJ 2008 has graded countries on their IT implementation. It has categorized them according to the implementation levels: very high, high, moderate and low levels of implementation. It accorded 44 points to systems having implemented all 11 types of functionality in 100 percent of all courts. A system with those functionalities in less than 10 percent of its courts scores only 11 points. Taking into account the problem with the full table on p. 269 mentioned earlier, there are still some observations to be made.[6]

Finland, Austria and the United Kingdom, but also Estonia, Slovakia and Hungary, are in the very high implementation group because they score more than 39 points (CEPEJ 2008 p. 87). High levels of implementation can be found in France, Germany, Sweden, Latvia, Bulgaria and the Netherlands. Belgium, Ireland and Croatia are in the moderate level group. In the low level group we find Cyprus, Ukraine and Russia. That is, if we assume this ranking was based on correct and accurate data.

In the very high level group, direct support for judges and support staff are fully functional, and countries in this group are ahead of the other groups with digital access and communication. They use web forms, special web sites and other forms of electronic communication more than the others. This is a general conclusion that the table on p. 269 allows. Austria has developed the Elektronischer Rechtsverkehr (ERV) or Electronic Legal Communication, a system that is updated periodically with new technical capabilities (Fabri 2003 p. 112-116). This system was initially developed for communication between lawyers and the courts, but it has gradually been opened up for other user groups. In England and Wales, a special court was set up to process small money claims for large claimants such as energy companies and banks. This procedure is now accessible to everyone living in England and Wales. It is used frequently by small businesses and the self-employed (Fabri 2003 p. 176). The functionality of this court, Money Claim On Line (MCOL), was extended to another simple procedure, that of repossession: Possession Claim On Line (PCOL). There is a more detailed discussion of MCOL in Part 3.

Implementation of functional technologies has been managed by most courts. Networking technologies seem to have been implemented in a fair number of courts systems. Different factors influence those levels.

One factor is early implementation. Early starters, such as the United Kingdom and the United States, have progressed further than later starters, like some countries in Western Europe. This, however, should be nuanced for the really late starters, for example in Central and Eastern Europe. Velicogna observed how countries newly adapting to automation moved very quickly because of reform pressures from the European Union and available funding and assistance (Velicogna CEPEJ p. 48). Another factor seems to be the approach that is chosen. Velicogna observes how in European courts, the more successful approaches to electronic administration of justice have been to choose simple procedures and to simplify more complex ones. Developing full online proceedings, where effort is centered on translating all the complexity of the paper based procedures into the electronic ones, has been characterized by never-ending piloting and mounting costs (Velicogna CEPEJ p. 48). There is a world of IT development experience behind these observations. That world is examined in the next chapter.

Chapter 2.2 Lessons on Developing and Implementing IT

This chapter looks at court IT from a different perspective than the previous chapter. Chapter 2.1 served as an inventory, listing what IT courts use for their business. The chapter you are reading now was inspired by reactions from judicial colleagues on early drafts of this study. The main concern they expressed was why getting the IT working in the courts is so difficult. Therefore, this study on IT for courts would be incomplete if it did not address that concern. Thus, this chapter examines what is needed to get IT into the courts. Conceivably, this is a question to be asked not before, but after deciding that IT will be implemented for specific areas of judicial reform. To a certain extent, that is right. This chapter would also have been well placed after Parts 3, 4 and 5. However, whether this chapter should come before or after the ones on judicial reform is something of a chicken-and-egg discussion.

In Part 2, dedicated to court IT, it serves two purposes at once: concentrating on IT in Part 2 means it does not distract from the topics in the parts on judicial reform. More importantly, studying implementation problems provides a clear argument for the relevance of the discussions in Parts 3, 4 and 5.

Before those major problems in judiciaries are addressed in the next parts, this chapter examines what is required if judiciaries want to develop and implement IT. In order to answer this question, it analyzes experience with IT development in courts and other organizations. It first studies two well documented IT projects for courts and justice institutions. It then analyzes experience with IT policy development in other organizations. From the findings, it extrapolates requirements for IT policy development in judiciaries.

IT development – learning from experience

IT projects are often unsatisfactory. In many organizations, and not just in courts and judiciaries, IT projects do not produce the results envisaged, on time, and within budget. These examples illustrate the point:

- More than 50 percent of all IT projects fail in some part, and between 4 and 15 percent fail completely, according to a report for the Dutch Parliament by the General Accounting Chamber (Rekenkamer A p. 9).
- Court IT projects in France and Italy are mired in difficulty, reports on IT developments in courts show (Velicogna CEPEJ 2007 p. 48).
- World Bank IT projects received a lower quality rating than World Bank projects overall, reports a World Bank quality study (World Bank 2006b p. 6).

Courts and judiciaries, in order to be successful in their adoption of IT to improve the quality of justice, may benefit by learning from experience. The need to learn is evident: either IT development activities are new to judiciaries, or the functionalities are new. It is in the nature of the activity of developing new IT for courts that what needs to be done has mostly not been done before.

They can learn from their own experience as well as that of others. Learning from others' experience can be done by observing successes and by studying failures. Others' successes may point the way, but their environments may not be similar. Learning from failures helps to avoid pitfalls, but it does not necessarily make clear how to do things right. Thus, the findings in this chapter will not provide hard and fast recipes for successful IT development and implementation.

This chapter studies documented IT experience.

First, there are descriptions of two IT projects in the justice sector. The projects are fairly representative of the approach to justice IT projects in the recent past. The descriptions highlight some of the problems the projects encountered. Next, there is an inventory of findings on IT development failures in a variety of non-judicial organizations. Both the inventory and the project experience are analyzed to draw some conclusions on the requirements of judiciaries wanting to use IT.

Two projects

This section examines two justice IT projects: the HBS project in the Netherlands and the Ontario Integrated Justice Project in Canada. Both projects were stopped before completion. These projects are relevant for four factors they have in common:

- They attracted a lot of attention.
- They illustrate a variety of learning points.
- They were audited by a third party, so there is an authoritative source for what happened. The audit reports are an important source of information for this section:
  - The external audit report of the Hoger Beroep Systeem Strafrecht (Criminal Justice Appeal System)) project submitted by the Netherlands Minister of Justice to the Second Chamber of Parliament in 2001 (Brouwer).
  - The audits, by the Ontario Auditor's office, of the Ontario Integrated Justice Project. These audits were conducted in 2001 and 2003 (Ontario 2001, 2003).
- They are no longer active projects, so their outcomes are known. There are many very interesting judicial IT projects in progress right now. Any of them would have been interesting for this study. However, they are difficult to judge because they are still in mid-course and their outcomes are not yet clear. Therefore, I chose to look at these two projects, which both closed some years ago.

The HBS project in the Netherlands is interesting because its level of technological ambition was high; it was the first court IT project in the Netherlands intended to implement work flow management and it severely tested the governance structure that was in place at the time. It is also interesting because it was stopped after it failed to deliver.[7] The Ontario Integrated Justice project is interesting because it is – to my knowledge – the single largest justice IT project ever attempted. It attracted a lot of attention because of the level of its ambition and scale. It subsequently attracted attention because it failed.

Project 1: HBS (Criminal Justice Appeal System)

The Hoger Beroep Systeem Strafrecht project intended to create the first electronic work flow management system for Dutch courts. Its goal was to develop a case registration and management system for the integrated case administrations of the appeal courts and the appeals prosecutors. It intended to develop a system that combined work flow management with the case registration database. It required designing a single business process over both the prosecution and the courts. Previously, each of the five prosecution offices and the five court administrations had their own paper-based administration. The timeline in Box 2 shows how the project's management was replaced several times. The project's governance structure was changed in mid-course. When the system as delivered turned out to have irreparable flaws, the project was stopped.

Box 2 HBS Project [8]

HBS project

Start: December 1996

Aim: To create one common information system for the case administrations of the offices of the appeals prosecutors and the appeal courts in the Netherlands.

Principal and budget holder was the Ministry of Justice. In 1999, the role of principal was instituted materially in a project steering committee, made up of three members from the prosecution, the appeal courts and the ministry.

Time line:

1997 – Q1 1998:	Feasibility study
April-October 1998:	Functional design, freeze because of doubts about the wide range of functional requirements
Projected delivery:	End of 1998
April 1999:	Second phase, with higher budget and new project management
2000:	Detailed design and actual building phase.
August 2000:	Detailed design completed
December 2000:	Technical delivery of the system
2001:	Testing and preparation of implementation started. Testing immediately uncovered problems, some of them extremely serious. The project management was replaced again. The problems turned out to be irreparable

October 2001:	Project was stopped
Total spending:	€ 12,7 mln or US$ 11.3 mln (estimated cost *f* 6 mln (€ 2.72 mln, or US$ 2.42 mln)

Source: Brouwer, and letters of the Minister of Justice to Parliament, October 2001, February 2002.

After it was stopped in 2001, the project was audited at the request of the Ministry of Justice. The external audit of the project examined risk management, project governance and control, responsibilities and leadership, and the main causes of the project's failure. It found (Brouwer p. 6):

- Expectations and points of departure were too ambitious in relation to the experience of the organizations involved.
- The feasibility study had already concluded the project was very risky. The risks had been identified adequately. Subsequently, the risks were not reduced and managed sufficiently.
- For the full duration of the project, the importance of change in the organizations and of integrating the user organization into the project were underestimated. As a result, the project did not achieve successful acceptance of the delivered system.
- Competences and responsibilities of those involved were not arranged properly for steering and controlling the project adequately.
- The chosen development methodology was not applied adequately during 1999 and 2000.

The Ministry of Justice acted as the principal for the project. Involvement of both the appeal courts and the prosecution made it politically complex. This meant the project was, in effect, run by three separate stakeholders, each with their own needs. The change in project governance in mid-course had to do with this political complexity because, as the audit phrased it, the responsibilities of those involved were not arranged properly for steering and controlling the project adequately. This phrase refers to the circumstance that the user committee, or at least the court representatives, had no clear mandate or strategy. They also could not refer back to an authority for guidance, since the appeal courts presidents did not have a strategy with regard to their IT.

The combination of functionalities envisaged, the case registration database with electronic work flow, had not been tried before. Therefore, the project was technologically ambitious. I recall being called upon to mediate when a problem arose after the national prosecution service and the judiciary had each chosen different products for their work flow functionality. It is an eloquent illustration of the kind of complexity integrated systems can face. The prosecution had chosen a system that encoded fully developed work processes for maximum control on integrity of information management. The judiciary, on the other hand, had chosen a system that would support developing different work flows and support experimentation. If we recall the typology of functionalities from Chapter 2.1, the judiciary chose a system that requires few complements and allows a large measure of freedom, and the prosecution chose a top-down system requiring full complements in terms of decision rights and centralized process control. This example shows how organizations can have different, and even opposing, needs. This circumstance added to the complexity.

The experience of the organizations involved with IT was extremely limited. The appeal courts, at the time, had no automated case registration system, and therefore no experience with anything beyond a paper docket. For the criminal divisions of the appeal courts and the appeal prosecution offices, this was going to be their first case registration system. They had no experience with IT, apart from word processing. The appeal courts and prosecution offices did not have experience with IT projects either, let alone projects of this complexity.

Project 2: The Ontario Integrated Justice Project

The Ontario Integrated Justice Project was regarded as a model project when it started in 1996. It was regularly presented at international IT conferences like the Court Technology Conferences of the National Center for State Courts in the United States. It was presented at the 2002 Technology for Justice Conference in Sydney, Australia in October, the same week it was scrapped.[9] Derek Freeman, chair of the Ontario Bar Association Integrated Justice Committee, presented the project. His presentation[10] and the 2001 and 2003 external audits of the project (Ontario 2001 and 2003) are my sources for this overview of the project.

In Ontario, the project was regarded as ground-breaking: "This is not fine-tuning or changing a process here; it is foundational and huge," said Deputy Solicitor General Virginia West, in February 2002 (Freeman 2002 slide 5). The project ended because its work term expired on October 8, 2002 when the ministries and the consortium of vendors, after 20 months of negotiations, were unable to renew their agreement to continue the project. The components were subsequently assigned to each component's most related ministries (Ontario 2003 p. 287).

When the project ended, the status of the work was as follows (Ontario 2003 p. 285):

- Police: Computer-aided dispatch, electronic records management system and offender tracking information system were implemented, but not with full functionality.

- Crown (prosecution): Case management was not completed.
- Courts: E-filing, digital audio court recording, electronic case management and scheduling were not completed and were not expected to be completed as originally envisioned.
- A common query system and common information services management were not achieved.

Box 3 The Ontario Integrated Justice Project

Ontario Integrated Justice Project
Start: 1996

Aim:

- Solve the problem of not sharing information on criminal justice
- Streamline the civil justice system
- Improve services.

The scope was to integrate all services and systems: courtrooms and court offices, the private bar, the judiciary, police services, prosecution, corrections and parole, and ministries of justice.
Police: computer-aided dispatch, electronic records management system
Crown (prosecution): electronic brief exchange, case management
Courts: e-filing, digital audio court recording, electronic case management and scheduling
Corrections (prisons): institutions case management probation and parole case management
Common query system
Common information services management
Savings through disintermediation, new efficiencies and new fees through increase and usage. E-filing for a fee was seen as a big cash tap.
Principal: Office of the Solicitor-General of Ontario

Time line:

1996-1998:	Plan project and define requirements
1999-2002:	Development and design
2000- :	Phased implementation, completion planned by August 2002

August 2002:	New systems had to be completed by September 2002.
October 2002:	Software had not been customized, there were policy issues, testing and developing were still going on, and the organization design was still in progress.
October 2002:	Project stopped. Parties will go their separate ways.

Total spending: March 1998 cost estimate was CAN$ 180 mln (€ 127 mln), with expected benefits CAN$ 326 mln (€ 230 mln). By March 2001 the cost estimate had gone up to CAN$ 359 million (€ 253 mln). Expected benefits were down to CAN$ 238 million (€ 168mln).

Sources: Ontario 2001 and 2003 (audits), Freeman 2002.

The audits of the Ontario project have a strong financial focus, but there are some observations about other aspects of the project as well. The 2003 audit sums up some of the basic problems that were outlined in this chapter from other evaluations:

- The original business case had "an aggressive schedule that was based on a best-case scenario [and] did not adequately take into account the magnitude of change introduced by the project, the complexity of justice administration – particularly that of the courts – or the ability of vendors to deliver the project's computer systems in the required time frames" (Ontario 2003 p. 283). That means that risks were underestimated. The main risks were the scale of the change involved and a lack of understanding of the complexity of the organization. That is, there was no understanding of the need for alignment with the business of the organizations involved, particularly that of the courts, and of implementation and what that involved.
- The financial benefits were overstated. Originally, benefits were estimated at CAN$ 326 million (€ 230 million on January 1, 2002[11]). More than half of those benefits, CAN$ 172 million (€ 121 million), were foreseen in the court. The main benefit, apart from staff reductions, was to be in e-filing of courts cases for a fee. Electronic filing of cases was expected to attract more business. Fees charged for this improved service were intended to make up a considerable part of the benefits of the project. By 2002, estimated benefits had been reduced to CAN$ 238 million (€ 168 million). This was still

overstated by CAN$ 57 million (€ 40 million), according to the 2003 audit.

Whereas the benefits were overstated, the costs went up as underestimated risks and unforeseen complexity materialized. Originally, the cost was estimated at CAN$ 180 million (€ 127 million); by October 2002, CAN$ 265 million (€ 187 million) had been spent.

- The project was politically and organizationally complex because it included applications for information exchange between the different parts of the justice information chain. If we look at the specific position of the judiciary, the Ontario Courts' Annual Report for 1999 says: "The integrated justice project is intended to create programs to allow information and evidence to be received and transmitted electronically at the counter and in the court room. A necessary component of the program is a court scheduling and case management system for all civil, criminal and family matters. Integrated justice has benefitted from the tremendous time and effort of the judicial committee in identifying the needs and expectations of the judiciary. The judicial committee has not stated how these needs and expectations should be met, as *this is a matter for the attorney general to determine*" (italics mine) (Ontario 1999[12]). A small piece of evidence of the organizational complexity is the circumstance that the attorney general, the minister of justice, determines how the needs and expectations of the judicial committee shall be met. The judiciary does not have the means to prioritize. However, that same judiciary was expected to deliver more than half of the estimated benefits, in staff reductions and new fees for new services.

Comparing the two projects

Both the scope and the scale of the HBS project were much smaller than those of the Ontario project. Otherwise, some similarities emerge from the audits:

- Both projects were overly optimistic about what the project results would bring. They were too ambitious and the Ontario project started out overstating the financial benefits.
- They both underestimated risks. Ontario had "an aggressive schedule on a best-case scenario." HBS "did not manage the risks identified."
- They both also underestimated the amount of change needed in the organization, and the need for integrating the users into the project structure.
- Both were politically complex. In both cases, the minister of justice was holding the purse strings. The judges and prosecutors expressed needs, but they had no means to prioritize. Competences

and responsibilities were not arranged for steering and controlling the project.
- The most striking commonality is the underestimation of the complexity of the projects.

Did the respective organizations learn from their experience? The Ontario project was taken apart and divided into smaller units. Each organization went on to develop its own systems. The HBS project produced some lessons. The governance structure of the Netherlands judiciary was already in the process of being reformed. In 2002, the Council for the Judiciary of the Netherlands took over the administration of the lower courts from the Ministry of Justice. As part of that reform process, IT policy making was positioned in the Council itself, thus enabling policy and financial control for the judiciary. A firm policy agreement was made to set up projects in such a way that results could be delivered within a calendar year. A comprehensive IT architecture project was started and then aborted. A project to develop a new case registration system was started. The pilot for this project was done in the same instance as the development of HBS. The project still has not delivered results after five years. Evidently, on the one hand, some lessons were learned, but on the other, there are still other lessons to be absorbed.

In order to find the most common lessons to be learned, the next sections will look at IT experience in other organizations. The most frequent failure factors in developing and implementing IT will be identified. For each factor, there will be an analysis of its implications for judiciaries.

Sources of experience

This section presents an analysis of lessons for courts and judiciaries wanting to improve their performance with forms of IT. To that end, it examines the experience of what went wrong in developing and implementing IT in various non-judicial organizations. It translates that experience into messages about IT for courts and judiciaries.

By now, there is a large body of experience with IT projects. In order to gain a broad understanding of that experience, this study will draw on several sources presenting such experience in consolidated form. This choice was motivated by several considerations, outlined below.

The most obvious and straightforward way to learn from projects is to look at what actually happened in those projects first, and then draw some conclusions from the information gained. This, however, may well present some problems. Project documentation is needed to study what happened. It is not always available, either publicly or on request. Then, there is the question of the accuracy of the documentation. In my experience, project documentation often does not provide the information needed because it was written for other purposes. A second option for learning from projects is to study their evaluations. Not all projects are evaluated in order to draw lessons from them. There can be any number of reasons for not evaluating projects: political sensitivity, lack of evaluation budget, and poor planning. Both options, learning from observing projects and studying project evaluations in order to acquire a representative picture, are not very feasible when time is limited. Besides, the perspectives gained from either operation are bound to be fairly limited because they will cover only a few projects. For all these reasons, I have chosen sources that present consolidated experience from evaluations of large numbers of government and other IT projects:

- The World Bank Quality of Information and Communication Technology Components in Bank Projects, Quality Assurance Group Assessment, July 2006 (World Bank 2006b). This study assessed IT components in World Bank projects. Projects to be assessed were selected as follows. Out of 215 operations, about half of which contain some ICT components, projects were selected with ICT components meeting the following three characteristics: enabling the creation of enhancement of an information system; enabling policy, administrative or institutional reforms; and being a key success factor for one or more project outcomes. Of the 31 projects selected, the 24 projects with the highest ICT expenditures were actually assessed. This report is interesting because of its wide scope and world wide overview.
- A report in two parts of the Dutch Algemene Rekenkamer (General Accounting Chamber) on government IT projects (Rekenkamer A and B). This report is of particular interest because it discusses the specific problems government IT projects encounter. Report A examines the underlying causes of problems with IT projects in national government and reporting about them to parliament. Report B analyzes the efficiency and effectiveness of expenditures on IT projects, and avoidable costs and delays since 2000 by studying five projects.
- A survey on lawyers' experience with failed IT projects in the Netherlands, summarized in a Top Ten of failure factors (Beenker). The survey questioned 13 law offices with experience in settling and litigating failed IT projects. The survey produced a long list of 90 failure factors. The report is fairly brief, but it is interesting because it consolidates experience with failed IT projects.

- Cap Gemini's Global CIO Survey 2008 focuses on the role of the IT function in business innovation (Capgemini). It explores the views and experiences of 425 CIOs and companies world wide on how access to new technologies and information is changing their role, and the role of their IT function.

The next section summarizes the findings from those sources and examines their messages for judiciaries and courts.

The strategic perspective

At first glance, it might seem that the most important cause of difficulties in IT projects is IT that does not work: inadequate performance of an IT application or system. However, if we look at the combined wisdom of our sources, the most prevalent reason why IT projects fail is strategic: it is in the relationship between businesses and organizations on the one hand and their IT on the other. The strategic perspective relates to the way organizations position themselves and plan with regard to their overall role and purpose.

Defects in the strategic link between the organization and its technology affect IT development and governance at every level.

Organization and technology fit

Capgemini's survey of the top innovative businesses in 2008 supports these findings. It finds that organizations where the IT function has a leading role in business innovation share a number of characteristics:

- The business leadership team thoroughly understands IT (77 percent against the average, 38 percent)
- Effective relationships between IT and the business (94 percent against the average, 67 percent)
- Strong delivery of fundamental IT services (83 percent as opposed to the average, 56 percent)
- The Chief Information Officer (CIO) reports to the Chief Executive Officer/Chief Operational Officer (CEO/COO) rather than to the Chief Financial Officer (CFO) (75percent against 53percent)
- Overwhelmingly (88percent) the IT function plays the role of partner to the business, as opposed to trusted supplier or utility player (Capgemini).
- The other sources report a similar experience:
- The strategy of any organization needs to provide a vision of what information is, and what its potential is for IT applications in the business (Beenker p. 3).
- The organization strategy and the ICT strategy need to be in line.
- Business is leading, and thereby responsible for budgeting and prioritizing (Rekenkamer A p. 31).

– Investments in IT projects need to be part of the project portfolio of the organization (Rekenkamer A p. 31).

Without this strategic alignment, business and ICT will be two different worlds. If reporting is only financial, the effect will be that the only reasons for prioritizing are economical ones. As a consequence, only increased efficiency will count as a valid reason for investing in IT. This does not do justice to the role of information and its potential to improve performance and processes.

In summary: Every organization, in order to benefit from IT, needs a vision of the role of information in its organization, and of the potential of IT applications. The business leadership team needs to thoroughly understand IT. The strategy in business determines the IT strategy. Hence, strategy also determines budgeting and prioritizing, in general and in the organization's project portfolio.

a What does this mean for judiciaries and courts?

In the case of the HBS project, the appeal courts, or the judiciary as a whole, had no vision of the role of information or a strategy with regard to information. This meant their representatives could not provide adequate guidance to the project for lack of understanding the direction in which it needed to go. The end result of this deficiency was that the project was unable to produce functionality according to user requirements. In Ontario, the judiciary had enunciated its needs, but the Attorney General decided about the means to meet the needs.

b Judiciaries and strategy

Courts are normally concerned with judging individual events that have happened in the past. Strategic orientation, looking forward over the longer term, does not come naturally to them. The skills needed for deciding individual cases, such as patience and attention to detail, do not prepare one for designing strategies for the future. The cases courts need to decide are always concerned with events that happened in the past. Moreover, the authorities used to decide the cases are the law, jurisprudence and precedent. Both jurisprudence and precedent derive their authority from the past. Consequently, thinking in general terms and looking forward is not a common activity in courts and policy. Strategy formation skills are not the prime requirement for judges and court staff. As an Australian report on IT in courts observed, the legal profession is historically conservative (Victoria p. 30).

Therefore, judiciaries that choose to use IT to improve the way they administer justice need to acknowledge this cultural background and the entailing limitations. This means they may have to make a major shift in thinking. A framework for policy formation and fit with IT needs becomes a necessity. For most judiciaries, this is a new situation. It may require changes in governance structure to provide for a policy formation function.

Moreover, the judiciary's leadership and the IT function - this includes everything having to do with IT, from development to managing systems and hardware - both need to understand how information works in their courts and what the implications for IT can be. Courts' business is to decide individual cases and to confirm norms. The international human rights instruments also set standards for the way courts administer justice. The role of information in court processes is very important: in internal processes, in communication with the environment. Understanding the role or roles of information is crucial for understanding the way IT can support improving courts in their performance. This requires training in what is already known, and research to generate new knowledge.

The leadership also needs to be able to prioritize in terms of funding and budget allocation. Reporting should focus on policies, not on spending. This may require changes to the reporting and budgeting systems.

Summing up, IT sets new requirements for judiciaries: (1) a policy formation function able to set a strategy, with (2) a corresponding budgeting and reporting structure and (3) understanding of the role of information in the work of the courts.

The project perspective

Projects are temporary structures set up to produce results. New processes and applications are actually produced at the project level. The overall strategy should determine what the projects' results should be. Strategy failure, consequently, also affects whether results are produced at the project level.

When there is no strategy setting a clear goal, it is difficult to determine what the system is intended to do. This means the project result cannot be defined. As a consequence, the project's management does not know what it is expected to produce. We already observed in the HBS project how the courts could not provide guidance to the project, resulting in irreparably inadequate functionality.

The next problem caused by a lack of strategy is a failure to understand how the products of the IT projects will effect change in business processes. This leads to inadequate change management. The business will jump to ICT solutions quickly, without considering the impact of an organizational change on IT (Rekenkamer A p. 19). IT projects are incorrectly assumed to be primarily technical challenges (World Bank 2006b p. 6). In the HBS project, the implications of electronic work flow for the business processes of the courts were not foreseen.

In Chapter 2.1, we have seen that implementation of enterprise technologies such as work flow requires a redesigned business process to be in place. Failure to recognize this requirement can lead to a situation where redesigning business processes is left to the IT specialists. They are trained to develop and implement technology, not for redesigning business processes. Their exclusively technical training means they look at the project from a limited number of perspectives. The IT lawyers observed that, because of their perspective, IT professionals do not take resistance to organizational change seriously enough (Beenker p. 3). This creates resistance to IT (Beenker p. 3). Leaving innovation solely to the technicians can also lead to an inadequate skills mix: isolated, unsupervised ICT operations working outside the established units (World Bank 2006b p. 7). The HBS project ultimately delivered a system that could not be used because essential functionality was missing. From the above, it is clear that this was due to a lack of strategic orientation in the courts, causing the project to fail.

In summary: IT project goals need to be clear. This requires that (1) they can draw on a strategic vision, and (2) their relation with business change is understood and managed. If the fit between business and IT is not understood and managed properly, process redesign risks being done from an exclusively technical perspective. Then, the redesign will be done by people who do not have sufficient business knowledge. This will generate resistance to both business change and IT.

What does this mean for courts? Judiciaries need to have a strategic vision of their processes as their core business and of the role of information and of IT in those processes. If processes need to be redesigned, that should be done in such a way that IT helps them instead of hindering them. This requires people who combine knowledge of court processes with IT to link IT development and court processes. Courts also need knowledgeable IT personnel who understand how IT supports those processes.

Learning through experimentation

Understanding how information works in courts and how IT can improve court information processes requires not just training and research. It also requires building experience through experimentation with functionalities. In Chapter 2.1, we have seen how users learn to understand and use functionalities that are introduced. They experiment to learn what the new functionality can do for their process. With stand-alone, functional technologies, it took years to develop and subsequently implement smart merge routines that could be used in the entire court system in the Netherlands. To be honest, it benefited greatly from an internal network in order to access the databases. At the time of writing this study, courts in the Netherlands are experimenting with forms of collaboration by judges and court staff on the intranets, to produce decisions by panels. No standards have emerged from this process yet. This type of experimentation resembles what Valerie Frissen calls bricolage (Frissen 2004 p. 15). Frissen contrasts bricolage, tinkering, with linear planning activity as done by engineers. User-bricoleurs can "tinker" with materials to make surprising new combinations and uses.

The need for experimentation will become more urgent as technologies affect work processes more profoundly. As we have seen in Chapter 2.1, digital court access beyond the European Union's stage 2 requires a business process suited to managing incoming electronic information. In fact, what characterizes interactivity at level 3 and beyond is the presence of an electronic business process that can receive and manage electronic information. The new processes need to be in place before the technology can be implemented. Because they need to be in place, there is little room for experimentation once the technology is implemented. Therefore, there needs to be room for experimentation *before* the innovation of two-way online communication with courts can be implemented. Consequently, fostering user experimentation can be an important source of learning. For process innovation, it is a necessity.

Government projects: Big solutions and perverse incentives

Judiciaries are constitutionally independent, but in practical terms they operate in the framework of government. The two projects show how IT for judiciaries is sometimes developed in a context involving other government organizations. Ministries, judiciaries, prosecution services, politicians and actors in other institutions have to work together in IT projects to produce the results needed. This complicates the problems already identified above. The Dutch General Accounting Chamber examined large government IT projects in the Netherlands at the request of the Dutch Parliament. It found that a combination of political, organizational and technical factors makes government IT projects too ambitious and too complex (Rekenkamer A p. 15-22).

The report signals the following clusters of complexity:

- Political complexity, engendering additional requirements and political deadlines
- Organizational complexity, related to the goals of the project
- Very complex cooperation between parts of the information chain, insufficiency of the chain's governance, broad and diverse variation in use of data, and massiveness of the primary business process
- Technical complexity of development and implementation.

In its examination of government IT projects, it found the following typical problems:

The parties (ministries, politicians, and IT vendors) all have an interest in large, ambitious projects, and they are all naturally inclined to think in terms of big solutions for big problems. They do not counterbalance each other. On the contrary, they hold each other captive, and this easily spirals inevitably into a complex project with the status of political fact, from which no elegant exit is possible (Rekenkamer A p. 23).

The big ambitions engender difficulties. They can cause a lack of restraint in project ambitions. This leads to too much made-to-measure, tailored work, where numerous exceptions from regulation are included in the system, making for complexity that is difficult to deliver. Lack of prioritizing as a consequence of big ambitions can lead to the concurrence of large IT projects that compete for the same IT staff (Rekenkamer B p. 52). An excessive level of ambition may lead to attempting a combination of ITcomponents and solutions that have not been tried within the organization before (Rekenkamer B p. 52). The Rekenkamer's advice is to reduce complexity whenever possible. Reducing complexity means to start small, and to move forward in small steps. Organizational complexity can be reduced by limiting the number of organizations involved, or by choosing an approach with pilots. Choosing standard software wherever possible will reduce technical complexity.

In summary: In government projects, complexity is compounded. There are few or no incentives to curb big ambitions. Too much complexity is allowed to go unchecked, leading to technically and financially unmanageable projects. Reducing complexity wherever possible should increase the success rate of government IT projects.

What does this mean for courts? The HBS and Ontario projects illustrate how insufficiently controlled complexity can make projects unmanageable and underproductive. Judiciaries, however independent, operate within the complex field of public government. Judiciaries usually get their funding from the public treasury. They work with other participants in information chains, like the prosecution, lawyers, probation services and social security agencies. They are part of information chains with complex mechanisms. Reducing political, organizational and technical complexity needs to be a major concern.

Reducing complexity: The example of Money Claim On Line

The Rekenkamer's advice is to mitigate complexity by reducing it and starting small and moving forward in small steps. This small excursion explores implications for judiciaries. Velicogna observes how in European courts, the more successful approach to electronic administration of justice has simple procedures and to simplify more complex ones (Velicogna CEPEJ p. 48).

I offer the development process for Money Claim On Line (MCOL) in the United Kingdom, one of the more successful approaches in Europe, as an example of ways to reduce complexity. The three most salient ways in which MCOL has reduced complexity are the following:

A simple procedure: MCOL has chosen to automate money claims, one single, simple procedure. Civil procedural regulation in England and Wales is less formal than in some other countries, which helps to reduce complexity. Filing a claim by sending it to a court institutes proceedings. A formal summons delivered by a bailiff, like in continental European systems, is not required. An attempt to develop a similar online small claims system for the Netherlands was unsuccessful. The formal requirements of the summons may have been of influence. A suggestion, put forward in the context of a general reconsideration of civil procedural regulation, to deformalize formal summons altogether and replace them with a request addressed to the court, was not followed up (Asser 2006 p. 101).

A dedicated court: MCOL has simplified organizational complexity by setting up a dedicated court, instead of creating a process that could be handled by all the competent courts.

Moving forward in small steps: The development process has spanned many years, and involved several distinct steps:

- Receiving claims, without completely automated processing in the court
- Processing undefended claims without human intervention.
- Supporting defense

Starting with one procedure and with one court reduces complexity. Doing what is known, by taking small steps, fostering experimentation and using information produced in the experiments for development, is an approach that limits the risks engendered by complexity. There is a more extensive discussion of Money Claim On Line in Chapter 3.3.

Other requirements

The changes required in the work processes prior to implementation of enterprise technology functionalities make implementation of functionality at this level particularly difficult. Work processes tend to differ from court to court. If they should be automated, they need prior simplification and standardization. This will require a centralized effort. Users in the courts will experience those efforts and the resulting changes as a loss of autonomy and discretion.

There also needs to be a clear vision of the degree of automation, as well as standardization, the work flow really needs. Velicogna's story about IT projects mired in difficulty for wanting to automate too many exceptions emphasizes this point (Velicogna CEPEJ p. 48). It has become common wisdom in IT development that 80 percent of a process can be automated with 20 percent of the cost and effort needed to automate 100 percent of the process. Automating the other 20 percent takes 80 percent of the cost and the effort. In this light, the extent to which court processes should be automated or streamlined in a work flow system is a matter of serious concern. What are the pros and cons of leaving the possibility of handling exceptions on an ad hoc basis open? The strategy needs to provide clear guidance on this point. Evidently, that guidance needs to be based on an understanding of the processes in question.

Conclusions for Part 2

Part 2 examined IT in courts. Chapter 2.1 inventoried IT functionality in use in courts, mostly in Western Europe and the United States Chapter 2.2 examined frequent problems in IT development and the implementation of IT.

Chapter 2.1 inventoried the court IT that is in use in different countries in the world, and uncovered how some court systems struggle with implementing IT. The IT most widely implemented mostly supports courts' paper based processes, word processing for document production and case registration to replace the paper docket. Networking technology, where it has been introduced, is mostly used internally and informally. External electronic communication is the edge where development by the forerunners is taking place. Work flow management and other enterprise systems do not seem to get much attention. Work flow technology was at the forefront of development ten years ago, and the CEPEJ survey results show it still is. It has not become a domesticated technology in courts. European court systems do not emphasize courtroom technology, contrary to U.S. systems.

The inventory also tells us something about development approaches. Attempts to translate the entire complexity of the court process appear to have been expensive, cumbersome and ultimately unsuccessful. Successful development has been incremental development of one simple procedure, or after simplification of a more complex procedure. The application is then opened up to other fields, or to new user groups.

In the HBS project story, there is an eloquent illustration of the kind of complexity integrated systems can run into. The prosecution had chosen a system that encoded fully developed work processes for maximum control on integrity of information management. The judiciary, by contrast, had chosen a system that would support developing different work flows and experimentation. If we recall the typology of functionalities from Chapter 2.1, the judiciary chose a system that requires few complements and allows a large measure of freedom, and the prosecution chose a top-down system requiring full complements in terms of decision rights and centralized process control. This example shows how organizations can have different, and even opposing, needs. The prosecution needs a system that supports accountability within its hierarchy. The judiciary's main need was a system that supports experimentation. Understanding those needs based on the role of information in the organization's processes, developing a corresponding strategy and managing the needs of the organization when implementing IT are essential activities for successful implementation.

Chapter 2.2 examined frequent problems in IT development and implementation. It concluded that some judiciaries may have to make a major shift in thinking and in their organization.

Experimentation in translating the needs of administering justice into IT applications needs to be institutionalized. The results of such experimentation are important for innovation. In this way, the IT function should learn from the users. Court systems can also learn from the experiences of other court systems and other organizations.

The judiciary's leadership and the IT function both need to understand how information works in the courts and the implications for IT. This requires both training and research. Redesigning processes, where needed, requires people who combine knowledge of court processes with IT in order to link IT development and court processes. Judiciaries also need knowledgeable IT personnel who understand those processes.

Changes in the governance structure may be needed to support strategy and policy formation and to support prioritizing funding and budgeting in accordance with the policies.

This chapter concluded that the most salient deficiency is that of strategy: a strategic vision of processes administering justice, shaped by knowledge and understanding of the role of information in courts. The next three parts of this study aim to improve that understanding. They examine the role of information in courts' and judiciaries' internal processes (Part 3), in external communication (Part 4), and in safeguarding integrity (Part 5)

Notes

1 Apparently, data from the survey are inserted into the report by hand, thereby leaving room for error. Email from Pim Albers of CEPEJ, October 3, 2008.

2 Special thanks to Elizabeth Wiggins of the FJC who arranged an invitation for me to attend the round table.

3 They use WordPerfect.

4 Interview in New Delhi, July 2005.

5 This discussion is limited to publicly available jurisprudence collections. It does not cover collections that are available only to subscribers.

6 I already pointed out there is a problem with the data in the report. According to the report, p. 269, the Netherlands should have implemented word processing in less than 100 percent of all the courts, less than in the 2006 report. Email (to my knowledge functional in 100 percent of the courts) is implemented in less than 10 percent of all the courts, according to page 269. The correct data for the Netherlands would lead to a score of 38 points. Turkey was placed in a very high group, but its points on p. 269 lead to a score of 32 points, which would put it at the bottom of the high level group. Therefore, the data on p. 269 cannot be used to draw conclusions.

7 At the time the HBS project was stopped, I was active in the Dutch Judiciary's IT field. I was not directly involved in the decision making surrounding the project. In order to avoid unverifiable judgments, my conclusions are based solely on the findings of the external audit report.

8 The exchange rates were calculated as of January 1, 2002 by Oanda, http://www.oanda.com/convert/classic?free=1

9 It is not difficult to imagine this caused some uproar.

10 http://www.aija.org.au/tech3/program/presentations/Ontario2002-2.ppt

11 The exchange rate was calculated as of January 1, 2002 by Oanda, http://www.oanda.com/convert/classic?free=1

12 The web version of the Annual Report has no page numbers.

Part 3 Case Delay

This part examines how IT can support reducing case delay. Excessive delay in processing cases is the most common complaint about justice system performance. There is an almost universal opinion that courts and judiciaries take too long to respond to users of their services.

The discussion of case delay comes in three chapters. From the starting point of delay, they examine case handling to uncover ways in which IT can support improvement in case handling processes in a broad sense.

This part starts with a chapter on delay itself. In the two chapters that follow, its scope extends to court processes in a wider sense and to a more detailed examination of some individual processes. It ends with some conclusions on how information technology can be leveraged to reduce delay. Consequently, there is more to this part of the study than delay.

This first chapter presents an overview of the traditional approaches to case delay. It explores how to establish whether there is delay, what its causes can be and where to find the most likely areas for remedies. The second chapter moves beyond the traditional approaches. In order to understand how information technology can support reducing delay, it is necessary to learn more about how delay occurs through the way courts handle cases. This chapter examines how case processing works as a process of information handling. The vehicle used for this purpose is a case study of civil justice in the Netherlands. This chapter presents a conceptual framework to aid the study of information handling in court processes. The third chapter, continuing the case study of civil justice in the Netherlands, applies this framework to look at case handling in more detail. It analyzes four different categories of court cases. It looks at the process in each category as an information process. For each category, it draws conclusions about IT functionalities that can help to implement improved case processing and innovative ways of handling information, leading to more timely and adequate judicial decisions.

Chapter 3.1 Case Delay

This chapter analyzes the dynamics of case delay. It examines current theory regarding the problem of case delay: the normative framework, diagnosing delay itself and candidate remedies for it. First, it will discuss current thinking on the impact of delay. Next, to facilitate a clear discussion of the issues involved in delay, it presents the most commonly used terminology. An analysis of the normative framework is next. After that, we look at ways to identify delay by measuring case disposition times and using standards. Finally, we will also examine the most common ways of combating delay and how effective they have been.

Case delay as a problem: A brief tour around the world

Probably the most famous adage in the culture of the justice world is British Prime Minister William Gladstone's "Justice delayed is justice denied" quote, with its French counterpart, the adage "justice rétive, justice fautive."[1]

Case delay has been a topic of debate for centuries. Here are some examples.

- In 1802, the City Council of Hamburg, now part of the Federal Republic of Germany, adopted a directive to shorten court procedures.[2]
- In the early 1970s, many U.S. states enacted legislation setting time limits for trials.
- In 1983, the Supreme Court of India quoted the Chief Justice of the Bombay High Court as saying that any "judicial system which delays disposal of cases or resolution of disputes over decades can be said to have outlived its utility" (Bharuka 2003).
- The European Court of Human Rights has difficulty dealing with all the complaints about late, overdue court decisions. 28 percent of its judgments found a violation on account of the length of the proceedings (ECHR 2009 p. 6).
- Today in Nigeria, court users, when comparing the issue of delays with other problems affecting the justice system, considered delays the most important obstacle to using the courts; the majority perceived the length of the process as the most serious problem. Business people also seemed generally unsatisfied with the time required for the dispensation of justice (UNODC 2006 p. 34).
- Only 44 percent of court users in the Netherlands, surveyed between 2005 and 2007, were satisfied with the duration of their procedure. They were also less satisfied than they were in a previous survey (Prisma 2008 p. 4, 26).

Nowadays, case delay is officially regarded as a very important problem to be addressed in many judiciaries:

- In the United States, it has been the focus of targeted case management reform as early as the 1970s (Steelman 2000 p. xi).
- Influenced by developments in the United States, court reform in Latin America has also focused on case delay (Hammergren 2007 p. 58).
- CEPEJ was created by the Council of Europe with the express brief to improve the efficiency of courts and judiciaries in the Council's more than 40 member countries.[3] CEPEJ has commissioned a number of studies that have produced very interesting results. Some of the results will be discussed below. Court delay is now recognized as the most important problem to be addressed in many European judiciaries (CEPEJ 2005 p.2).

In the literature, the issue of court delay has been addressed fairly widely in the United States, Canada and Australia, less in Europe and even less elsewhere in the world. A few technically very complex studies have been done in the Netherlands, focusing on civil procedures. The results of these studies will also be discussed below.

This small sample illustrates two things: case delay is believed to be a problem, and it is also considered important.

Hammergren notes from extended experience working in countries in Latin America, and in which delay was first identified as a major problem, that:

- The incidence of delay was exaggerated.
- Its causes were not as claimed.
- Its impacts were different than imagined (Hammergren 2007 p. 71-78).

Hammergren's point is that claims require verification, and verification may turn up some surprising findings. We will first look at some of the impacts of case delay that have an empirical foundation. In order to verify that delay is a reality, and not just a belief, we then go on to look at the incidence of delay with a discussion of how to measure it. This chapter ends with an analysis of causes and remedies.

Some impacts of delay

Timely justice is not just an abstract right. There is always a risk that justice will be denied when proceedings drag on. As time passes, certain legitimate interests may be adversely affected. Delay directly affects the parties to a case. Moreover, delay affects the administration of justice itself, as well as society in a wider sense.

Delay has many different impacts. First of all, there are impacts on the *parties* to a case:

- The value of any awards that they eventually receive will be reduced by delay.
- Further costs are incurred when delay occurs, which the parties may sometimes be unable to bear.
- Long case duration may mean that a party to a money claim case may not survive. This puts particularly small and medium enterprises at risk (Felsö p. 88).
- Delays in criminal cases can cause severe hardship on victims and on those under suspicion or accused of crimes. Lengthy pretrial detention is only one of those hardships.
- Access to justice is obstructed for those who cannot bear the cost of delay.
- Delay can also be an incentive for parties to settle a dispute.
- Next, there are impacts on *the administration of justice* itself:
- Evidence disappears and sometimes new evidence has to be adduced.
- Witnesses disperse.
- Witnesses lose credibility as time elapses.
- Defendants and suspects may disappear.
- Justice can be avoided when investigations and trials are extended beyond the statute of limitations.
- Corruption is encouraged by delay because delay creates opportunities to request bribes to speed up case processing or to hold off attention to a case (Reiling 2007 p. 71).
- There is also the *wider impact* of case delay. Good performance of the judicial infrastructure, of which timeliness in courts is an important aspect, boosts economic growth (Van Velthoven 2005 p. 31), lowers transaction costs for business (Van Dijk 2003 p.1), and lowers the business cost of crime (Van Velthoven 2005 p. 20). Research on the situation in the Netherlands has shown that particularly lengthy procedures lead to problems in all areas of the law. Conflicts remain unresolved longer, which adversely affects social stability and leads to inertia. The damage increases as dispute resolution takes longer. Long procedures hamper effective crime reduction. They lead to delay and sometimes abandonment of activities, long-term uncertainty, damage through continued illegal activities and cash flow problems. The direct social cost to Dutch society of unnecessarily long processing times was cautiously estimated at € 450 million annually (Van Dijk 2003 p. 2).

However, although delays can have negative impacts, a sufficient amount of time is essential for proper inquiries to be conducted, all the questions of law elucidated and relations between the parties settled, and for the court to arrive at a reasoned conclusion (CEPEJ 2006 p.16; World Bank 2006a p. 48-49).[4]

In summary, case delay negatively impacts the parties to a dispute as well as the larger society.

The normative framework

Everyone is awarded the right to have their case disposed without undue delay or within a reasonable time by a number of international human rights conventions:

- The International Covenant on Civil and Political Rights (ICCPR), article 14, states that in the case of criminal charge, cases must be disposed by courts without undue delay. Disposal includes commencement, end and judgment in the case.[5]
- The African Charter on Human and People's Rights, article 7, states that every individual shall have the right to have his cause heard, comprising the right to be tried within a reasonable time.
- The American Convention on Human Rights states in article 8 that every person has the right to a hearing with due guarantees and within a reasonable time.
- The European Convention on Human Rights (ECHR), article 6, accords inhabitants of the member states of the Council of Europe the right to a fair and public hearing by an independent, impartial tribunal, within a reasonable time. The Court of Justice of the other European organization of states, the European Union, has recognized the ECHR as an important source of law and takes article 6 into account when considering issues that have to do with reasonable time.

The core business of the courts is to handle everyone's case, and to do so without undue delay and within a reasonable time. This is a standard that is authoritative for courts in countries that are signatory to one or more of these conventions. Those courts need to comply with this standard. In itself, the standard is not very practicable as a standard because it is not very concrete. We will come back to the topic of standards after the discussion on diagnosing delay. Once we have discussed how to measure delay in courts, we come back to standards to establish whether the disposition times found in the measurements are excessive.

Diagnosing delay in two steps

Delay occurs when a given time exceeds a standard. If the law stipulates a certain term for a court decision to be finalized, and the decision only comes after the expiration of the term, we can say that there is delay. Therefore, measuring the time it actually takes a court to dispose a case is the first step in diagnosing delay. The next step is to determine whether the actual time found exceeds a standard.

Terminology for case delay

The terms most frequently used in the context of case delay are timeliness, delay, backlog and congestion.

Timely generally refers to an absence of delay.

Delay refers to a task being late or deferred. It is something that should have been done, but has not been. There is a normative component to the term delay. Delay is something that exceeds a standard.

Backlog is another term frequently used in the context of case handling. It means an accumulation of tasks to be handled. It is things piling up without getting done. If delay is what court users experience when their cases do not get handled in time, the courts experience backlog when they do not process cases at the same rate as they are filed.

Congestion describes the situation where the number of tasks is so great that it interferes with completion.

An important distinction is that between the time a case spends in court from the time of filing to the final disposition, and the time someone actually does something with the case. In the literature on case delay and case management, the terminology found is not consistent. In this study, the following terms are used consistently:

Disposition time is the time that goes by between the filing of a case and the time it leaves the court, by a judgment or otherwise. Disposition time is usually measured in calendar days.

Processing time is the time during which someone actually does something to a case. Processing time is usually measured in minutes or hours.

A preliminary step in the diagnostic process is to determine what data are available. Only a few justice systems have statistical records available that enable the easy calculation of these figures for specific stages or for the entire trajectory of a case. In most countries, real statistics for these cases are not readily available. Most judicial reform assistance projects operate in countries where working statistics offices for courts are scarce. In those cases, other mechanisms will have to be used. They are discussed below.

It is common for justice assistance projects to introduce computers in courts, and subsequently develop a case registration and management system. Such a system, when implemented in an entire court system, will make the types of measurement discussed below easier and potentially more accurate. It can also enable comparisons across courts within the system and maybe even across systems.

The next section will first discuss ways of measuring disposition times with or without automated case management systems. In step 2, we will examine what standards there are in order to assess whether the times measured are excessive and can therefore be qualified as delay.

Step 1: Measurement

The first step is to measure disposition times. For assessment purposes, representative figures are needed. The mathematical average is the measure that is most commonly used. It is generally used as an indicator for an ordinary, run-of-the-mill case. As such, it is often an effective indicator for that purpose. The average is the measure normally used in annual reports. However, when most cases are processed relatively quickly but a few cases take an extremely long time, the average does not tell us much about ordinary cases. Here, case distribution is skewed. In case of skewed distribution, the median is a better indicator. The median is the central measurement in a series of measurements. If we look at case disposition times in civil cases, one-half of the cases take less time than the median, the other half takes longer (Eshuis 2005 p. 19, Eshuis 2007 p. 144). The measure of dispersion also is informative. It makes an enormous difference if most scores are clustered around the mean or median, or if the "average" hides a wide range of scores. For example, there is a telling difference between 90 percent of cases being processed in 6 months versus a 6-month average composed of times ranging from a few days to several years (Reiling 2007 p. 63, Eshuis 2007 p. 144). In order to express this, the 90th percentile is usually the measure. It means the time within which 90 percent of all cases are disposed. This is the measure used in the U.S. Trial Court Performance Standards, discussed below.

Distinguishing types of cases is also necessary in order to compare cases that are actually comparable. It is more informative to know the average time for a bankruptcy case, a simple debt collection proceeding, or a dispute over unfair dismissal than just the average time for processing civil cases in general. As we will see in the discussion of ECHR jurisprudence, disposition is more urgent in some case types than in others. Moreover, measures to reduce processing times can be identified only for specific procedures. In criminal cases, the most common distinctions are between simple misdemeanors, major felonies, and complex investigations of suspected corruption or other white collar crimes. Such a categorization is relevant for several reasons. For instance, the parties involved in a certain type of case have a specific interest in the timely resolution of their case. Moreover, proportionality requires that case types are handled commensurately with their importance. Finally, if an eventual reform is meant to focus on reducing delay, this kind of analysis early in the process is a necessity because it helps to draw attention to possible points for reform.

National Center for State Courts (NCSC) CourTools

The most common methodology for measuring case disposition is described in CourTools, a methodology developed by the U.S. National Center for State Courts.[6] This methodology was developed to help U.S. state courts wanting to measure their performance with setting up their own measuring system. The methodology is described in very clear, understandable terms. CourTools explains how courts can set up their own measuring system to suit their own needs. It explains how to measure court performance in ten aspects:

- Access and fairness
- Clearance rates
- Time to disposition
- Age of active pending case load
- Trial date certainty
- Reliability and integrity of case files
- Collection of monetary penalties
- Effective use of jurors
- Court employee satisfaction
- Cost per case.

The system presumes there is a categorization of types of cases. The methodology is based on the American Bar Association's Trial Court Performance Standards (TCPS), to be discussed below in the next step.

CourTools measures 2, 3, 4 and 5 have to do with case delay. The discussion in this study is confined to those measures. They are discussed in depth in Box 4. The time measurement methodology can provide a framework to measure case processing times in other systems than the U.S. system as well (Steelman and Fabri, p. 31). *Time to disposition* is the most immediately relevant measure. It measures the time a case is in court from the time of filing to the day judgment is entered, in calendar days. *Clearance or disposition rates,* measure number 2, measure whether a court is keeping up with its case load. *The age of the active pending caseload* of a court, measure 4, measures how long the existing case load has been on the court docket since the cases were filed. *Trial date certainty,* measure number 5, is a measure that is important for systems that conduct trials. It measures the number of times a case was set for trial. The *congestion rate,* not part of the CourTools measurements, is a simple rate that expresses whether a court is building up a backlog. Box 4 also explains how to calculate case load congestion.

Box 4 Time Measurement Methodologies

Time to disposition is the time it takes a court to dispose a case (of a certain type) from the day of filing to the day of disposition, measured in calendar days.
The clearance or disposition rate measures whether a court is keeping up with its case load. The clearance rate expresses the number of outgoing cases as a percentage of the number of incoming cases. If the clearance rate is less than 100%, the court is building up a backlog (Dakolias 1999 p. 10-17).

The CourTools methodology
Time to disposition expresses the percentage of cases disposed or otherwise resolved within established time frames. Those time frames can be the local, state or national guidelines for timely case processing, for instance the ABA and the COSCA standards (Table 7).
Clearance rates measure outgoing cases as a percentage of incoming cases. Outgoing cases can be cases that have been decided or cases that leave the court in some other way. Incoming cases can be new cases or cases that are reopened or reactivated, depending on the court system in question. The clearance rate is calculated by dividing the sum of outgoing cases by the sum of incoming cases. If the result is 1, or 100 percent, the court is keeping up with its caseload. If the result is less than 100 percent, the court is building up a backlog. The clearance rate methodology itself does not take an existing backlog into account.
The age of the active pending caseload of a court, measure 4, measures the age of the active cases that are pending before the courts, measured as the number of days from filing until the time of measurement. This measurement is again related to the ABA and COSCA standards in Table 7.
Trial date certainty, measure number 5, is a measure that is important for systems that conduct trials. It measures the number of times cases disposed by trial are scheduled for trial. A court's ability to hold trials on the first date they are scheduled to be heard is closely associated with timely case disposition.

Source: NCSC CourTools.

The case delay measurement methodologies we have seen in this section all measure disposition time. If few data are available, there are some proxies that can be used for diagnostic purposes. Analysis of random case files is an approach for situations in which no data are available at all. Where those data are available, time to disposition, disposition rates and age of case loads are useful information on how well a court is keeping up with its case load. Since there are many different types of cases, categorizing them is very informative as to whether the disposition is timely. This is particularly relevant when we look at the standards because the standards mostly apply to specific categories of cases. The next step is to look at standards to see whether the results found in the measurements exceed them.

Step 2: Standards

The second step, after acquiring quantitative data on disposition times, is to determine whether the acquired disposition times exceed any standards.

Thus, standards are needed to determine whether there is delay. The problem is that, in practice, there are very few standards for case handling. The standards that do exist are either unclear or volatile. Some countries have set time limits for case processing in their laws, for instance in their procedural codes. These standards have legal relevance because they are in the law. Nonetheless, for diagnostic purposes, their value is limited because (1) they are fairly general and abstract, and (2) there may also be a gap between the law and actual practice. In summary, standards will need to be identified first.

A special problem sometimes raised is whether standards apply to judiciaries, given that judiciaries are independent. Issues have been raised about the concept of standards for judges and judiciaries. First, the independence of the judiciary is sometimes regarded as a bar to setting or imposing standards. Second, there is the question if, and how, standards should be enforced.

The first problem is not as serious as it might look at first, because solutions to the problem of authority have been found. If we look at standards that have emerged in judiciaries, they can be classified according to their source of authority.

One type of standard is that of *self-imposed* goals. An example is the United States where the accepted standards are the Trial Court Performance Standards developed, adopted and published by the Conference of State Court Administrators, the Conference of Chief Justices and the ABA. Judges are generally members of the ABA. The standards are promulgated as illustrations. Each state court system is gently encouraged (cf. the text in Table 6) by the National Center for State Courts to use or modify the standards. The Netherlands has recently adopted a time standards system, based on the TCPS and on data about actual case processing times. The Dutch system is displayed in Table 7.

Another type is the standards that *emerge from jurisprudence on undue delay*, like the one from the European Court of Human Rights. This court hears complaints about undue delay in the member countries of the Council of Europe. The Court has ruled that, for criminal cases, two years is a reasonable disposition time, counting from the moment the reasonable suspicion arose to the decision in the first instance. It has by now developed an extensive jurisprudence on what is reasonable and what is not when it comes to disposition times. This jurisprudence is discussed below because it offers important pointers on what are the relevant factors in the issue of case delay.

A third type of standard is that of *emerging from actual practice.* It is closely related to the first type Research into disposition times can lead to knowledge about average practice, and this knowledge can become a basis for standard setting. An example of a comparative approach that could become a potential source of such a standard is the World Bank's Doing Business database, discussed below as well.

Knowledge about actual practice can lead to turning actual practice into the norm. It can also lead to setting more stringent standards, as happened with the ABA norms. In conclusion, judicial independence is not a barrier for courts and judges to adopting standards to measure their own performance.

That leaves the question of enforcement. Courts in the United States are "gently encouraged" by the National Center for State Courts to use the standards. Courts in the Netherlands are encouraged to conform to their own standards by the Council for the Judiciary, their governing body. The European Court of Human Rights can order a member country to pay punitive damages because of case delay.

Self-imposed goals as standards: The ABA

The ABA has set time disposition standards for cases of different types in U.S. courts. For general civil cases, for instance, the standard is that 90 percent of all filed general civil cases should be disposed within 12 months after filing, 98 percent in 18 months, and 100 percent in 24 months. Table 6 also gives the more generally phrased standards adopted by the Conference of Chief Justices and the Conference of State Court Administrators. Both sets of standards can be applied in measurements according to the CourTools methodology (Box 1).

Tables 6 and 7 show how different types of cases are considered as different levels of urgency. Those involving juveniles who may need to be kept in detention are considered the most urgent.

Table 6 *Case Disposition Time Standards in the United States*

Time Standards Adopted by the Conference of State Court Administrators (COSCA), the Conference of Chief Justices (CCJ) and the ABA

	CCJ and COSCA	*ABA*
Case type		
Criminal		
Felony	180 days	90% in 120 days 98% in 180 days 100% in 12 months
Misdemeanor	90 days	90% in 30 days 100% in 90 days
Civil		
Jury trials	18 months	
Non-jury trials	12 months	
General civil		90% in 12 months 98% in 18 months 100% in 24 months
Summary proceedings, small claims, landlord/tenant		100% in 30 days
Domestic relations		
Uncontested	3 months	
Contested	6 months	
All cases		90% in 3 months 98% in 6 months 100% in 12 months
Juvenile		
Detention/shelter hearings	24 hours	24 hours
Adjudicatory/shelter hearings	15 days	15 days
1. In a detention facility	15 days	15 days
2. Not in a detention facility	30 days	30 days
Disposition hearings	15 days	15 days

COSCA adopted its standards in 1983, CCJ and ABA adopted theirs in 1984.
Criminal cases: time from arrest to trial or disposition.
Civil and domestic relations cases: time from filing to trial or disposition.
Juvenile detention and adjudication or transfer hearings: time from arrest to hearing; juvenile disposition hearings: time from adjudicatory hearing to disposition hearing.

Note from NCSC: These case disposition standards, which have been promulgated by professional organizations in the field of judicial administration, are provided in the CourTools methodology only for illustration purposes. Each court or state court system that has not already adopted case disposition time standards may wish to consider using or modifying these standards as a means of regularly evaluating its case management performance.
Source: National Center for State Courts 2001.

The Netherlands courts have a time standards system that is derived from the U.S. Trial Court Performance Standards, adapted on the basis of Dutch case processing statistics over the years.

Table 7 *Case Disposition Time Standards in the Netherlands*

Case type	*Case category*	*Court*	*Time standard*	*Input at*	*Output at*
Commercial, defended	102/103	district	70% within 1 year 80% within 2 years	First hearing	Issue of decision/ removal from record
		local	75% within 6 months 90% within 1 year		
Commercial, undefended	105	district	90% within 1 month	First hearing	Issue of decision/ removal from record
		local	90% within 15 days		
Requests	106		90% within 3 months	Request received	Decision sent/ withdrawal after hearing
Summary proceedings and provisional decisions	301/302	district + local	90% within 3 months	Draft summons received	Final decision
Divorce	201	district	50% within 2 months 95% within 1 year	Request received	Final decision sent/ withdrawal received
Alimony	1596/1597/ 1600/1601	district	90% within 1 year	Request received	Final decision sent
Juvenile: authority and visiting rights	1595/1598/ 1602	district	80% within 1 year		Final decision sent
Juvenile: supervision and shelter	203	district	90% within 3 months	Request received	Decision sent/ withdrawal received
Dissolution of labor contract, settled decided	107	local		Request received	Decision sent
	2606		90% within 15 days		
	2607, 2608, 2709		90% within 3 months		

Source: Netherlands Judicial Council Quality Standards project, final report, November 16, 2007.

The standards laid down in this report have emerged from actual practice. They are self-imposed. In a number of categories, actual practice is even timelier than the standards. We will come back to this point in the next chapters.

The same picture, but with some differences, emerges from the European jurisprudence discussed in the next section.

Jurisprudence as a standard: The European Court of Human Rights' jurisprudence on undue delay

Article 6.1 of the Convention deals with timely justice by stating the right to justice without undue delay. Article 13 states that member states must have a remedy in the national system for those who have not been given the right to justice without undue delay. As a subsidiary measure, the European Court of Human Rights hears complaints from those who feel the national remedies were insufficient to address the violation of their right to timely justice. They can apply for a ruling of the Court on violations of the European Convention on Human Rights. The Court can order the member state in question to pay compensation to the applicant, if it finds there has been a delay that was undue, and thus a violation of article 6.1. The Court's decisions also have a broader authority, because they are a source of authority on the proper administration of justice guaranteed in the Convention. For example, the case of Brogan[7] against the United Kingdom led to a major reform of the Dutch procedural rules for pretrial detention.

When judging claims of undue delay, the Court generally allows a duration of two years for a case in a single instance. It then applies four more individualized criteria to judge whether there has been a violation of article 6.1: [8]

- The complexity of the case
- The applicant's conduct
- The manner in which the matter was dealt with by the administrative and judicial authorities
- What is at stake for the applicant – some cases need to be expedited, such as labor disputes involving dismissals, compensation for victims of accidents, cases in which the applicant is serving a prison sentence, police violence cases, cases where an applicant's health is critical, cases of applicants of advanced age, cases related to family life, and cases with applicants of limited physical state and capacity. Such situations make up what are termed priority cases.

The starting point of the calculation the Court makes is different in civil, criminal and administrative cases. In administrative cases, it is the date on which the applicant first refers the matter to the administrative authorities. In civil cases, it is normally the date on which the case was filed in court. In civil cases, the end date is when the decision becomes final, but the court also takes into consideration the length of enforcement and other implementation procedures that are viewed as integral parts of the proceedings. In criminal cases, the starting point may also be the date on which the suspect was arrested or charged, or that on which the preliminary investigation began. The Court regards the date on which the final judgment is given on the substantive charge or the decision by the prosecution or the court to terminate proceedings as the final date of the proceedings.

Analysis and comparison of the large number of cases the court has decided in this matter has led to some indications of the Court's approach. The resulting indications are still fairly general (CEPEJ 2006a p. 6).[9] Table 8 provides the full list.

Table 8 *ECHR Jurisprudence on Reasonable Time*

Type of case	*Issues, case type*	*Length*	*Decision*
Criminal	Diverse	More than 5 years	Violation
Criminal	Normal	3y6m (total in 3 instances) 4y3m (total in 3 levels + investigation)	No violation
Criminal	Complex	8y5m (investigation and 3 levels)	No violation
Civil	Complex	More than 8 years	Violation
Civil	Simple	1y10m in first instance 1y8m on appeal 1y9m Court of Cassation	No violation
Civil	Priority	1y7m in first instance (labor) 1y9m on appeal 1y9m Court of Cassation	No violation
Administrative	Priority	More than 2 years	Violation
Administrative	Complex	More than 5 years	Violation

Source: CEPEJ 2006a p. 6.

This is the general trend:

Generally, a total duration of *up to two years* in normal non-complex cases was regarded reasonable.

In *priority* cases, the court may find violation even if the case lasted less than two years.

In *complex* cases, the court may allow more time, but pays special attention to periods of inactivity that are clearly excessive. The longer time allowed is rarely more than five years and almost never more than eight years of total duration.

The only cases in which the court did not find violation in spite of manifestly excessive duration of proceedings were the cases in which the *applicant's behavior* had contributed to the delay.

Standards emerging from comparison: Doing Business

If there are no standards against which the actually measured disposition times can be judged, comparing actual practices is a help in developing standards. This section will take the Doing Business data – even though they are not actually measured disposition times - to illustrate how this can work. The *Doing Business* (DB) methodology (World Bank 2006a, 2008) gathers and compares data and information on the business climate in most countries in the world. Doing Business has a network of informants in all its participating countries. In 2007, 178 countries participated in the data gathering. The Doing Business process is explained in detail in Box 5.

There are two reasons for using this example. First, it is a widely used tool for developing countries to compare their performance with regard to the business climate, including that of the justice system. Second, it does not depend on the presence of a statistical function of any sort in the justice system in question. That makes it a useful tool when assessing court performance in the context of developing countries. Chapter 1.3 discusses the DB methodology in general, as well as its limitations.

It works as follows: Every year, it asks informants in all its participating countries to provide information on the performance of a number of institutions relevant to doing business, such as the tax office, customs, and also the justice system. With regard to contract enforcement, lawyers in all its participating countries are asked to provide their estimates on the pursuit of a commercial contract enforcement case: the disposition time, the cost and the number of steps that need to be taken. The time counted begins at filing and ends at completion of enforcement. The lawyers who are DB's informants in the country estimate how long, in calendar days, a case would take in their courts. DB averages the times estimated by the lawyers. The time is specified for three specific activities: (1) filing and service, (2) trial and judgment and (3) enforcement.

Here is a methodological illustration: In 2006, the time in days needed to process a claim in the Netherlands, displayed in the DB index, changed from 48 to 408. This is not a typo, nor does it reflect that 90 percent of the Dutch judiciary has suddenly become incapacitated. The Doing Business team confirmed that they have changed the case in the questionnaire put before the correspondents. The new case (Box 5) was constructed to make the results more comparable across countries. Consequently, the procedure for the claim has changed. The new number of days, including 50 days for enforcement, tallies with the Dutch judiciary's statistics. This change means we can no longer compare the data over time if we want to go back beyond 2006. The other limitations are in the fact that the data provided are not primary source data, but estimates.

Box 5 Doing Business Database – Methodology for Contract Enforcement Scores

Indicators on enforcing contracts measure the efficiency of the judicial system in resolving a commercial dispute. The data are built by following the step-by-step evolution of a commercial sale dispute before local courts. The data are collected through study of the codes of civil procedure and other court regulations as well as surveys completed by local litigation lawyers (and, in a quarter of the countries, by judges as well).

Assumptions about the case

- The value of the claim equals 200% of the country's income per capita.
- The dispute concerns a lawful transaction between 2 businesses (Seller and Buyer), located in the country's most populous city. Seller sells goods worth 200% of the country's income per capita to Buyer. After Seller delivers the goods to Buyer, Buyer does not pay for the goods on the grounds that the delivered goods were not of adequate quality.
- Seller (the plaintiff) sues Buyer (the defendant) to recover the amount under the sales agreement (that is, 200% of the country's income per capita). Buyer opposes Seller's claim, saying that the quality of the goods is not adequate. The claim is disputed on the merits.
- A court in the country's most populous city with jurisdiction over commercial cases worth 200% of income per capita decides the dispute.
- Seller attaches Buyer's goods prior to obtaining a judgment because Seller fears that Buyer may become insolvent during the lawsuit.
- Expert opinions are given on the quality of the delivered goods. If it is standard practice in the country for parties to call witnesses or expert witnesses to give an opinion on the quality of the goods, the parties each call one witness or expert witness. If it is standard practice for the judge to appoint an independent expert to give an expert opinion on the quality of the goods, the judge does so. In this case the judge does not allow opposing expert testimony.
- The judgment is 100% in favor of Seller: the judge decides that the goods are of adequate quality and that Buyer must pay the agreed price.

- Buyer does not appeal the judgment. The judgment becomes final.
- Seller takes all required steps for prompt enforcement of the judgment. The money is successfully collected through a public sale of Buyer's movable assets (for example, office equipment).

Procedures
A procedure is defined as any interaction between the parties, or between them and the judge or court officer. This includes steps to file the case, steps for trial and judgment and steps necessary to enforce the judgment. This year, the survey allowed respondents to record procedures that exist in civil law but not in common law jurisdictions, and vice versa. For example, the judge can appoint an independent expert in civil law countries whereas both parties in common law countries send a list of their expert witnesses to the court. To indicate the overall efficiency of court procedures, 1 procedure is now subtracted for countries that have specialized commercial courts and 1 procedure for countries that allow electronic filing of court cases.

Time
Time is recorded in calendar days, counted from the moment the plaintiff files the lawsuit in court until payment. This includes both the days when actions take place and the waiting periods between. The respondents make separate estimates of the average duration of different stages of dispute resolution: the completion of service of process (time to file the case), the issuance of judgment (time for the trial and obtaining the judgment) and the moment of payment (time for enforcement).

Cost
Cost is recorded as a percentage of the claim, assumed to be equivalent to 200 percent of income per capita. Only official costs required by law are recorded, including court and enforcement costs and average attorney fees where the use of attorneys is mandatory or common.

Source:
http://www.doingbusiness.org/MethodologySurveys/EnforcingContracts.aspx

The *Doing Business* approach of using estimates by local lawyers entails a risk. Where there are no statistics from courts or other sources, there is no way of checking their accuracy. How much accuracy is required depends on what we need to do with the figures. If, for example, the average estimated time in days is 285, and we want to compare that to the ECHR general standard of 2 years, the level of accuracy is sufficient for the purpose. Actual court statistics, provided they are reasonably accurate, would most probably not make the outcome of this comparison any different.

Table 9 *Doing Business Database Contract Enforcement: Time in Days*

	Time in calendar days including filing, service and enforcement in 2007	*Time in calendar days for trial and judgment*	*Overall ranking on contract enforcement in 2007*
Benin	720	375	166
Georgia	285	100	42
Macedonia	385	280	84
Nepal	735	365	123
Netherlands	514	442	36
Romania	537	365	37
Sri Lanka	1318	1000	133
United States	300	180	8
Singapore (lowest number of days)	120	88	4
Hong Kong, China (best overall ranking)	211	176	1
Timor-Leste (highest number of days, lowest overall ranking on contract enforcement)	1800	1500	178

The lowest number of days for all three phases found by Doing Business for 2007 is 120 for Singapore. The highest number is 1,800 days, for contract enforcement in Timor-Leste.

The final column in Table 9 shows the ranking of each country in the list of 178 participating countries. Thus, Hong Kong, China ranks top performer on contract enforcement and Timor-Leste, in place 178, is at the bottom of the list.

The reason for describing the DB database here is to show how comparing national figures can play a role in developing standards, in this case for case processing in court. Doing Business has existed in its present form for only a couple of years at the time of writing (2008). It has become a widely used source of information on the business climate in most countries in the world. It contains a wealth of information. This information cannot always be verified. Reality has been modeled to a great extent to make the scores comparable. That may mean it no longer reflects actual practice. For instance, in the Netherlands the number of cases in which witnesses are heard is less than 2 percent of the total number of civil cases. A seller who wants to enforce a contract will turn to summary proceedings rather than a full trial. This does not provide the information needed to track problems in courts because that would require information on disposition times at the court level. Showing an average number does not reflect whether there are extremes and their share in the average disposition time. A large share of extremes may be a signal of problems.

DB's greatest value is for those situations where no other information is available. The point this section aimed to illustrate is the fact that these estimates are available to serve as a basis to reflect on what disposition times are acceptable, and which are manifestly unreasonable. This way, it can serve as a basis for setting standards.

Comparing results to standards

In order to provide an illustration of the methodology developed in these chapters, we can now compare the estimates from Doing Business with the standards, trends and indications discussed earlier. The case constructed for the DB purposes is a general civil case of no particular urgency. For this type of case, the ABA, CCJ and COSCA standard is 12 months or 365 calendar days for non-jury trials (see Table 6). The ECHR's general indication is 2 years, or approximately 730 days, for a simple civil case.

The U.S. DB result of 180 days for trial and judgment is well within the ABA, CCJ and COSCA standards of 12 months for non-jury trials. The Netherlands result of 442 days for trial and judgment exceeds the ABA standard of 365 calendar days but is within the ECHR jurisprudence's framework. Romania's result of 365 days for trial and judgment is well within those limits. Courts in all countries in the list except Sri Lanka and Timor-Leste have estimated disposition times that fall within the most current standards.

It is also possible to make a world wide comparison for a general civil case: If the phases of service and filing and enforcement take on average 135 calendar days, that is, 4½ months, courts in 72 of 178 countries are estimated to perform within the ABA standard. Courts in 135 of 178 countries are estimated to perform within the indicative standards that emerge from the ECHR jurisprudence. This raises the question whether, if a majority of courts' estimated performance falls within a widely accepted standard, the belief that courts are slow is justified for this particular case type.

How do these observations relate to Hammergren's conclusion above that case delay is exaggerated? If the DB estimates are approximately correct, and if the ECHR standards are applied, that conclusion is more or less justified. With the stricter time standards of the ABA, more disposition times would qualify as delays. This could serve as a starting point for a debate about case delay that is based on facts rather than beliefs.

Some preliminary conclusions

Case delay is recognized as a major problem in the administration of justice. Delay negatively affects parties in a case, society in a wider sense, and the administration of justice itself. Case delay means taking so long to process a case that it is considered excessive. Delay needs to be measured in order to establish whether it exists, whether it is as serious as claimed, and to identify remedies. In order to answer these questions, we do quantitative measurements. We do not measure delay itself but proxies, such as time to disposition, age of case load and clearance rates. In order to see whether there is an undue delay, the results of these measurements need to be gauged against standards. Hard and fast standards for case disposition times are not generally available. Existing standards have emerged from factual evidence about actual practice. That evidence is used to establish self-imposed goals for what the system wants to achieve. Jurisprudence deciding whether there has been a violation of the reasonable time rule is a source of standards too. Existing time standards differ for different case types: some types of cases require more expedient disposition than others because the parties involved have a more urgent need for a judicial decision. Case disposition times differ widely across the world.

The next section looks for causes of delay that may explain some of those differences.

Identifying causes

Courts may, if they have measured their disposition times and possibly compared them with standards, find that the times indicate unreasonable delays. This may bring them to the conclusion that delay is a significant problem for them. In order to find ways of reducing the disposition times, the next challenge is to identify the causes of delay. Identifying these causes has been approached in different ways. One is to look at variations disposition times between courts and factors that may explain those variations. There is research into factors explaining variations in disposition time. The scope of this research is limited because it is almost entirely American. The approach the research usually takes is that of comparing differences in case disposition times between courts on the basis of a theory regarding which factors are relevant. The next step is to identify those factors that emerge as significant in explaining these differences. The results of this research are diffuse (Eshuis 2007 p. 28).

Another approach is to look at interventions to reduce disposition times and how effective they have been. Solid empirical research into the workings and the results of concrete remedies against disposition time problems is very scarce, but there is some information on interventions to reduce disposition times and how effective they have been. Most of the examples below come from the 2002 *World Development Report* (WDR 2002). They are an aggregate of experience from judicial reform projects around the world. The value of these findings is also limited, for two reasons: (1) the interventions did not take place under well controlled circumstances, and (2) the results of the interventions were – both beforehand and afterward - not very well defined. Drawing conclusions about their effectiveness would be tentative at best. Drawing general conclusions from practical experience in an international context would also be problematic because of the important differences in the setup and scope of procedures, resource levels and a host of other factors.

With all those caveats, the discussion below looks at four groups of factors and interventions: case load, procedural factors, organizational factors, and cultural factors and other incentives. If the findings on both factors and interventions point in the same direction, the assumption will be that the factor in question effectively influences case disposition times.

Caseload

The most common explanation for delay is the size of a court's caseload: a court with more cases will take longer to process them. Caseload size alone does not determine delay. Only in relation to the human and other resources available to dispose it does caseload have meaning when it comes to disposition times. Case influx in the courts is determined by different factors:

- Legislation regulating which disputes or matters (for example divorce, property disputes, criminal sanctions) need to be brought before a court
- Incidence of these matters in society
- A large number of cultural and other factors influencing whether cases or matters actually come before a court (Genn 1999 p. 252).

These factors can all change. Congestion, backlog, and delay are inherent risks for organizations that face uncontrolled demand, while their resources are limited and inflexible. This kind of disconnect is very common for public service institutions, and the institutions in the justice sector are no exception. In principle, anyone can take a case to court, and the factors influencing the decision to do so are largely outside the court's control. For instance, the demand for commercial court cases will fluctuate inversely with the economy. If more people and businesses are unable to pay their bills, more claims will be filed with the first instance courts. The demand for criminal court cases may well vary with the political climate and public sector priorities in a country. The actual caseload is also influenced by the types of cases that have to be dealt with. A rise in more complex cases, for example when a country decides to prosecute more fraud or corruption, may not be reflected in the numbers, but it will constitute a greater demand on resources.

The caseload is sometimes regarded as the basis for differences in work distribution and cultural differences. However, a study of courts in the United States found that differences in the cases, in a court's case mix or in the percentage of jury trials did not explain variations in disposition times (Church p. 79). At first glance, it may seem that caseload is a factor that is not easily influenced. Timely and reliable management information reports and the use of modern case flow management techniques were found to be important factors in reducing backlog (Mahoney p. 19).

Backlog reduction programs were reported as effective in the short term. However, to reduce disposition times over the longer term, it is necessary to tackle the more fundamental causes (Eshuis 2007 p. 282).

Framework regarding procedures and processes

There is strong evidence of a significant relation between higher levels of procedural complexity and longer disposition times (Djankov c.s. p. 25, Botero c.s. p. 73). In countries with more complex procedures, case processing generally takes longer. It is important to differentiate between the procedural complexity, which has to do with the steps that need to be taken, and the substantive complexity of the case or dispute at hand, like the number of issues that need to be resolved.

With regard to remedies, the primary area to look would be in procedural simplification. The 2002 WDR lists different forms of simplification that have improved court performance:

Simplifying procedural rules is reported as successful by the WDR (WDR 2002 p. 127). Its beneficial effect is reported to increase with the degree of complexity of the older rules. An example is to reduce the possibility to appeal interim decisions and to limit appeal to the final decision only.

Alternative dispute resolution (ADR) is, according to the WDR, an alternative for badly functioning courts. It is important to distinguish ADR as a means to resolve disputes, and ADR as a means to relieve the courts of disputes that can be resolved alternatively in order to reduce the caseload and help courts to process the cases that need a court decision more quickly. As a concentrated form of dispute resolution, ADR can well be regarded as both a type of simplification, as well as a kind of procedural specialization. Genn reports that ADR has not had much impact on the way members of the public seek to resolve their justiciable problems[10]. Genn predicted in 1999 that this may change as courts encourage parties to try mediation to resolve their disputes (Genn 1999 p. 261).

The presence of *summary proceedings* was found to be significant in explaining variations in disposition times (Eshuis 2007 p. 28). The introduction of summary proceedings is reported as successful in reducing disposition times by offering a simpler procedure to resolve some disputes much faster (WDR 2002 p. 128). In the Netherlands, summary proceedings (*kort geding*) are a popular and effective means of acquiring a judicial decision in a short time.

Small claims courts, with a simpler procedure proportional to the size of the claim, were by far the most successful measure in reducing disposition times (WDR 2002 p. 126). However, it must be noted that there is not an overwhelming amount of evidence for this observation.

The degree of *specialization* of judges in some U.S. courts was found to be not significant in explaining the variation in processing times (Eshuis 2007 p. 28). However, the WDR reports that *specialized courts* were a successful measure for improving court disposition times and other aspects of court performance. Specialization in the sense of differentiating case streams is a popular remedy, although evidence for its efficacy is rather slim (WDR 2002 p. 126).

Early interventions in individual cases, either in court or just before the case comes to court, were mentioned as effective in reducing disposition time (Eshuis 2007 p. 299, Goerdt p.56). They generally serve to reduce the complexity of a dispute at the start of the court case. There are positive evaluations of this approach in Australia and the United Kingdom.[11] *Court conferences*, a form of early intervention where the judge plans the way a dispute will be handled with the parties and/or their representatives, have been found to reduce disposition times.

Practices and structures

This section is a mixed bag of various factors and remedies having to do with court practice and court structures.

Lack of resources is frequently put forward as a cause for longer disposition times. Resources were found to affect the length of disposition times in some studies in some U.S. courts, but in others they did not turn out to be significant. One study found that long disposition times are caused by lack of resources in the courts. A lack of resources may mean a relatively low number of judges. A lack of judges entails a higher caseload per judge, and that brings us back to the relative caseload as a factor affecting disposition times. The numbers of judges and staff were found to be related to disposition time in one study (Eshuis

2007 p. 28). Raising budgets and funding as an isolated measure does not lead to longterm improvements, according to experience reported in the WDR (WDR 2002 p. 128-129).

Methods of planning and control, caseload planning and guarding and enforcing time limits have all proven to be significant explaining in variations in disposition times in U.S. courts.

A study of courts in Argentina and Venezuela by Buscaglia and Ulen published in 1997 found that the use of *computerized word processing* is strongly correlated with faster disposition, particularly in the sentencing stage in courts in Venezuela and Argentina (Buscaglia 1997 p. 290).

Differences in organization and the ways the courts work were found to be relevant in explaining differences in case disposition times. Case management, keeping track of each individual case in order to ensure its expedient resolution, was found to be an important factor. Case management systems and keeping track of disposition times are two of the instruments used in case management. In a comparison of specific methods of management, the results were diffuse. Another study found a court's management characteristics, planning methods or goals not to be significant factors explaining its case disposition time (Mahoney p. 6, Eshuis 2007 p. 28).

Correct production statistics and *awareness of disposition times* are both proven factors leading to reduction in those times. This raises the question about causality: how, and whether, correct statistics contribute to delay reduction. We will come back to this question later. Research also shows that U.S. courts have adopted the ABA standards only under external pressure. Moreover, standards are a useful instrument for courts that seriously try to shorten disposition times (Eshuis 2007 p. 32).

The WDR reports that making individual judges responsible for cases is an improvement compared with master calendars (WDR 2002 p. 125). This reflects similar findings by Church (Church p. 72). Master calendars list cases that are in court, but have not been assigned to an individual judge. There is evidence that assigning cases to a judge early helps its prompt disposition. Lack of *oversight* at all stages of the proceedings is another contributor to delays.

More publicity in the form of information about judicial conduct and court hearing observation makes administration of justice faster and fairer, according to the WDR (WDR 2002 p.125). The presence of television cameras in the court made case disposition 30 percent speedier, and the quality of judgments went up. Observation by civil society organizations who evaluate judges is another example put forward by the WDR.

Insufficient implementation: where implementation of interventions to speed up case processing was insufficient, it was unsuccessful. Shortening disposition times is a long term exercise requiring longer periods of implementation. In the change processes, leadership is considered a factor. External pressure is an important factor to move local court systems (Eshuis 2007 p. 33).

Culture and other factors

Established expectations, practices and informal rules of behavior of judges and attorneys do explain variations in disposition times in a study of some U.S. courts (Church p. 50).[12] Efficient work orientation was also found to be significant in explaining variations in disposition times in some U.S. courts (Ostrom p. 108-9). Local expectations as to whether speedy procedures are generally considered important were found to be relevant for disposition times. However, there is no solid empirical evidence for the idea that they influence disposition times significantly (Eshuis 2007 p. 28). Finally, explanations can be sought in a series of perverse incentives. There are benefits to case delay too, for instance for the party who wants to defer payment. Defendants may have an interest in trying to hold off or prevent decisions against them. Lawyers may want to string out cases as a means of increasing their fees. A court itself may want to have a backlog as an argument for more resources.

This section analyzed which factors and interventions have proven to be effective in reducing case delay. The picture is not very clear. If we start looking for areas with factors (1) that have turned out to significantly influence disposition times, and (2) where interventions have helped in reducing disposition times, the following areas present themselves:

Increased transparency, such as correct measurement and awareness of actual disposition time, and of standards, can be regarded as positive factors in reducing disposition time. They have the potential to change the local legal culture posited by Church. As Church phrases it: “The crucial element in accelerating the pace of litigation in a court is concern on the part of judges with the problem of court delay and a firm commitment to do something about it” (Church p. 81). This is confirmed by Goerdt: “Delay can be reduced where there is commitment to expeditious case processing” (Goerdt p. 57). Information about actual practice can be a first step in fostering that awareness and change culture.

This is a hypothesis than can actually be tested. Taking the data on IT implementation from CEPEJ and the estimated disposition times for general civil cases from Doing Business, we can see whether the presence of case registration and case and court management systems bear any relation to those disposition times. I divided the countries reporting to CEPEJ into two groups: those reporting that they had implemented case registration systems, case management systems and court management systems in all courts, and those that reported they had not. In the first group, DB's disposition time estimates varied from 210 days for Lithuania to 515 days for Spain. The median disposition time for general civil cases for all countries in this group is 386 days, and the average is 388 days. Estimates for the second group of countries ranged from 237 days for Azerbaijan to 1,210 days for Italy. For all countries in this group, the median disposition time for general civil cases is 561 days and the average is 577 days.

For general civil cases in the Netherlands courts, average disposition time was 608 days in 1996, and 420 days in 2007. Simplification of case processing in the form of early intervention, specialization of case streams and simplification of procedures are also positive factors in reducing disposition time.

The area of court resource management presents itself as well, but it is outside the scope of this study on primary judicial processes. Courts and judges have often, and often with good cause, been accused of not paying attention to the issue of court resource management. Nevertheless, the issue is not part of this study because it focuses on the judicial process in itself.[13]

Therefore, increasing transparency and simplifying case processing, which both stand for a number of more specific activities, are areas that should receive special attention when we move on to the next chapters.

Conclusions for this chapter

This chapter took a first look at the question of how IT can support delay reduction in courts. It examined a number of aspects of case delay.

Outcomes of the research on causes of delay and interventions are diffuse. They do not provide hard and fast guidelines for reducing backlog or delay. Local culture, awareness of actual practice and the need for expedient case processing present themselves as factors affecting delay. Procedural complexity and simplification emerge from the research as likely areas for reducing delay. Specialization is reported as an effective remedy. It comes in many forms: summary proceedings, small claims courts and simpler procedures. Early intervention is also reported as effective.

IT as a factor affecting case delay in courts has not been studied empirically, except in some isolated cases.

One IT factor arises from this study: database technology used in case registration and management systems producing case processing statistics. Having data on case disposition and processing available facilitates both measuring actual disposition times and developing standards. The first standards emerged in the early 1980s in the United States, where technology was implemented in courts earlier than in most other countries. Apparently, database technology has been a factor in the development of standards. It has also been a tool in studies on factors affecting case delay. As a foundation for a debate about standards, case handling statistics have the potential to affect court culture.

According to the DB estimates regarding ordinary civil contract enforcement cases, courts in 58 of 178 countries dispose those cases within the ABA standard, and courts in 135 of 178 countries stay within the ECHR jurisprudence of what consists a reasonable delay in ordinary civil cases. Such a result provides a basis for discussion as to what a reasonable delay actually is. Such standards help to determine whether delay is a problem that needs to be tackled. They also help in reducing delay by providing a target. Self-imposed standards do not conflict with the constitutional independence of the judiciary. This is still true if the standards were adopted under external pressure because the obligation to provide timely justice is an obligation laid down in the Conventions. Jurisprudence on compliance with those standards, like that of the European Court of Human Rights, is a source of standards as well. Standards like the ones from the ABA can emerge from the study of actual practice, either in one country or in cross country comparisons like in *Doing Business.*

Looking at most other sources, IT is usually discussed in a very generic way: using IT will reduce processing times. Programs aiming to reduce processing times frequently refer to IT as a means for doing so. However, there is very little empirical foundation for this claim. One exception is the finding that the presence of word processing systems speeded up case disposition in Argentina. Apparently, experience-based research has not identified the implementation of IT as a very successful factor in reducing case disposition times. Various explanations for this observation are possible. Maybe the issue has not been studied, or maybe the results of studies that were done were inconclusive or negative. Possibly, it is hard to study because after implementation, no control group is available. Or maybe implementation of IT in courts has not yet led to changes in work processes that result in more expedient disposition times. After all, most courts are still paper based, and their interactions with the parties have, so far, not changed fundamentally.

In summary, the question of how IT can support reducing case delay has not received a satisfactory answer yet. Therefore, this study will need to take a different approach. In the next chapters, it will look at court processes themselves in terms of information handling. We need to know more about those processes in order to gain a deeper understanding of what IT can do. From the above, we have an indication of which interventions may benefit from using IT: increasing transparency and simplification. We will look at those interventions in terms of information processing. Writing about IT easily risks becoming speculative. To avoid this risk, a concrete, practical example that can be tested is necessary. Therefore, civil justice in the Netherlands will be the object of study in the next chapters.

Chapter 3.2 Case Processing as Information Management

This chapter examines information handling in case handling processes. It develops a conceptual framework for examining those processes. The next chapter tests the framework in a case study of civil justice in the Netherlands.

The following chapters will be mainly concerned with what courts do – deciding cases, producing titles, providing legal protection, and confirming norms –in terms of processes (Susskind 1996 p. 83). Thinking productively about those activities and processes in terms of information requires a conceptual framework. That framework will be unfolded in this chapter. It was first developed as a picture of first instance civil justice for a reappraisal of civil justice in the Netherlands in the first years of this century. That model, with a more extensive explanation of the thinking behind it, is presented in this chapter. Subsequently, I used a much more detailed version of the model to explain civil case processing to the information experts developing information architecture for the Netherlands judiciary. Both can be found in two articles I wrote. The first one appeared in the *Netherlands Legal Weekly* (Nederlands Juristenblad) (Reiling 2003). I later wrote an English language version of it for *Information and Communications Technology Law* (Reiling 2006). That version, now updated, is presented in the next chapter. I have found it to be a useful tool. Below, I will explain the thinking behind the model as it developed over the years.

We will take up the conclusions from the chapter on case delay again here. One important conclusion from the previous chapter is that *knowledge about what goes on in a court helps us to understand what can be improved.* A case registration system using a database and producing information about cases and how they are handled is a tool for courts that want to improve their performance. The adage about measuring is that what gets measured gets done.[14] This chapter and the next one will illustrate, in different ways, what can get done once the measuring is done.

Another observation from the discussion of case delay in the last chapter is that *it is uncertain whether the introduction of forms of information technology has reduced case delay in courts.* Understanding how information technology can contribute to reducing case delay may be more effective with a different approach. If we want to learn how information technology can support improvement in case processing, we will do well to consider the roles of information in the judicial process. This chapter examines court processes themselves in terms of information management, and largely independent of the legal substance of the cases in question. The analysis will draw on non-legal disciplines, such as sociology, information science and organization science.

The plan for this chapter is as follows:

The first step will be to introduce the theory behind the model that will be presented: Basic concepts about processes, products, roles and information. The roles of the judiciary are confronted with the theories about products and processes. This analysis leads to a conceptual framework in the form of a matrix

Next comes practice: A case study of civil justice in the Netherlands, applying the matrix framework developed in the first step and using statistics about civil case processing.

In the concluding part of this chapter, we will confront the findings with some common approaches to civil justice reform in the recent past.

Theory: Case processing as an information process

What does it mean to look at case processing as an information process?

The parties take a case to court. What they take to court, in terms of information, is information concerning their view of the issues in their case. Some of the information can be qualified as legal, most of it relates to the factual situation. Courts, judges, and juries process cases on the basis of information. From here on in this chapter, I will use the term "court" to include courts, judges and juries for the purpose of this discussion on processes. The information courts use to decide a case is both legal and factual. It comes from different sources: the parties, as well as sources of substantive and procedural law and other sources. In court, the information is processed and transformed into new information. The transformation is a process that involves all parties to the case as well as the court. The court output is information that the parties can subsequently use to pursue their goals.

This analysis of the use of information in court processes will use concepts from different disciplines. Therefore, those concepts need to be defined clearly and unequivocally, in order to make them understandable to readers from different disciplines. These concepts will be needed when we look at the court processes in more detail later in this chapter and in the next ones.

Then, we will look at the roles of the judiciary. Judiciaries around the world have been awarded similar roles, but there are some differences depending on the national context. The roles will be analyzed from various perspectives.

The next step will be to identify the products and outputs that correspond to the roles we found earlier.

We then move to the processes that produce these outputs and products. The processes will be examined as ways of handling information, not according to their legal substance.

Basic concepts

Here are the basic concepts used in the rest of this chapter and the next ones:

Role: A role is a function performed especially in a particular operation or process.

Process: Organization science, more specifically business process theory, provides the notion of process: a process is a collection of activities that takes one or more kinds of input, adds value and creates an output that is of value to the customer (Hammer p. 38). A process is a structured, measured set of activities designed to produce a specified output for a particular customer or market (Davenport p. 5). This output can be called the product of the process. In an information processing business, the process takes information as the input, processes the information and adds new information. The resulting product is new information the customer can put to use.

Product: The term product, also from organization science, will be used here for "that which is produced" by the court process. It will usually be a judicial decision. The product is distinct from the output.

Outcome: In this chapter, the term outcome is reserved for the content of the court's decision: the claim is awarded, the defendant is not guilty, the government has wrongly taken a decision, the divorce is granted.

Output: In the same framework, the term output is used for that which is produced in a process, and that is *of value to the customer.* Here, this term will be reserved for that which is the value of the court product for the customer. Court decisions can have different values for the customer: an end to a legal debate, a document to register a divorce, an entitlement of some sort, a document to enforce a claim, or the execution of a prison sentence.

Thus, the court process produces a decision (product) with content (outcome) that has value for the user (output). Processes are determined first and foremost by what they produce. Both the process and the product are related to the role of the producer. Hence, the outputs and products of the judiciary are closely related to its roles. What are those roles?

Court roles (1)

If a role is a function performed especially in a particular operation or process, and the role affects the processes and products, we first need to examine how the role of the judiciary can be described. Court users, judges, the legal profession, socio-legal studies and society in general all have their own perspective on the role of courts. These perspectives are described in Chapter 1.2. Here is a brief summary.

Court users, the "customers" for whom courts produce value, perceive the courts as an institution providing concrete legal protection to the individual, ensuring that the individual will not be jeopardized beyond the limits of the law. *Judges* differ in how they view their role. First instance judges regard resolving disputes as their role. Final court judges give priority to safeguarding the unity of the legal system.

From the *legal point of view,* under the rule of law, the role of the court is determined by the law. Court tasks as attributed by the law may differ from country to country.

Most legal sociologists consider dispute processing the central judicial role (Cotterrell p. 220). Court decisions as judgments are, in most sociologists' perspective, both a resolution to a dispute or concrete legal protection, as well as an assertion of normative order, or abstract legal protection.

For the purpose of this discussion about the courts' processes, the product of those processes is defined as "decisions." Those decisions are not just any decision, but the decisions that are specific to the court's role in society. Courts are not the only instance in society producing decisions. Government agencies decide about policy, civil servants decide about entitlements, arbiters decide certain disputes. What characterizes the court's role is that it produces decisions that can be enforced with public means: bailiffs, the police force. Judicial decisions sanction the use of official force, whether it concerns enforcing sanctions or auctioning off assets. In this perspective, the role of producing enforceable decisions distinguishes judiciaries from all other organizations producing decisions and resolving disputes. Those decisions are also affirmations of norms in the broader sense of abstract legal protection.

Court roles (2)

In this section, the roles perspective is narrowed down in order to focus on the court processes. The role of the court in general is to produce enforceable decisions, in other words: to provide title. The product is consequently an enforceable decision. In this role, the question can be asked: What is the output of the judicial process? Output, as we have seen, is the value for the customer produced by the processes. How are the enforceable decisions produced of value to the customer? This is the next question we explore.

The framework used here to explore customer value related to court roles was introduced by Blankenburg in a comparative study of German and Dutch courts in the light of access to justice and alternatives to courts (Blankenburg 1995). I have adapted it by reversing the horizontal axis in order to model the relationships between the court processes and their outcomes more adequately. However, the roles allocated to the court remain the same (Blankenburg p. 188). For each role, we can determine which products and outputs are brought forth. Next, we can determine the characteristics of the processes that produce them. The descriptions below are ideal types of each role. In reality, cases will resemble one of the types to a certain degree, and they may at the same time have some of the characteristics of another type. Here are the ideal types of each role:

a Title provision

Overall, title provision is the role of the court as attributed by the law. It is to provide parties with the output, the formal decision they need to proceed with their business: with a judicial decision in hand, they can go to a bailiff for contract enforcement, to impose criminal sanctions like fines and prison sentences, or to have administrative decisions revised. This role includes the affirmation of norms in a more general sense. Apart from being the general role of a court, it is also the role associated with undefended claims. This is how it will be discussed in the rest of this chapter.

Three other specific roles can be identified that will help us understand the information processes in courts and judiciaries.

b Notarial role

This role resembles that of a public notary. The parties submit an arrangement to a court for approval: an agreement on how to conduct their divorce, who will exercise parental authority, or how they intend to terminate a labor contract. Judicial control ensures the arrangements proposed by the parties are within the limits of the law. The judicial decision formalizes the arrangement. In this role, there is only marginal control of what the parties have arranged and now submit to the court. The parties will generally need this decision for a next step in a bureaucratic process, such as having their divorce registered with the civil administration.

c Settlement

This is a role that is often stressed in socio-legal literature. The settlement role is gradually becoming an accepted modality in courts. More and more, courts are encouraged to help parties settle their differences, rather than pursuing their differences to the full. Settlement occurs, for instance, when the parties agree to settle their differences in an agreement, instead of letting the judge decide.

d Judgment

This role is considered the judicial role par excellence. The full legally relevant scope of a dispute is dealt with by the court, and the court case ends with a judicial decision. The decision is reached with legal reasoning.

The roles cannot always be distinguished quite so sharply in actual practice. Case processing may contain elements of more than one role, but in most cases it is possible to identify an overriding role.

Now that the roles we will be examining have been identified, the next step is to look at the products and outputs that come with each role. The term "product" describes what the court actually produces. The term "output" is reserved to describe what it is that is of value to the customer. Finally, the term "outcome" describes the content of the judicial decision.

Products, outputs and outcomes

Each of these roles brings with it a specific product and output. The product will, in most cases, be a judicial decision of some sort. The output, as we have seen, will be a title. In the notarial role, it is also a confirmation that can be used for the next step in some bureaucratic process: registering a divorce in the civil register, applying for a social security benefit. This is the output that is of value to the court users. The settlement role is an exception because, at least in the Netherlands, the product here is not a judicial decision but a court report containing the provisions of the settlement. The report is full proof of the settlement.

What makes the roles and the products relevant for our discussion is that they affect the way information is used in the primary judicial process.

Two factors affect court processes in a major way:

A major factor affecting a process is the *unpredictability of the outcome*. The outcome of a process can be completely predictable from the outset. For example, in the case of a factory, the process is set up to produce a predetermined object, for instance bicycles of a certain type. Alternatively, the outcome can be more or less uncertain at the outset. This can be the case in a design process, for example, of a new model bicycle, with participants influencing the outcome during the process. Events happening along the way can affect the outcome. In our case of court processes, the outcome is the content of the decision: the divorce arrangement is in keeping with regulations, the claim is unfounded.

In terms of information: the information available at the outset of the process can be either sufficient to produce the outcome, or insufficient. In that case, other factors, including added information, may affect the outcome while the process is going on.

Another important factor is the parties' interest configuration: it can be one party's loss and the other party's gain at the same time, or the outcome can be a gain for both parties. In terms of game theory, the result is either zero-sum or win-win. In game theory, zero-sum describes a situation in which a participant's gain or loss is exactly balanced by the losses or gains of the other participant(s). In zero sum, it is irrelevant whether the parties maintain a good relationship. A win-win game is a game that is designed in such a way that all participants can profit from it one way or the other. In conflict resolution, a win-win strategy is a conflict resolution process that aims to accommodate all the disputants. In win-win, cooperation by the parties is vital toward producing the best result for each of them.

Figure 1 shows this concept in a matrix

In this matrix, the role of the court and the ensuing products are arranged along two axes: the relative uncertainty of the outcome from left to right, and the relationship between the parties in terms of zero sum and win-win from top to bottom. In showing court roles in this way, I also want to make the point that, regarded from this perspective, individual cases are on a continuum, both vertically and horizontally. A

Figure 1 *Matrix of Judicial Roles*

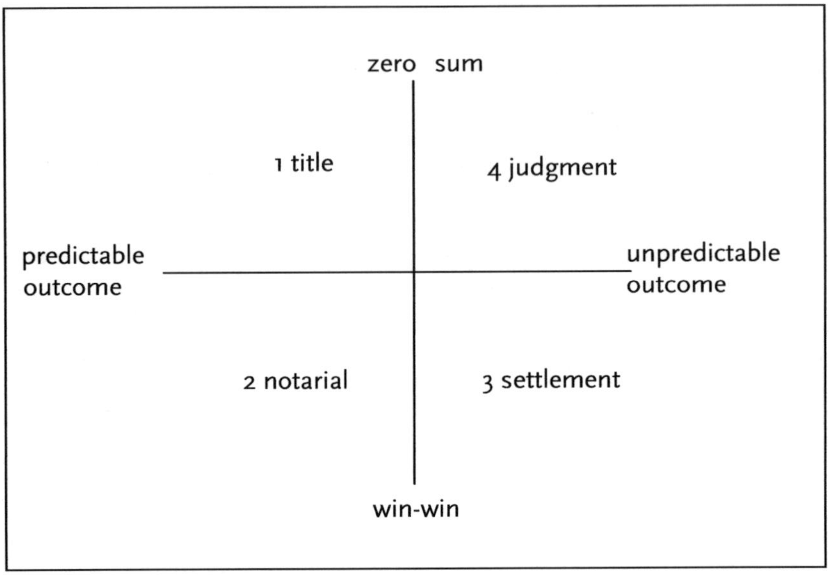

case or a decision can be mostly notarial with a little judgment, or mostly judgment with a little settlement.

The next step will be to explore how court cases fit into the groups.

Introducing the groups and their characteristics

This next section works toward categorizing court cases according to the use of information in each group. This is relevant for subsequently determining what forms of information technology can support them. The matrix above is the vehicle used for this purpose. Below, each group is identified and its most relevant characteristics are discussed.

Providing title is the role in the first group. As we have already seen, the product of the judicial process is always a title, in the sense that it is an enforceable decision that can be used to take possession, to effect imprisonment, or perform any other act of enforcement. But it is the output of this group in particular. Here, we deal with a process that does no more than producing that title. The case is "cut and dried" (Galanter 1983b[15]). The outcome is zero-sum because one party gains and the other party loses. The process in this group is characterized by a very low level of uncertainty. Undefended money claims come to mind as an example.

The *notarial role*, group 2, produces an affirmation, a formal declaration that the arrangement proposed by the parties is legal. It also entails little uncertainty. The outcome is win-win. By cooperating, the parties can achieve an optimum result. This process is also characterized by low uncertainty. Ideally, parties propose an arrangement they have worked out among themselves. The arrangement is examined by the court only marginally. Family cases and plea bargaining are some of the examples for this group.

The *settlement role*, group 3: here, the overriding objective is for the parties to reach agreement. This agreement is the output. The outcome is win-win. The process is characterized by uncertainty about the outcome, and by communication and negotiation. Very complex information, needed to help the parties to reach agreement, can be the object in this process.

The *judgment role*, group 4, is widely regarded as the judiciary's main function. The outcome of the process is dependent on all sorts of events that may occur during the process. The parties are in opposition. The court decides. This process may involve large amounts of complex information. It should be noted here that the difference between groups 1 and 4 is relative, in the sense that the outcome is more or less unpredictable. If no or almost no legal issues need to be decided, the case is regarded as a title group case. As the number of legal issues to be decided increases, the case moves in the direction of the judgment group. The cutoff point between groups 1 and 4 is whether the case is defended or not. However, there can still be legal issues that need to be decided in group 1 cases.

In the next section, we will take the actual caseload of civil justice in the Netherlands and sort the cases into the groups according to the model developed above. We can determine the relative share of each group in the total caseload, the average processing and disposition time, some other statistics. The answer to these questions is primarily important to determine where efforts at implementing IT can be most effective.

Practice: A case study of civil justice in the Netherlands

The next step in our exploration is to apply the matrix to civil justice in the Netherlands. The Netherlands has a legal culture in which settlement plays a substantial role.[16] Civil procedural law instructs judges to attempt settlement before deciding a case on its merits. Each country will most probably have its own legal culture in this regard. It will be interesting to see whether other legal cultures have demonstrably different patterns, and whether those patterns show up in the matrix. Such an exercise requires intimate knowledge of case types and court roles in the context of the legal culture of the country involved. For instance, it requires a solid database with case management data with sufficient differentiation of case types. Hence, it should not be undertaken lightly.

However, finding such patterns in other legal cultures is not the purpose of this chapter. It is to learn how different processes use information in order to understand what they need by way of specific IT functionality.

Reasons for choosing civil justice
There are a number of reasons for choosing civil justice. First, in thinking about information technology in court processes, civil justice has, in my experience, turned out to be the most accessible area of law. This may have to do with the real or presumed equality of the parties. The reason for choosing the Netherlands for this case study is that categorizing cases into the groups is an exercise that requires in-depth knowledge of the local legal culture and its practices. Having been a practicing civil judge in the Netherlands for many years, I am familiar enough with civil justice to make the judgments needed to make the conclusions robust, and this study useful.

The other reasons are more objective in nature.

Civil justice is *statistically* of relatively large importance in Dutch administration of justice: 45 percent of all disposed cases are civil.

The second is its *economic* importance: 1 in 4 cases of insolvency is due to late payments. 35 percent of these payment delays are deliberate late payments; they are not due to financial problems of the debtor, or of a dispute over performance, or even administrative inefficiency.[17]

This section starts with an overview of civil justice judicial institutions in the Netherlands. Then, we look at the statistics of disposed cases. Those cases are put into their groups in the matrix quadrants. In the next chapter, we look at each group, and how information plays out, in much more detail.

Some statistics about the Dutch court system

The Dutch court system has some of the characteristics of the classic Napoleonic civil justice (as opposed to common law) system. It has three tiers of jurisdiction. In the first instance, there are 19 district courts working in sectors: a civil law sector, a criminal law sector, an administrative law sector and a local courts (*"kanton"*) sector. The civil law sectors deal with major money claims, family matters related to divorce and civil juvenile matters. They generally have a specialized commercial matters unit and a unit for summary proceedings. The formerly more than 60 local courts were administratively integrated into the district courts in 2002. They deal mostly with money claims up to

€ 5,000, traffic violations, minor family matters, and employment and rent contract matters. They also have summary proceedings in their civil law fields. For the purpose of this study, they will be called "local courts" and "civil courts," respectively. There are five appeal courts that hear appeals of civil, criminal and some administrative cases. For civil and criminal justice, the apex court is a court of cassation known as the Supreme Council.

With 19 first instance courts for 16 million inhabitants, the rate of courts per inhabitant is a little less than 1 court to a million inhabitants. With 2,280 judges totaling a full-time equivalent of 2,072, the rate of judges to inhabitants is 13 judges to 100,000 inhabitants. Looking at the results of the CEPEJ study on court efficiency, both those rates are very low compared with those in most other member states of the Council of Europe (CEPEJ 2006b p. 61, 62). In 2002, the total case influx was 1,330,500 with total production at 1,450,000. In 2007, the case influx had gone up to 1.733,600 and production was at 1.726,000 (2007 Annual Report of the Dutch Judiciary, p. 79-80).

Table 10 *Civil Justice: Disposed Cases in Three Instances*

Year	*1st instance local court*	*1st instance civil sector*	*Appeal*	*Cassation*
2002	502.030	201.880	9000	488
2003	580.590	208.480	11940	490
2004	671.090	225.610	13000	466
2005	695.170	230.570	14370	452
2006	685.430	232.600	14310	463
2007	680.100	236.120	14710	475

Source: Netherlands Judicial Council Annual Reports, Supreme Court Annual reports

Table 10 shows the number of disposed civil and family cases for 2002-2007.[18] More than 700,000 civil cases were disposed in the first instance in 2002. Almost 500,000 of these were disposed in the local court sectors of the district courts, the other 200,000 in the other civil sector or sectors in the district courts. Approximately 9,000 cases got a review in the appeal courts.[19] Finally, the Supreme Council reviewed 488 civil cases.[20]

By 2007, the numbers for the first and appeal instances had gone up to more than 900,000 and 14,000, respectively, but the cassation numbers remained at around 500 annually. Evidently, from these quantitative data, the appeal and cassation instances' numbers are extremely low compared with the first instance. Statistically, they do not influence the distribution in the groups we will be looking at below. That is why, from here on, only the statistics for the first instance of civil justice in the Netherlands are taken as our object of study.

Cases into groups
The first step is to find out how many cases are in each group.[21]

To that end, actually disposed cases are counted, based on the reports of disposed case by the courts to the Council for the Judiciary. The count follows the detailed case categories the Dutch courts use for their production reports, as reflected in Table 11.

The counts were done as follows:

Group 1: Final dispositions and summary dispositions of undefended money claims, both for the local court and the district court.

Group 2: Dispositions in parental authority, supervision and settled employment termination cases in the local courts, and dispositions in divorce related family cases in the district courts.

Group 3: Cases withdrawn at the parties' request or struck off the record.

Group 4: Final dispositions of contested civil claims, including those going through a phase of fact-finding by hearing witnesses and viewing locations, for both local and civil courts.

Table 11 *Detailed Count of Groups, with Case Category Numbers*

Group	*Local court*		*Civil court*	
1	105	Final dispositions in undefended claims	105	Final dispositions in undefended claims
	302	Final dispositions in undefended summary cases	302	Final dispositions in undefended summary cases
2	204	Decisions instituting supervision	201	Divorce dispositions
	299	Decisions instituting guardianships and parental authority	204	Other family cases including maintenance, adoption, parental authority after divorce, visiting rights, other dispositions in family cases, reclaiming social assistance
	2606	Settled employment terminations		
3	301 399	Defended cases Withdrawn or struck off the record at parties' request, both summary and non-summary cases	1568, 1570-1573, 1635, 2560, 2565 399	Defended cases withdrawn, struck off the record at parties' request
4	1686, 1691, 1692	Final dispositions in defended cases	1589-1593	Final dispositions in defended cases

Group	*Local court*		*Civil court*	
	2607	Non-settled employment terminations	1631	Final dispositions in defended summary cases
	1727, 1728	Final dispositions in defended summary cases		

The numbers are the case category numbers known as Lamicie categories after the commission that first developed them; in italics: more detailed case category numbers, where applicable.
Source: Netherlands Council for the Judiciary.

Figure 2 shows the matrix with the distribution of cases over groups, as a percentage of total civil case dispositions in 2007.[22] The numbers vary slightly over the years, with group 3 showing a little growth from 2002 to 2007 and the other three groups small reductions. Civil case production itself grew by 76 percent during those years, but the variation in distribution is not significant. The numbers are for 2007.

The distribution of caseloads over the groups presents a different picture. Group 1 is the largest with 35 percent of the total case production. Group 2 is only somewhat smaller at 30 percent. Groups 3 and 4 are much smaller. Group 3 is 9 percent of the total caseload and group 4 is the smallest, at 8 percent. Cotterrell observes that it is well known that courts handle large numbers of routine matters as well as disputes

Figure 2 *Matrix of Judicial Roles and Caseloads*

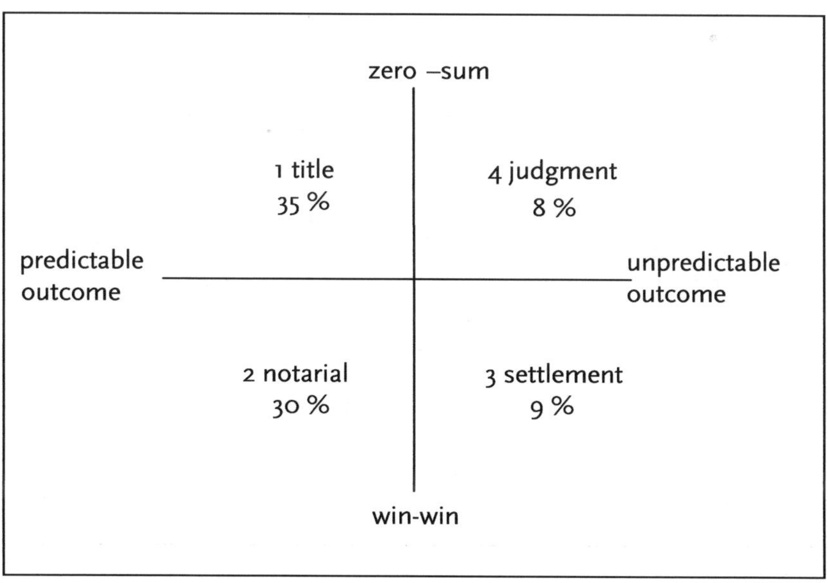

(Cotterrell p. 224-225). Group 4, in which defended cases are decided by the court, is normally considered judicial work *par excellence.* Yet, it is only 8 percent of the case production.

This diagram tells us a few things that are useful for automation (electronic processing): the title group is the group that is easiest to automate because it is zero-sum and the outcome is predictable. It is also the largest group. That makes this a good candidate to start automation, developing routines for electronic processing. The notarial group comes in a close second.

In the next chapter, each group will be discussed in more detail.

Conclusions for this chapter

This chapter took a first step in analyzing information handling in case handling processes. It developed a conceptual framework for examining those processes.

The main topic in this chapter was the matrix showing the different groups of civil cases that flow through the court. The groups reflect judicial roles as well as case characteristics and processes. The cases can be sorted according to the level of predictability and the party configuration of zero-sum and win-win outcomes. That leads to a number of conclusions:

The different roles of courts determine the processes and products that can be identified for each of the groups. Offering legal protection, providing a way to enforce rights and affording fair hearing, resolving disputes and dispute processing are the roles most often found. In a different perspective, courts fulfill four major roles.

In the majority of the cases processed in the Dutch civil jurisdiction in the first instance, there is no dispute resolution because there are few disputes to be found there. Titles are provided for undefended claims (role 1), arrangements in family situations are marginally tested (role 2), and settlements are encouraged wherever possible (role 3). In those cases where there is no dispute, the information available at the outset is sufficient to finalize the case and produce a decision.

Relatively few cases, less than 20 percent, need more information during the court procedure in order to bring a resolution of the dispute closer.

Half of those cases are most probably resolved with a settlement (role 3).

What is left after that is a small fraction of the total caseload in which disputes are decided by a judicial decision (role 4). The role of dispute resolution, most often mentioned by the different stakeholders, is not the most prevalent one if we look at its share in the total caseload.

These conclusions can be drawn because – as observed before - the relevant statistics are available from the case registration systems.

We can put these findings into the context of some common approaches to civil justice reform in the recent past. Zuckerman's study on Civil Justice in Crisis in 1999 was an attempt at a comprehensive approach to the reform of civil justice. In this approach, the three aspects of time, cost and truth are central. Zuckerman observed in 1999 that a reassessment of the balance between those three was going on in many parts of the Western world, with the emergence of the ideas of proportionality and a just distribution of procedural resources (Zuckerman p. 48). The study for a fundamental reconsideration of the Dutch civil procedural system posited the basic principle that a dispute can best be resolved where that can be done at the lowest possible social expense: it should be accessible, cost efficient, use modern means of communication, be open to alternatives and have acceptable disposition times (Asser 2006 p. 19). By now, ten years later, we should be able to see Zuckerman's trends in action. Whether and how courts and judicial systems have started to use forms of information technology to support effective dispute resolution within a reasonable time should also be discernible by now. These questions will provide guidance for the next chapter.

Chapter 3.3 Judicial Roles in Detail

This chapter examines each group in the matrix in more detail, in order to identify how IT can support reducing case delay in each of the groups. It takes a closer look at civil justice in the Netherlands. For each group in the matrix, we first collect some statistics. Then, we examine the role of information in the process in question. From those findings, we look for the IT potential in each group. This potential will be determined by the roles of information we discovered looking at the process. We also examine some examples of the use of information technology in other court systems. The chapter ends with conclusions about possibilities for IT in each of the groups, framed in terms of the wider debate on civil justice and case delay reduction.

Methodology

For each group, the first item is its main statistical characteristics. These come from the courts' own case administration systems. The courts report the numbers of their caseload and disposed cases with the help of their information systems.[23] The figures shown in each group below are those reported by the courts to the Council for the Judiciary:

- Percentage of the total caseload as an indicator of the importance of the group. This figure is calculated from the counts of disposed cases from the last chapter. The statistics are for 2007.
- Average disposition time in calendar days. Disposition time is the length of time a case is in the court administration, from filing to final disposition. The disposition time is the actual figure usually shown in the statistics. This figure comes from the court statistics for 2007. For some groups, the figure is an average of very diverse case categories.
- Processing time. This is the time someone is actually performing some action in a case file. Actual processing times are not available, but the case processing time standards are. They are updated every three years to reflect actual practice. They are the best proxy available. Processing times are expressed in minutes, for both the judge and the support staff. The most recent update as shown here is from 2005.

Starting from this information about Dutch court practice in each group, each process is examined to understand the implications of its characteristics. How do their characteristics affect handling the information involved? What are the consequences for supporting and improving the process with IT? Examples of proven technology and of changes in business processes that enable new technological solutions are analyzed. Each discussion of a group wraps up with conclusions for information technology support for that group.

The chapter as a whole will close with a discussion of information technology support for civil justice, and about the activities needed to make that support work.

Group 1 – Title role

The outcome of the cases in this group is both zero-sum as well as highly predictable.

Facts

The title group consists of the final dispositions and summary dispositions of undefended money claims, handled by both local and civil courts.

In the local courts, about 46 percent of all civil cases are undefended. In the civil courts, the percentage is only 5. Therefore, this is an important group for the local courts, but not a priority category for reform in the civil courts.

Table 12 *Case Categories in the Title Group*

Group 1		*Local court*	*Civil court*
Percentage of total civil caseload		46%	5%
105	Final dispositions in undefended claims		
	Time standard	90% within 15 days	90% within 1 month
	Average disposition time for 2007	1 week	5 weeks
	Work load standard processing time for 2001	Judge 1 minute Staff 45 minutes	Judge 15 minutes Staff 90 minutes
	Work load standard processing time for 2005	Judge 1 minute Staff 19 minutes	Judge 9 minutes Staff 98 minutes
302	Final dispositions in undefended summary cases	Time standard not available	Time standard not available
	Average disposition time for 2007	30 days	48 days
	Work load standard processing time for 2001	Judge 1 minute Staff 45 minutes	Judge 15 minutes Staff 90 minutes
	Work load standard processing time for 2005	Judge 1 minute Staff 45 minutes	Judge 15 minutes Staff 90 minutes

The numbers are the case category numbers.
2005 is the most recent year for which practice-based processing time standards are available at the time of writing in 2008.

Source: Netherlands Council for the Judiciary.

The *local courts* process default cases in a disposition time of 8 days on average. The workload standard for processing time for 2001 was 1 minute of the judge's, and 45 minutes of the support staff's time. By 2005, processing time had dropped to 19 minutes of the support staff's time per case. The judge's task is usually limited to signing the decision that has been prepared by the court staff following judicial instructions. Because self-representing parties can appear in person in the local courts, they handle these cases in an orally conducted roll session.

In the *civil courts*, the disposition time of ordinary, non-summary undefended cases was on average 37 days in 2007. The workload standard for processing time per case for the judge was 15 minutes in 2001, and it came down to 9 minutes by 2005. The support staff's time for 2001 was 90 minutes. That time went up to 98 minutes for 2005. Clearly, in the civil courts, there is more judicial involvement with individual cases than in the local courts. Processing those cases also takes the civil court support staff longer.

Process and information analysis
The outcome in this group is mostly or completely predictable from the outset. The outcome does not depend on any cooperation between the parties. This is what happens: A claim is filed, and the defending party files no defense. There is a check whether it is complete and in conformity with the law. This check of the lawfulness of the claim may require the attention of a judge in some individual cases. Otherwise, court staff members process these cases on the basis of instructions from the judges. The claim, provided it is complete and lawful, is granted because it is undefended. In the local court, the work the judges do on individual cases is 1 minute on average, as opposed to 9 minutes in the civil courts. Local court staff time, 19 minutes, is also much more limited than the 98 minutes for civil court staff.

Cases also involve decisions about other issues, such as costs. Costs, as a general rule, are borne by the losing party. The part of the judicial decision awarding those costs is mostly handled routinely because collection costs, procedural expense, most legal representation fees, and court fees have been standardized in a tariff structure. The tariffs are the product of working groups or committees in the National Association of Magistrates (Nederlandse Vereniging voor Rechtspraak, NVVR). Some courts, by way of incentive, produce decisions more quickly for parties who claim collection costs according to the tariff (NVVR 2002[24]).

Because the outcome is predictable and zero-sum, generally speaking the information that is available at the outset is sufficient to decide the case. It seems reasonable to assume that this process should be the easiest one to automate. Automation means: creating a process that can be handled by a machine without human intervention. In the context of IT, this means the process runs electronically. This does not mean that the entire process needs to be automated. It is also feasible to automate parts of a process, for instance for fixing procedural cost compensation as discussed below. Automation means translating policies and routines into programs for electronic processing. Those programs operate as follows: if x, then y. For example, if there is a tariff for collection costs, the program does the following: if the claim amount is a, or between a and b, or more than c, depending on the tariff, then the collection cost according to the tariff is x, or y or z, and an amount of x, y or z is awarded as the collection cost. Thus, the claim amount needs to be entered into the program. This concept needs to be standardized enough to serve the purposes of fixing cost compensation amounts for all cases. We have to be certain that the claim amount is (1) always composed of the same elements so that it (2) produces the same sum of collection costs. So far, this is the same for automated and non-automated processes alike. But when the process is automated, the computer needs to know, so to speak, what the amount of the claim is. Hence, in the database that contains the case data, there is a data field containing the amount of the claim. If data are provided by an outside source, like the bailiffs, there needs to be a recognizable data field with the claim amount using the same concept. The data need to be structured in order for the computer to recognize them. This is what is meant by structured data. Structured data do not necessarily have to be in electronic form. A paper form with boxes or numbered questions and dotted lines for the answers is also structured data. Therefore, the availability of structured data is a necessity because the programs transform the structured data that constitute the input into a product.

The more the input into the court can be done as structured data, the less human activity is needed for the product. Even less human activity in the court is needed if those data can be supplied to the court in electronic form, and online.

In summary, there are two opportunities in this group. The opportunities are closely related. One is the interaction with the parties submitting cases, the other is internal processes. If the parties file their cases by submitting structured data electronically, and the internal court process receives those data, manual data entry by court staff is avoided. If court routines are translated into programs to handle those data, the titles that are the product of this process can be produced (almost) without human intervention.

Examples

In this section, we look at some examples of applications for (nearly) automated title provision in actual operation.

a Example 1: Online claims in the United Kingdom

An example that is relevant for group 1 cases comes from the United Kingdom[25]. It consists of three online systems: the Claims Production Centre (CPC), Money Claim On Line (MCOL) and Possession Claim On Line (PCOL). These systems are the best known examples of online title provision.

It took a long period of time for them to get to the present level of functionality. What started out in the early 1990s as a simple processing center for processing large amounts of electronically filed claims from frequent users (CPC) now accepts individual claims for money (MCOL) or repossession (PCOL). First, here are the most significant steps in that development:

A dedicated center (the CPC) was set up at Northampton County Court as a service to large returning court users like energy companies and banks. It was set up in the early 1990sto handle large numbers of routine civil cases. Freeing up the staff of the other local courts for other tasks, the CPC is a central point for receiving monetary claims. The CPC was set up long before the emergence of the Internet. It has been in use for many years. Large returning customers, such as energy companies and banks, use it to file large amounts of claims. They file those claims, batched, electronically, with structured data. Originally, they would send in only data tapes. Today, the transmission is also done online. After receiving claims, a next step is to process undefended claims.

The feature to actually process undefended claims was subsequently added to the court. At that stage, if claims were defended, the claimant could request referral to the court that is competent according to the normal rules (Timms 2002).

In February/March 2002, *Money Claim On-Line* (MCOL) was added as the Internet mailbox for the court.[26] MCOL is governed by a practice direction contained in the Civil Procedural Code.[27]

Entering a defense online has been possible via the MCOL system for all claims issued via either MCOL or the CPC since December 2002. If claims are defended, they are automatically transferred to the court that is competent according to the normal rules.

In October 2006, *Possession Claim Online* (PCOL) was launched (HMCS Annual Report 2006-2007).[28] As reported in the HMCS Annual Report for 2006-2007, it enables property owners to apply electronically for repossession when rent or mortgages are not paid. Defendants can also issue a defense online. This addition to HMCS' online service portfolio makes claiming far simpler and faster: fees are paid electronically, claims issued straight away and hearing dates scheduled automatically.

Box 6 Online Services in the United Kingdom

MCOL - Money Claim On Line
Internet based system - can be used for any specified money claims provided that the particulars of the claim can be summarized within 1,050 characters.
Claimants can make individual claims over the internet.
Allows parties to make or defend a claim, and/or request a judgment and warrant.
It is available 24 hours a day, 7 days a week.
Guaranteed issue within 24 hours.
Fees can be paid by credit or debit card.
Where a claim is defended, it will transfer immediately to the defen-

dants local court for a hearing.
Fees = £5-£35 (depending on the value of the claim) cheaper than local county court.

PCOL – Possession Claim On Line
Internet based system for simple mortgage or rent arrears claims where there is a postcode.
Claimants can either make claims individually on the Internet or in bulk using a dedicated interface.
Allows users to access court forms and review and check the progress of claims online.
Fees can be paid by credit or debit cards and, for registered organizations, direct debit.
Hearing dates and correct jurisdiction are allocated automatically
Guaranteed issue within 24 hours.
Guaranteed hearing date within 8 weeks of the date of issue.
It is available 24 hours a day, 7 days a week.
Users can opt for all system generated correspondence to be sent by email - in which case they will receive instant and guaranteed communication.
Fees = £50, cheaper than issuing at local court.

Source: Her Majesty's Court Service, debts and housing branch

There are some particular features in civil procedural law in England and Wales that enable, or at least facilitate, the use of online claim processing:

No summons: In England and Wales, no formal summons is needed to start a civil claim. The claimant sends his or her claim to the court, and the court notifies the defender by mail. For the Dutch courts, a formal summons is a requirement.

No obligatory court competence: The users themselves can decide whether to use the Northampton court or not because the relative competence of courts (where to go to with one's case) is not obligatory.

No lump sum court fees: Court fees are charged for each requested activity separately.[29]

It is the U.K. Government's overriding aim to avoid cases coming to court unless absolutely necessary. It is not the intention that provision of online services will extend access to new users. When MCOL was launched, the intention was that the users would be claimants in person, or small businesses that do not have the volume or technology to do bulk processing, and it seems that these are the ones that are using it. Research in 2006 suggested that 95 percent of those using MCOL had issued fewer than 10 claims. Whenever a service is "opened up" by making it available on the web, there is always a risk that this will encourage users who might have shied away from manual methods, thus introducing a new market. However, this does not appear to have happened for MCOL, as the number of small claims issued has remained fairly static since before MCOL was launched (1.4 million claims issued in 2000, pre MCOL, and 1.4 million in 2007, 7 years after its launch), with a few small differences along the way, which are probably more attributable to market forces.[30]

With those figures, changes in user numbers may be difficult to track because the total number of claims is so high. I would still like to point out an effect that, according to the presentation in 2002, was seen in the early pilot phase of MCOL. Self-employed individuals started using MCOL on a regular basis. This group had made very little use of the court system until then. This group was responsible for almost the entire growth of the labor market in England and Wales in the first five years of the new century: the "white vanmen." They are self-employed, small entrepreneurs with not much more than a van and a computer (Timms 2002).

b Example 2: The Mahnverfahren *in Germany*

The *Mahnverfahren* in Germany is another example of a procedure to acquire an order of payment online. This procedure was introduced successively from state to state, and is now available in all the *länder* or states of the German federation. This procedure produces a title, but without a judicial procedure. Apart from the classical application in writing, there are various ways available for filing an application for a Mahnbescheid, the title for execution of payment.

For example, using the bar code procedure; the application is filled out on the web site of the central title court. After data entry, it can be printed out at home. On the last page, the data are printed in coded form in a bar code. The application must be signed. All printed pages are then sent to the court by ordinary mail.

Using a diskette requires specific software and an identification number. This enables transmission of more than one application at the same time. The applications will be processed on the day they are received. This modality requires an authorization to debit the applicant's account.

Submitting a claim online requires downloading a software module and Java Webstart, which are both available without charge through the Internet. It also requires a card reader and a smart card with a qualified digital signature. Here, filing is immediate upon transmission. The applicant is billed online.

In 2003, more than 90 percent of nearly 9.5 million orders for payment in Germany were processed automatically (Šijanski and Barber p. 1).

c Comparing the two examples

There are some significant differences between MCOL and the Mahnverfahren.

The Mahnverfahren was introduced in 1982 as a paper based procedure. The electronic procedure was, so to speak, put on top of it. Money Claim On Line was developed for electronic processing.

Identification of the applicant: A new MCOL user registers with the court and provides a credit card number for fee payments. The Mahnverfahren requires different modes of identification depending on the transmission modality: an identification number or a smart card with a qualified digital signature.

Payment: The Mahnverfahren does not use credit card payment at all. The court fee is due upon filing. The claimant is billed for the court fee and expenses when the order for payment is issued.[31]

d Example 3: A pilot in the Netherlands

In the Amsterdam local court, the largest local court in the country, a pilot was done in data transmission in a specialized case stream. The pilot was an initiative of an Amsterdam bailiffs' office. The bailiffs could transmit case data from their own databases, received from their clients, in electronic form on a CD-ROM. The data were received in a central location and transferred to the local court overnight. Cases were regarded as undefended until a party announced a defense. In practice, decisions were printed out in all cases on the assumption that the vast majority would remain undefended, which it did. If someone appeared at the first hearing with a defense, the decision was simply struck off, and the cases processed as a defended case. This considerably shortened both disposition and processing times for undefended cases. The functionality tested in this pilot was never implemented widely. The bailiffs in the Netherlands say they can supply processing information to the courts electronically, provided an interface for supplying the data is set up (Struiksma p. 202).

IT for the title group

In these zero-sum, low unpredictability cases, there is no dispute. Consequently, there is also not much judicial dispute resolution activity in this group. Judicial activity in individual cases is very limited.

The case volume in this group can be quite a large part of the total caseload. In the local courts, it is a large part of the total civil caseload. For civil courts, this group is very small compared with its share in the caseload in the local courts. Hence, it is probably not a priority for civil courts. For local courts, however, it is a group worthy of attention.

The information that is available at the outset is usually sufficient for producing the final product. The IT processing activity in this group is mostly merging data with text to produce decisions. That activity is supported by office automation, such as word processing and case registration databases.

The information opportunities for such zero-sum, low unpredictability cases are in:

- Online case filing and/or data entry by court users, including data transfer from frequent users,
- Internal processes that can process the data without the need for human intervention.

The opportunities have been developed in different ways in some systems in Europe. The differences have to do with variations in rules, competences and payment usage in each country. In Germany, an existing process was refitted to accommodate automated processing. There, functionality differs for different user groups. Frequent users are given the opportunity to supply data on a diskette or using their identification. One- time users can download a form. In the United Kingdom, a completely new process was devised using the possibilities of IT and credit card payments. It involves a back office designed to process large volumes from frequent users electronically, and a web site with online electronic forms and a help function. In both Germany and the United Kingdom, the development process took many years. The development process has involved different steps.

The Mahnverfahren was piloted in one *land* (state), that of Bremen, and then implemented gradually in the other states.

From the MCOL development process, which took place over many years, we can identify the following stages: (1) receiving claims, without completely automated processing in court; (2) processing undefended claims without human intervention and (3) supporting defense. Each subsequent development built on the previous one. Such phasing of development is important, taking into account the regulatory framework, local customs and the possibilities of the system. It involves learning from experience, and mobilizing the new learning for the next step. It is also important to observe that setting up a service like MCOL for individual users to file their claims requires close attention to user support. This will constitute a major shift in orientation for most court systems. That shift, and other aspects of increasing access to courts, is discussed in Part 4, on access to justice.

Group 2 - Notarial role

The outcome of the cases in this group is mostly win-win and highly predictable.

Facts

The notarial group includes dispositions in parental authority, supervision and settled employment dissolution cases in the local courts and dispositions in family cases in the district courts.

Cases in this group do not involve a real dispute. The outcome is highly predictable. Parties submit a proposal to the court. The proposal is reviewed only marginally. As a rule, no hearing is held. This group is the second largest group.

In this group, we find, for instance, most of the 33,000[32] divorce requests. More than half of these requests are filed jointly; the rest of the applications are filed by a one party. Legal representation is required for divorce requests. These matters can become complex in two ways: (1) they can be contested, and (2) there is an estate to be divided. About 25,000 requests are uncontested and do not require estate division. About 6,500 divorce requests are contested. The disposition time of divorce requests is on average 113 days. The median is 46 days.

Many of the 126,000 family cases in the local courts can also be included in this category. The local court judges appoint guardians for minors in a number of situations. Unmarried parents can be given joint parental authority at their request.

Table 13 *Case Categories in the Notarial Group*

Group 2	*Local court*	*Civil court*
Percentage of the total civil case load	31%	25%
201 Divorce dispositions	Time standard 50% within 2 months, 95% within 1 year	
Average disposition time for 2007		16 weeks
Workload standard processing time for 2001		Judge 90 minutes Staff 300 minutes
Workload standard processing time for 2005		Judge 82 minutes Staff 367 minutes
204 decisions instituting supervision	Disposition time standard not available	
Average disposition time for 2007	4 weeks	
Workload standard processing time for 2001	Judge 10 minutes Staff 60 minutes	
Workload standard processing time for 2005	Judge 12 minutes Staff 138 minutes	
204 other family cases		Disposition time standard not available
Average disposition time for 2007		22 weeks
Workload standard processing time for 2001		Judge 90 minutes Staff 360 minutes Judge 99 minutes Staff 485 minutes
299 Decisions instituting guardianships and parental authority	Disposition time standard not available	
Average disposition time for 2007	4 weeks	
	Judge 10 minutes Staff 60 minutes Judge 2 minutes Staff 56 minutes	
2606 settled employment terminations	90% within 15 days	
Average disposition time for 2007	2 weeks	
Workload standard processing time for 2005	Judge 55 minutes Staff 190 minutes	

The numbers are the case category numbers.
2005 is the most recent year for which practice-based processing time standards are available at the time of writing in 2008.

Source: Netherlands Council for the Judiciary

In the local court, the applications for dissolving employment contracts on the basis of article 6:785 of the Dutch Civil Code are a significant part of the caseload. This particular case type will be discussed in much more detail later in this chapter. Here, a brief description will suffice: Both parties to the contract can request the court to dissolve the contract. The court can set a sum to be paid by either party as equitable compensation. The parties can agree to have a dissolution settlement confirmed by the court. The disposition time of such applications is on average 15 days. The number of settled dissolutions is very sensitive to the economy; it doubled from 2001 to 2002. It has since decreased because of a change in social security policy: the decision is no longer necessary to claim unemployment benefits.[33] At the time of writing, in the second half of 2008, it is too early to tell whether this change in legislation will have an effect on the caseload or other aspects of the procedure.

Process and information analysis

In this group, unpredictability is low and the outcome is win-win. The parties can achieve the best result by cooperating with each other.

Cases in this group come to court in the form of requests. The procedure for requests is less formal than that for money claims. There is no formal summons by a bailiff. The court sends a copy of the request to the interested party or parties. For some cases, a hearing is standard procedure; for the majority, there is no hearing. The court product is a decision, but not a formal verdict.

The first salient point is the low unpredictability this group has in common with the title group. This indicates similar opportunities for automated processing, ideally based on data entry by the parties.

The win-win aspect points to a new opportunity: guidance for the parties to help them achieve the best result in working out the terms of the request to the court. If the parties can file a proposed arrangement that is correct the first time, that will save everyone involved time and effort. This is best achieved if the courts can specify what information they need, and what criteria they use to judge incoming requests.

The opportunity that presents itself for this group combines both data entry and guidance: online forms for filing both data and substance.

Example: Employment contract dissolution in the Netherlands

This example demonstrates a number of interesting aspects of the opportunities for this group. It shows how an effort to increase legal consistency can simplify issues and procedures, and support out-of-court settlement. It also shows how information technology can provide support, although it is not a direct example of innovative technology use.

It is about the process and effects of simplifying a particular procedure. The most striking finding is that a significant number of judgment group (group 4) cases moved to the notarial group (group 2) as a result of this reform. The description is quite detailed because this example so clearly illustrates some of the most relevant, important points involved.

Here is, in brief summary, what it involves. Dissolving individual labor contracts in case of irreconcilable differences is attributed to the local courts. They can award compensation based on equity. The local court judges' association has developed guidelines for compensation on the basis of existing equity practice. The guidelines consist of a formula to determine the amount of compensation easily if there are no unusual, special circumstances. The formula is public, available on the Internet and free. Such a public information service can facilitate that parties can present a complete and correct contract dissolution proposal to the court, making the judicial process a routine matter.

a Background

The statistics in Box 7 provide some background on employment protection in the Netherlands[34].

Box 7 Employment Protection in the Netherlands

The working population of the Netherlands is about 7.5 million –of a total population of 16 million. Between 700,000 and 1 million people change jobs every year. About 100,000 of those changes require permission from the labor office or a court decision.

In the Dispute Resolution Delta in the Netherlands, of a total of 1,870 justiciable problems, 313 are related to loss of a job. Job loss is considered the most serious labor-related problem, rated at 3.5 of a possible 5 (Van Velthoven 2004 p. 206).

The employment protection regime in the Netherlands is, according to OECD figures, about the OECD average. Employment protection is much stricter in Turkey, and much more lenient in the United States.

Employment protection is thought to be good for "insiders," those who are securely employed. It is believed to lead to longer duration of employment. Employment duration in the Netherlands is relatively low, at about 6.5 years, with the EU average a little over 8 years.

Employment protection is believed to be bad for "outsiders," people who are not securely employed. It is believed to lead to relatively high unemployment. The unemployment rate for 2007 in the Netherlands was 3.3 percent with the EU average of 7.9. The OECD average standardized unemployment rate was 7.1 for Europe, and 5.6 overall. The

OECD standardized unemployment rate for the Netherlands was 3.2 in 2007, down from 4.5 in 2005.
Employment protection is also believed to be bad for labor mobility. In the Netherlands, mobility is relatively high. Sixty percent of people expect to change jobs in the coming five years, with the EU average at 40 percent (OECD). The proportion of permanent jobs in the labor market is nearly 80 percent. About 8 percent of jobs are flexible and 15 percent can be considered self-employment.

Source: Symposium on labor protection at http://www.deburcht.org on November 7, 2007.

About 90 percent of people who leave their jobs do so without recourse to any of the employment protection instruments. Of the rest, less than half lose their jobs with permission from the social security authority CWI. Fewer than 6 percent come into contact with the judicial procedure described here. Between 1995 and 2005, an average of about 50,000 dissolution cases per year came to the local courts. In 2007, the total number was nearly 30,000. 26,000 were settled. These requests make up the bulk of group 2 cases in the local courts (Van Velthoven 2005 p. 22).

b The law

Article 7:685 of the Netherlands Civil Code says the local court judge can dissolve an employment contract at the request of one of the parties and determine an equitable compensation. Thus, the law does not give anything much by way of criteria for setting the compensation. This request has its own procedure laid down in the law: the procedure is initiated by a written request from either party, but in most cases from the employer. The resulting decision is an order. Because the legislature considered the underlying situation urgent, there is no possibility for appeal, except on grounds of wrongful application of the law. Grounds for dissolution are reasons sufficient for immediate dissolution (they can be summed up as gross negligence on either part), as well as changes in circumstances of such nature that in equity, the contract should end immediately or in a short while. If the contract is terminated because of changes in circumstances, the judge can determine an amount of compensation if this appears to be equitable in light of the circumstances of the case.

The procedure has been quite popular, at least partly because it does not take a long time. Since the end of the 1970s, criticism has focused mostly on the amounts of the compensation because they were quite different from one judge to another (Van der Meer p. 7). From a legal point of view, the procedure is weak. Because there is no appeal, consistency is not safeguarded by a review option. The professional legal press compared the procedure, because of its inconsistent outcomes, with a tombola.

In the 1990s, some of the local courts experimented with a common approach, but only within their own court. This approach consisted of a common way to calculate the amount of the compensation. The national association of local court judges took the initiative to try and create uniformity for the entire country. Its labor law committee was charged with this task.[35] The committee surveyed all local court judges in the Netherlands with a questionnaire asking about their approaches to the procedure and to setting compensation. On the basis of the survey results, the committee drafted recommendations. The recommendations were debated and adopted unanimously in the assembly of the local court judges association on November 8, 1996.[36] The recommendations cover both the procedure and the way compensation is calculated when applicable. The feature that attracts most attention is the so-called "local court formula," or *kantonrechtersformule.*

From a legal point of view, the recommendations do not have the status of law. That means non-observance is not a valid ground for appeal.

The recommendations and the formula are managed by the association's labor committee. In 2008, the committee was in the process of amending them. After an internal evaluation, about 15 theses were put to the vote in the association's full assembly. Most of the votes were unanimous. The recommendations will now be amended based on the outcome of the vote.

Box 8 Simplified Labor Dissolution Procedure

How does the procedure work?

Procedure

A dissolution in the notarial group based on a settlement between employer and employee is decided without a hearing. The time standard is 15 calendar days disposition time. The decision in writing is a confirmation of the settlement, in conformity with the formula.

For an opposed judgment group dissolution, there is a concentrated procedure: request, reply, oral hearing and decision. Its disposition time standard is 56 calendar days. Usually, the discussion during the hearing will focus on either party's negligence as a cause for the termination: the formula's c factor explained below. The decision needs to be sufficiently reasoned. No witnesses are allowed. There is no possibility for appeal.

The *formula* is very simple. It looks like this: (a + b) x c= x,
where a is the gross salary per month. The definition of the salary has been streamlined and kept very simple.
b is the employee's age and number of years of service. Both factors weight in the end result according to how they are thought to influence the employee's career expectations and his or her chances in the labor market.
c is a correction factor. In studies of actual cases, factors a and b were found to not adequately explain the variation in amounts awarded. The extremes were mostly caused by serious negligence by either the employer or the employee. That explains the correction factor c, which accounts for variations according to circumstances in the individual case
x is the resulting amount of compensation.

c Impacts

The most important intended impact was to get rid of the tombola, and create a legal standard for the judges themselves. A foreseen but not intended impact was to get a larger proportion of negotiated and settled dissolutions, through improved legal unity.

The most striking impact has been that employment contract dissolutions, formerly settlement or judgment group cases, were mostly settled by the parties and became largely notarial group cases.

Figure 3 shows the number of cases processed between 1996 and 2007. The baseline in this chart is 1996, the last year before the new approach was implemented. In 1997, 24 percent of all cases settled. In 2003, the percentage of settled cases had gone up to 86. In 2007, it was 82 percent. The absolute number of cases increased from 14,901 in 1996 to 72,961 in 2003 and back to 27,395 in 2007. A couple of circumstances were at work here:

- A downturn in the economy
- A backlog in the Work and Income Centers (Centra voor Werk en Inkomen, CWIs), which deal with employees' social security. The CWIs can also sanction labor dissolution contracts. They are, in a way, competitors of the local court judges.

A decision from the CWI or the court used to be compulsory for claiming unemployment benefits. In 2007, this requirement was abolished. Hence, demand for this type of decision is expected to decrease in the near future.

This requirement was dropped in legislation adopted in the course of 2007. Therefore, it does not affect the statistics shown in Figure 3.

Figure 3 *Impact of Labor Contract Dissolution Standards*

Source: Netherlands Council for the Judiciary research database.

Figure 4 *Labor Contract Dissolution Disposition Times*

Source: Netherlands Council for the Judiciary research database.

The disposition times in calendar days are between 10 and 18 days for settled cases, and between 39 and 49 for opposed cases. The courts adhere to the standards that were set in 1996 quite accurately. The data from the years before 2000 are not very accurate because registration was inconsistent. However, it looks as if in 1996 the courts were already adhering to the standards they set themselves at the end of that year.

Where is the IT?

The IT for the internal processes is word processing, possibly combined with data merging.

Externally, the IT is mostly the Internet. Most organizations involved in providing legal information on labor issues to the public have it on their web sites.[37] The formula is quite straightforward and can be used by anyone seeking to find out what his or her compensation could be, provided the correction factor is neutral. The formula is an interesting example in this context because the legal issues involved have been simplified to the extent that they can be largely automated. An important point is how routine and policy development is a prerequisite for using IT to its full advantage.

Some lessons on developing routines and policies

There are some lessons on developing routines and policies to be learned from this example. An important lesson is the impact of judicial policy: it was not developed to reduce either disposition time or the level of quality, justice or fairness, but to create a legal framework for the judges who had little guidance from the law to go on. The guidance for parties wanting to settle was actually a by-product. Nevertheless, the policy as guidance for settling parties has turned out to be one of its most important impacts. The procedure gives the parties an informed choice. Where the parties value their relationship, there is a premium on settlement. If they are unable to agree, the more elaborate but still quite fast procedure in the judgment group will give them a fair hearing as before.

The second lesson concerns the process of policy development. From the report above, the steps needed for developing a routine or policy can be identified (Box 9).

Box 9 Steps to Develop a Policy

Steps taken in developing the process and the formula:

1. Problem identification
2. Ownership and leadership by the body involved
3. Pilots in local courts
4. Survey of judges
5. Draft recommendations
6. Consultation
7. Agreement
8. Implementation
9. Periodic evaluation

Box 9 lists the steps taken when the formula was developed and implemented.

Innovation of this kind requires a professionally operating organization. The list of steps is a clear demonstration of this lesson. Ownership of both the problem and the solution, and leadership in the development process, are crucial. The formula is managed by the local court judges association, whose general assembly voted it into existence in 1996. As a guideline developed by a private association, it is not considered law. Non-application is not a valid ground for appeal.

From the first chapter on case delay, we have learned that simplification can be an effective way of reducing case delay. In this example, we see that mechanism at work. The guideline and its formula have limited the number of points that have to be addressed in case of dissolution of employment under the article 6:785 rule. Eighty-five percent of cases are processed within 15 days of filing.

IT for the notarial group

In the notarial group, there are two main opportunities for applications of information technology.

The first opportunity already emerged in the title group: it is in chain automation. Let users fill in the case database, and less time consuming data entry work needs to be done.[38] Moreover, parts of case processing can be automated once standardized processing for them has been developed. This will result in cases moving to the left in the matrix.

The second opportunity is web functionality: communicating to parties what information the court needs to deal with the case as quickly and expediently as possible. In the case of employment contract dissolution, the parties are guaranteed delivery of the decision in 15 calendar days after filing, if they provide the court with all the information needed. The Internet is a vehicle for giving the parties this information. The possibility of online forms presents itself. This information is one-sided; it is pushed to the users. However, the information may also help them settle their differences. This opportunity will be discussed in more detail in the chapter on access to information.

Group 3 – Settlement role

In the settlement group, the outcome is relatively unpredictable. The outcome is largely win-win. There is a dispute. But if the parties cooperate to settle it, they may be able to produce an outcome that is beneficial for both, and their relationship may be saved. The dispute need not necessarily be resolved exactly according to the rules of the law.

Facts

How many of the present cases fall in this group is difficult to determine with great accuracy. They are not registered as such by the court administrations. I have included all cases that leave the court without a judicial decision into group 3. Counted this way, it is similar in size to judgment group 4.[39]

Table 14 *Case Categories for the Settlement Group*

Group	*Local court*		*Civil court*	
3	301 399	defended cases withdrawn or struck off the record at parties' request, both summary and non- summary cases	1568, 1570-1573, 1635, 2560, 2565 399	defended cases withdrawn, struck off the record at parties' request

The numbers are the case category numbers; the numbers in italics are more detailed case category numbers where applicable.

Source: Netherlands Council for the Judiciary.

This group comprises about 9 percent of the total civil caseload. It consists of very diverse cases that are either withdrawn or struck off the record before or after a hearing. More detailed statistics for this group are not readily available.

Processing times for settled cases are between 5 and 15 minutes of staff time if they are withdrawn without a hearing. Obviously, if they are withdrawn after a hearing has taken place, they also take judicial time. There are no figures readily available for those situations.

Process and information analysis

The Netherlands have a long tradition of settlement. We have seen it described by Voltaire in the 18th century: The civil procedural code instructs judges to try settling a case before resolving it in the legal manner. There is considerable experience with mediation, court annex and otherwise. The difference between group 2 and group 3 cases is that in group 2 the parties need court approval for their arrangement, and in group 3 the parties are free to settle their dispute themselves.

Shapiro presents the image of dispute resolution as a triad: two parties who have a dispute and a third party to help them settle it. The triad is an imbalance, as the third party needs to take the side of one party or the other in order to resolve the dispute. Thus, one party will be the losing minority. In order to avoid this imbalance whenever possible, judges the world over will always attempt to reach as much consensus with the parties as possible (Shapiro p. 11). Hence, there is a strong preference for consensus over zero-sum dispute resolution.

In recent years, court practice has focused on ways of dispute resolution that are less formal than evidence production and judicial decisions. We will discuss the outcomes of this process in the judgment group. In such a practice, the gap between dispute resolution by courts and less formal mechanisms like mediation narrows.

Internationally, various informal and formal ways of court-supported dispute settlement are in practice. They can be found in different places on the scale of informal to formal dispute resolution:

Conciliation is the most informal, most party-focused variety.

Mediation requires a third party, but only to facilitate the process.

Neutral case evaluation requires a third party to evaluate the dispute on its legal merits, but leaves it to the parties what they want to do: settle the case, take it to court, or abandon the venture altogether.

These less formal modalities lend themselves best to disputes between parties who value continuation of their relationship. To that end, fostering cooperative behavior and keeping issues to a minimum are important activities. Less informal dispute resolution mechanisms are not always voluntary. Some systems require parties to participate in mediation before a case is admitted in court.

There is no scientific evidence suggesting that mediation in general is a better way of dealing with disputes than a court procedure (Asser 2003), as is sometimes claimed. Neither is there a hard and fast rule about which disputes lend themselves to settlement or not. Eshuis observes that early intervention in the form of early hearing did not increase the settlement rate in the Dutch courts between 1994 and 2003 (Eshuis 2007 p. 212).

In *The Future or Law*, Richard Susskind suggests that publishing general rules of thumb as to how things can be arranged and resolved in general may prevent disputes from breaking out (Susskind 1998 p. xlviii). This kind of information can also guide solutions in case of settlement.

Examples

In the Dutch system, attempts to settle a case are part of the civil procedure in court. Particularly in countries with an Anglo-Saxon legal system, much effort goes into preventing a case from ever coming to court. We have seen MCOL and PCOL as examples of this in group 1. In group 3, facilitating informal dispute resolution and mediation are also used as a way of keeping the parties out of court as much as possible.

a Example 1: Australia – Adelaide Magistrate's Court

An example of the use of prelodgement notices comes from Australia (Cannon 2002). The procedure described here was introduced in 1999. The Magistrate's Court (in this example that of Adelaide) provides a form for a final notice of claim by the plaintiff to the defendant. This notice is a final warning that proceedings against the defendant are about to be filed at court and once that happens the court is likely to award costs to the plaintiff. The parties have 21 days to voluntarily negotiate a resolution without further involvement by the court. Only after the expiration of the 21-day term is the plaintiff entitled to file the claim in the court. The court offers mediation free of charge. Mediators provide their services free of charge on a pro bono basis. The court also offers the option of technical advice from an independent expert from the court office. Technical advice can narrow the issues to be settled. The court decided to support this new procedure with forms available on its web site. The final notice and an Enforceable Payment Agreement (EAP) can be downloaded from the court's web site. Having the forms available on the Internet is a great benefit to claimants who can access it from any computer at any time. After a slow start, use of the forms increased exponentially. Between June 1999 and September 2002, the facility was used more than 14,000 times, 5,300 of these between September 2001 and September 2002. In the first 18 months, 59 mediations took place, more than half of which ended with a settlement. Research also shows that nearly 60 percent of the defendants paid the debt owed when they received the final notice, making it a cheap and effective means of trying to collect debt. If the plaintiff will not negotiate and the defendant admits the claim, but cannot afford to pay, the defendant can serve a notice that the debt is admitted and avoid the costs of a court claim being commenced. Later, one criticism of the form was that it could be taken for the actual claim form. The form was amended to describe the plaintiff as the sender and the defendant as the recipient.[40]

b Example 2: Singapore's e@dr negotiation

The Singapore subordinate courts offer the possibility of electronic alternative dispute resolution: an amicable, cost-free avenue to initiate negotiations with the other disputing party. There are two conditions for starting an e@dr process:

(a) The party involved has not commenced any court proceedings

(b)The party has an email account and the email address of the other party.

Some examples of results of the e@dr process:

A Singaporean purchaser of online goods from the United States managed to obtain a refund of additional delivery charges deducted, as the other party agreed that he was not aware that a certain classification of his goods required re-direction fees.

A claim for unpaid administrative services of more than $1,000 was settled, even though prior to e@dr there were numerous reminders and phone calls.

A request for reprint costs of a newsletter was directed and negotiated with the correct party, thereby allowing a recovery of more than $2,000 and a waiver of late interest payment.

By using the e@dr process, a claim for refund due under a car grooming service was resolved.

c Example 3: Online dispute resolution mechanisms outside courts

In e-commerce, new online forms of dispute solution come up where parties can negotiate supported by a computer program. Thus, the online auction site eBay has developed a settlement system called www.SquareTrade. SquareTrade is a free-standing service offering a guarantee for online purchases in general, providing insurance and claims handling. If a problem occurs, a claim can be filed with SquareTrade. By supporting assisted, automated negotiation, it facilitates participants' independent resolution of the problem with the other side. Two other major examples of automated negotiation are http://www.smartsettle.com and www.cybersettle.com. Since 2004, the City of New York has piloted using Cybersettle for settling claims cases filed against it.

IT for the settlement group

The Singapore example shows support for negotiation, where parties themselves resolve their dispute. It uses email, asynchronous communication, between the parties. The court acts as a go-between. Asynchronous communication may give parties time to think. However, it does not particularly favor cooperative behavior.

The Adelaide example shows another way of preventing cases from coming to court. The ability to have mediation and expert advice prior to a formal claim being lodged with the court means that an ADR process can occur earlier than the involvement of the court in a conference/ directions hearing phase. The advantages are:

- Early intervention in the dispute
- Costs contained
- Reducing the possibility of entrenchment
- The parties still have control of the resolution.

This example uses the court's web site and online forms. Access to the service with online forms proves to be successful in Adelaide Magistrates Court. Offering free mediation and expert advice requires funding on the part of the court. In some societies, this would be considered a flaw in the market for legal services.

These examples show how, using the functionalities of email or a web site with information and online forms, a potential dispute is moved down, as well as to the left in the matrix. The result contains costs and avoids a complex, lengthy procedure. These opportunities do have a limit in that communication over distance may not be enough to foster cooperative behavior, so face-to-face contact may still be necessary to broker an agreement.

Another potential opportunity in this group is the shadow of the law in a new shape: guidance for parties who are negotiating a settlement. Susskind pointed this out as a powerful opportunity (Susskind 1998 p. xlviii). We have encountered it in the notarial group, with the example of the labor cases in the Netherlands.

Group 4 – Judgment role

In the judgment group, the outcome is unpredictable. The outcome is also zero-sum. There is a dispute. The parties are in opposition. The case is decided on legal merit. The court decides. Events during the process influence the outcome. To learn more about processes in this group, we look at the ordinary, non-summary cases.

Facts

In 2007, the local courts decided about 70,000 cases in this group, about 10 percent of their total civil caseload. The civil sectors decided approximately 9,370 cases in this group, about 4 percent of their total caseload. From statistics about South Australia, we know that the magistrates' courts there also process about 10 percent defended cases (Cannon 2002). The work in this group is generally considered the epitome of judicial work.

Table 15 *Case Categories for the Judgment Group*

Group 4	*Local court*	*Civil court*
Percentage of total civil caseload	10%	4%
1589-1593, 1686, 1691, 1692 final dispositions in defended cases	Disposition time standard 75% within 6 months 90% within 1 year	Disposition time standard 70% within 1 year 80% within 2 years
Average disposition time in days for 2007	16 weeks without evidence 43 weeks with evidence	60 weeks with/without evidence
Processing time standard, 2001	Judge 170 minutes Staff 300 minutes	Judge 660 minutes Staff 600 minutes
Processing time standard, 2005	Judge 118 minutes Staff 411 minutes	Judge 807 minutes Staff 619 minutes
Including evidence, 2005 only	Judge 516 minutes Staff 605 minutes	Judge 1726 minutes Staff 998 minutes
1631, 1727, 1728 final dispositions in defended summary cases	90% within 3 months	90% within 3 months
Average disposition time in days for 2007	4 weeks	6 weeks
Processing time standard, 2001	Judge 180 minutes Staff 420 minutes	Judge 190 minutes Staff 675 minutes
Processing time standard, 2005	Judge 122 minutes Staff 153 minutes	Judge 122 minutes Staff 787 minutes
2607 defended employment terminations	Disposition time standard 90% within 3 months	
Average disposition time in days for 2007	7 weeks	
Processing time standard, 2005 only	Judge 47 minutes Staff 116 minutes	

The numbers are the case category numbers; numbers in italics are more detailed case category numbers where applicable.
2005 is the most recent year for which practice-based processing time standards were available at the time of writing in 2008.

Source: Netherlands Council for the Judiciary.

These cases have basically three case processing modalities in increasing complexity: decisions without hearing, decisions after a hearing, and decisions after evidence production, in civil and local courts in the judgment group. Decisions after evidence production happen only in non-summary cases.

No hearing: this means the case is decided on the file as produced by the parties.

Hearing: If a hearing is held, its purpose can be to attempt a settlement (in which case they become settlement group cases if the attempt is successful), to acquire more information from the parties and/or to examine possibilities for producing evidence of disputed points. If the last activity leads to evidence production, the case moves to the final stage.

Evidence: In the cases that involve producing evidence, the evidence needed will be decisive for the outcome. Therefore, evidence production will be ordered by the court. It can involve witness hearing, a site visit, or an expert opinion.

Process and information analysis

In this group, both processes and substance can be complex. The outcome is zero-sum. It is also unpredictable.

Cases in this group take up the most judicial time. Time to disposition is considerable. There is some indication that the percentage of cases in which the different courts order evidence production varies considerably, and that this variation is associated with the length of disposition time.

Reducing substantive complexity is the main activity in the processes in this group: finding the points on which the parties are in agreement, the points they disagree on, those that will be decisive for the outcome, and how they should be dealt with procedurally. For some of those issues, handbooks on the law and case law and jurisprudence are consulted for clarification. Then, the judge in the case decides whether to have a hearing with the parties, and/or to order production of evidence (mostly witnesses) or some other form of verification of facts or an expert report. Hartendorp analyzed judicial decision making in this group. He observed court hearings in this group and notes that most of the time of the first instance judges in judgment group cases is spent on understanding the facts, not on applying the law (Hartendorp p. 197). Eshuis, studying disposition times and how they are affected by reform, observes there is a fairly strong correlation between early hearings and reducing disposition times (Eshuis 2007 p. 212).

Judgment formation is a very complex process. Two activities can be distinguished: understanding facts and interpreting norms. Hartendorp observes there is very little empirical research into how judges form their judgment.

Examples

As we go up the scale of complexity in civil cases, examples of IT use in courts become more difficult to find. Some U.S. courts have introduced electronic case files for difficult, complex cases involving many parties or large amounts of information.

Experience with electronic files for complex cases in the Dutch courts was – until recently - limited to a pilot in the criminal courts. Obviously, this example does not involve civil law. I report on that pilot here because its findings are relevant for processing civil cases as well. The district courts of Amsterdam and Rotterdam have piloted the use of digital files in criminal cases. While the Amsterdam pilot looked at high volume routine cases, the Rotterdam team specifically tested applications for use in high complexity, large criminal case files. The Rotterdam pilot used a common off-the-shelf application for structuring the information in the files. The results indicate that digital files have a great advantage in the case of large quantities of information. Some of the advantages mentioned by participants in the pilot:[41]

- Easy structuring of complex information: Information in the file can be electronically flagged during hearing preparation using a program indexing the text files. During the hearing, the flagged passages are retrieved easily in the screen file.
- Increased efficiency: A hearing in a tribunal can be prepared by one person structuring the information. This may save the other participants a lot of preparation time because they do not have to read redundant or irrelevant documents.
- Flagged passages can be retrieved for inclusion in the decision. An electronic file on the court network gives access to all concerned at the same time. With paper files, a lot of time is lost because the original file is not always accessible for all the participants in the process.
- Increased accuracy of information: Digital files can also include video and audio recordings and still images. Examples from the pilot mention recordings of actual wiretappings and video recordings of arrests.

Experience with the use of electronic files in the United States confirms the experience recorded here.

IT for the judgment group

Judgment group cases are complex to very complex. Their outcome is unpredictable. A case is decided by the judge or the court. This section explored the information process and some examples of IT to support them. Most activity serves to reduce the complexity of the information in the case file. It mostly deals with the facts of the case. The description given here is still very rudimentary. I regard it as a first attempt at developing an approach to capture the judicial processes more adequately. So far, not much is known from empirical research about the way judges form their judgment. An approach from the perspective of information science should also be attempted to shed more light on this important topic. More research into the information processes in this group is needed. More empirical research in this field will help to increase our understanding of how judges use information. Subsequently, it will be possible to identify information needs and forms of technology that can support this judicial process with more accuracy.

There is an expressed need for structuring complex information. Electronic case files are a functionality that could be helpful in this group. They can be used to structure large quantities of information with the help of electronic search capability. Electronic case files also open the opportunity for multimedia evidence. So far, in Dutch court practice, witness statements and location inspections must always be reproduced in writing for paper files. Witness statements are summarized and dictated for the paper file. This inevitably reduces the complexity and richness of the information. It is also inevitably less accurate. Thus, information is lost.

Knowledge management systems are the other obvious functionality for this group. Two forms of knowledge management some courts already have experience with are jurisprudence databases and decision support systems. The most common form is case law and jurisprudence databases. They help judges take legally correct, consistent decisions.

Case law or jurisprudence is traditionally published on paper. Nowadays, it is also published electronically. That has improved search possibilities with full text search. Jurisprudence databases can facilitate policy formation. However, for this purpose, the collection needs to be a representative reflection of what the "average judge" has decided. Judicial decisions can fulfill this role better if they are more structured than simple text files. If they are publicly available, they support the shadow function of the courts: facilitating out-of-court dispute resolution.

Decision support systems help with decision making by providing guidelines reflecting some consensus about the way in which relatively objective criteria can be applied to apply norms that are relatively open. The way determining the labor dissolution compensation was simplified is a striking example. Thus, decision support systems serve as the "front end" of judicial policies. They can make deciding cases more consistent and more transparent. That helps to increase both access and integrity.

Case-by-case knowledge management, where the expertise relevant for an individual case is presented to the judges and their legal assistants on the basis of case characteristics, is a further opportunity in this group. It requires a system for determining which information is presented with which case configuration.

It remains to be seen, however, what types of knowledge management are best suited to this group's needs. We do not yet know very much about the processes in the judgment group.

Conclusions for Part 3

These chapters set out to analyze IT support for reducing case delay. Chapters 3.2 and 3.3 looked at information processing in courts using a matrix on process outcomes. Cases were grouped based on case outcome, in order to identify information technology needs and opportunities. From these chapters, we can draw some lines on:

- The role of information management in civil justice reform
- What courts have achieved with regard to IT for case processing
- What needs can be identified
- What opportunities are in store
- What needs to be done in order to make those opportunities work to improve the administration of justice.

Civil justice, case delay and information technology

Judicial decision making can be an extraordinarily complex process. Many different models were developed to capture this complexity: Shapiro's triangle of dispute resolution, the continuum of dispute resolution modes, Zuckerman's triangle of time, cost and truth (Shapiro p. 2; Zuckerman p. 48). I have developed my matrix to capture judicial roles and court case loads. It helps to make visible how both relate to the need for information technology.

In Shapiro's triangle, the role of the third person helping the first two people with their dispute goes from helper to decider, related to the degree of consensus in the resolution. As the third person can achieve the most balanced result by striving for the highest degree of consensus, *moving cases down in the matrix* whenever possible suggests itself in this framework. In Zuckerman's triad, there is a trade-off between time, cost and truth: this suggests that reducing time and/or cost will result in less truth. I do not find the suggestion that less complexity means less truth totally convincing. After all, dispute resolution is largely reducing complexity. However, what does present itself from this image is that *moving cases to the left in the matrix* will result in less complexity and faster processing.

Case processing as information management

Looking at case processing as a process of information management helps to see opportunities for information technology applications in order to improve case processing. We have uncovered some actions that will result in cases moving to the left and/or down in the matrix.

Simplification: Creating routines and standards will move cases to the left. Thus, the number of individual decisions that need to be taken in each case is reduced. This reduces unpredictability through reducing the number of individual decisions that have to be taken in each case. In the example of the labor contract dissolution, a majority of cases moved from the judgment group to the notarial group. The main activity is simplification: By standardizing the concepts of salary and contract duration for the purpose of determining compensation more equitably, complexity was reduced. With the formula itself publicly available on the Web, the parties become capable of resolving most cases on their own. Therefore, cases may even be moved out of the court when the parties are given enough information to resolve their dispute by settlement. Thus, policy formation encourages problem solving by the parties. If, like the Dutch peacemakers in Voltaire's letter in the footnote above, we think time and cost can be saved by keeping dispute resolution away from the legal realm, and helping parties to settle their differences is a socially desirable objective, it is useful to find ways to move cases in the direction of the bottom half of the matrix.

Early intervention: Early intervention in individual cases can have two effects: it simplifies the case in question, which moves it to the left in group 4; or it facilitates settlement, which moves the case toward group 3. The example of the online pre-action protocols illustrates how a complex, lengthy process is avoided. A potential dispute is moved down, as well as to the left in the matrix to such an extent that it never gets to court.

IT for case processing: What has been achieved?

Most of the effort in implementing court IT has gone into streamlining and routines; in other words: simplification and process control. The lengthy treatment of group 1 underlines this point. This fits into the general trend in IT use, which appears to support large scale control by manipulating large amounts of information. It is an indication that proportionality is at work.

Not letting cases come to court is a trend. However, it is a trend that raises questions about how time, cost and truth are being rebalanced. Does it raise the barriers to access to justice? Are people not getting the justice they seek and deserve? What is the level of justice if legal protection cannot be invoked? These are questions that will be examined in Part 4.

Communication with the users, both one-way and interactive, is a way of helping them with solving their own problems. Much of the information technology identified, in order to be successful, involves or requires standardization of court practices or policy formation with regard to judicial decision making. These activities require active work on the part of courts and judiciaries.

Resolution of complex problems and innovative problem solving are not supported by IT to any great extent yet. The results of this study do not indicate that automating judicial reasoning for purposes of dispute resolution is a perceived need.

Databases

This study has used a lot of statistics to examine court processes. Those statistics are available where courts use database technology for their case administration. The U.S. courts were the first to start developing case processing standards. They have implemented technology to register and administer cases since the 1970s. That gave them an instrument to generate information and knowledge about their processes. It also provided them with a tool to check the implementation and progress of the Trial Court Performance Standards.

To my mind, the finding of the effect of electronic case administration is one of the most interesting: our ability to know our processes has increased enormously because databases keep the data we have fed them for us and make them available in ways we can use. Databases can produce correlations that we could never find otherwise. Justice Bharuka, then chair of the Indian Judiciary's IT Commission, told me how he first tracked case delay in Bangalore by using a self-constructed database.[42] The jurisprudence of the European Court on Human Rights on case delay was analyzed with a database. With the support of databases, we can learn what we do and how and where the problems are. After we develop and implement solutions, we can track changes in order to ensure that our solutions are working. For the policy research needed to develop routines, databases to compare and analyze are an indispensable tool. These examples are an illustration of the potential for changing culture with regard to timeliness in disposing court cases.

IT needs and opportunities

From the courts' perspective, internal information needs and external information provision are the two vectors that drive information management in cases. The matrix demonstrates how different cases require different processing. The cases can be divided into four groups. Each group has specific IT support needs. Those needs point to opportunities for IT support to reduce case delay:

For all groups, electronic filing is an opportunity that will save processing time. Most claimants are firms that have clients in an automated administration. Moreover, most claims are filed by either law firms or bailiffs. They will mostly have their clients in an automated administration. If they could deliver those data to the courts, as is done in the bulk claim center in the United Kingdom, the extra step of re-keying the data in court can be eliminated. Procedural rules affect how this can be achieved.

In the notarial group, an additional opportunity is in web functionality. Information on the court web site, online forms and information for settlements can be ways of stimulating the parties to work together to resolve their own disputes.

In the settlement group, information service on the Web to help parties settle their own disputes is also a good activity. Moreover, we see the use of communication technology, such as email or dedicated software, to help parties settle disputes with a less predictable outcome.

In the judgment group, the foremost need is for managing complex information. The opportunity of electronic case files presents itself here. Electronic files open up new opportunities themselves with multimedia storage of evidence and hearing recordings. The other need is for legal information service.

Electronic filing of claims, online data entry and electronic case files will reduce processing time, and possibly disposition time, for all cases. Automating routines can speed up processing for the title group. Internet functionality for public information and electronic forms supports the notarial group. Likewise, public information and software supporting negotiations can support processing specifically for the settlement group. Electronic files and knowledge management are the main tools specifically for the judgment group.

Interaction with the parties

Forms of electronic interaction between courts and their users present themselves as an opportunity for preventing cases from coming to court and for more expedient processing for the cases that are filed. Information on the Web and forms of increasing interactivity are explored in Part 4, on access to justice.

What needs to be done?

Major shifts in the way courts and judiciaries work are required if they choose to use the opportunities that are presented by forms of information technology effectively. Both require changes in organization as well as major shifts in thinking.

The first one is a shift toward generating knowledge from the court decisions and practices for the purpose of developing routines and policies. Developing routines and policies must become a standard activity. That is a big change for an organization geared to process individual cases. It is explored in the chapter on managing change.

The other one is a shift toward providing court users and the general public with information. This requires both organizational and attitudinal changes. Courts, in order to provide information to court users, need to develop an attitude that does not routinely rely on intermediaries like lawyers and bailiffs. The topic of communicating and interacting with court users is explored in Part 4, on access to justice.

Notes

1 Late justice is defective justice.
2 Hamburg, City Council of (1802) Verordnung über die Abkürzung der Prozesse, Directive on shortening court procedures of the City Council of Hamburg, May 21, 1802.
3 Resolution Res (2002)12 of the Committee of Ministers of the Council of Europe, adopted on September 18, 2002.
4 In the Intiba v. Turkey judgment of May 24, 2005, § 54, the Court stated that although Article 6 of the Convention required proceedings to be conducted with due speed, it also embodied the more general principle of good administration of justice (judgment in French only).
5 General Comment 13, United Nations Human Rights Website - Treaty Bodies Database - Document - General Comments -
6 http://www.ncsconline.org/D_Research/CourTools/tcmp_courttools.htm
7 Decision of November 29, 1988. Brogan and others v. United Kingdom 11209/84;11234/84; 11266/84; 11386/85. The issue involved here was whether the detention, under the Prevention of Terrorism Act, 1984, of Mr. Brogan and others from September 17 to September 22, 1984, was a violation of article 5 of the European Convention (prompt hearing by a judge). The Court found that there was a breach of article 5

para. 3. This decision prompted reform of the criminal procedural code in the Netherlands, regarding hearing by a judge after arrest.

8 The system as it developed over the years is explained by the Court in its decision of March 29, 2006 on the case of Mostacciuolo v. Italy (No. 1), 64705/01.

9 The author of the report observes she has established that the Court was reluctant to establish clear-cut rules, arguing that every case must be considered separately.

10 Genns work on justiciable problems is discussed at length in Part 4. She did not define the term justiciable problem, but she defined a justiciable event as "a matter(...) which raised legal issues (...).

11 For an example, see http://www.aija.org.au/tech3/program/presentations/Prelodge.ppt.

12 I recall how, in 1993 when I moved from my old court in Alkmaar to the local court of Amsterdam, my idea of active case management was dismissed with the statement that "in Amsterdam, that is impossible".

13 Special thanks to David Steelman for pointing out the trap courts and judges may fall into when not paying attention to court resource management as a factor in delay.

14 The original adage is in Dutch: "*meten is weten.*" Literally translated, it means: to measure is to know. Until now, my quest for a similarly elegant expression of this important principle in English has been in vain. Two candidates have presented themselves: "what is measured, improves," and "knowledge is power."

15 This article by Marc Galanter in the *UCLA Law Review* has no page numbers.

16 Settlement appears to be a very old Dutch custom. Here is a quote from Voltaire in which he praises enlightened court practice in Holland in the 18th century:

« La meilleure loi » selon Voltaire

Voltaire évoquait dans une lettre en 1745, une pratique judiciaire des Pays-Bas, de magistrats dits « faiseurs de paix » : « *La meilleure loi, le plus excellent usage, le plus utile que j'ai vu, c'est en Hollande. Quand deux hommes veulent plaider l'un contre l'autre, ils sont obligés d'aller d'abord au tribunal des juges conciliateurs, appelés faiseurs de paix. Si les parties arrivent avec un avocat ou un procureur, on fait d'abord retirer ces derniers, comme on ôte le bois d'un feu qu'on veut éteindre. Les faiseurs de paix disent aux parties : vous êtes de grands fous de vouloir manger votre argent à vous rendre mutuellement malheureux. Nous allons vous accommoder sans qu'il vous coûte rien. Si la rage des chicanes est trop forte dans ces plaideurs, on les remet à un autre jour, afin que le temps adoucisse les symptômes de leur maladie. Ensuite les juges les renvoient chercher une seconde, une troisième fois. Si leur folie est incurable, on leur permet de plaider, comme on abandonne à l'amputation des chirurgiens des membres gangrenés ; alors la justice fait sa main.*

«The best law» according to Voltaire

Voltaire, in a letter in 1745, recalled a judicial practice in the Netherlands, of magistrates called « peace makers »: *The best law, the most excellent custom, the most useful I have seen, is in Holland. When two men want to plead one against the other, they are obliged to first go to the tribunal of the judge conciliators, called peace makers. If the parties come with a lawyer or an attorney, the latter are made to leave, like one draws the wood from a fire one wants to extinguish. The peace makers say to the parties: you are great fools to want to eat your money by making each other mutually unhappy. We are going to help you and it will not cost you anything. If the rage of chicanery is too strong in the pleaders, they are deferred to another day so time can soften the symptoms of their illness. Then the judges refer them a second and a third time. If their folly is incurable, they are allowed to plead, just as limbs with gangrene are left for amputation by surgeons; thus, justice takes its course.*

17 Economic rationale for EU Directive combating late payment in commercial transactions (98/C/168/09).

18 Annual reports of the Netherlands Council for the Judiciary, 2002-2007, available on www.rechtspraak.nl.

19 The figures for the appeal courts in the annual reports differ between the various reports. I have displayed the figures for all years from the 2006 annual report. The differences are small: 10 percent for 2003, and less than 1 percent for 2004. They are not relevant for the rest of this study.

20 Annual reports of the Supreme Council of the Netherlands 2002 - 2006 available on www.rechtspraak.nl.

21 In many countries, courts also keep various registers, like the commercial register or the land register. It is safe to assume that the register role is an area in which use of information technology can be of great help to improve performance. However, case processing, not the register function, is our subject here, so we will not look into this category of court work.

22 The remaining 23 percent cannot be categorized meaningfully for the purpose of this study. The remainder includes bankruptcies, juvenile justice, other case groups that are very small but very diverse, and various supervision activities. Most of them are not dispute resolution in any sense of the word.

23 There is a full list of the case categories that make up each group of the matrix in the previous chapter.

24 Report of the working party of the Netherlands Association of Magistrates on extra judicial costs, as amended in November 2002.

25 Presentation by Perry Timms of the U.K. Court Service in 2002 at the Netherlands judiciary IT conference, and at the 2003 NCSC Court Technology Conference, CTC8. A copy of the Power Point presentation is in my possession. The information was updated with the contents of the Court Service web site http://www.hmcourts-service.gov.uk in March 2008.

26 https://www.moneyclaim.gov.uk

27 http://www.justice.gov.uk/civil/procrules_fin/contents/practice_directions/pd_part07e.htm#IDASCNLD

28 http://www.hmcourts-service.gov.uk/cms/files/HMCSAnnualReportAndAccounts-2006-07.pdf

29 The fees can be viewed on the HMCS web site at www.hmcourtsservice.gov.uk/infoabout/fees/county.htm.

30 The information in this paragraph was provided by the Ministry of Justice and Her Majesty's Court Service in the United Kingdom.

31 A possible explanation is that credit cards are not used as widely in Germany as in the United Kingdom.

32 The absolute number of divorce cases has remained stable at around 35,000 for years.

33 Interview with Herman van der Meer, then secretary of the Association of Local Court Judges and chair of the committee; validated interview notes in my possession.

34 This overview is a compilation of materials presented at a symposium on labor protection at http://www.deburcht.org on November 7, 2007. The percentages do not always add up to 100 %.

35 As a member of the association, I was present at most of the meetings discussed here. The historical data given here are also based on an interview with committee member Herman van der Meer. He validated my notes from the interview.

36 The event was hailed in the legal press as "a small miracle."

37 These are the first three sites found by Google after entering kantonrechtersformule as the search term on August 13, 2008. http://www.ontslag-krijgen.nl/berekenen/kantonrechtersformule.html and http://www.goudenhanddrukwijzer.nl/gouden-handdruk-kantonrechterformule.html allow the user to enter the data and calculate his or

her own compensation. http://www.rmu.org/index.php?paginaID=219# only gives an explanation with some examples.

38 Technically speaking, users do not have direct access to the live case registration database. Data entry is done through an extranet where data are checked before they are allowed to populate the database itself.

39 That tallies with the intuitive notion that half of all contested claims lend themselves to settlementof some sort.

40 This information is originally from a 2002 presentation by the court's Chief Magistrate Andrew Cannon. He updated the information in an email in April 2008.

41 Interview with the panel of judges who tested the application in March 2003.

42 Interview in New Delhi, July 2005.

Part 4 Access to Justice

Plan for the next three chapters

The next three chapters examine ways in which information technology can support improving access to justice.

The first chapter discusses the relevance of the concept of access to justice to the broader theme of judicial reform. It analyzes methodological difficulties of studying access to justice. It discusses the normative framework for the issue of access to justice. It then examines the main barriers to access to justice that have emerged from different sources.

The second chapter examines impediments with regard to information and knowledge. It ends with a list of information and knowledge needs people with justiciable problems experience. Those needs should be addressed to improve access to justice.

The third chapter takes up the conclusions from the other two chapters to look at courts and how they can improve access to justice using forms of information technology, and particularly the Internet.

Chapter 4.1 Access to Justice

Relevance and context

This section discusses how the concept of access to justice relates to the broader discussion on judicial reform.

Access to justice has become a major theme in the broader judicial reform agenda, as is shown by the following, fairly random, examples: In the Western world in the 1970s, a movement started toward making information about rights more accessible to the general public. Funding legal aid and legal representation became an area for government policy. Donors of development assistance fund projects focusing on access to justice in developing countries. Its place on the reform agenda means it is relevant as a topic for study in the framework of judicial reform. Whether access to justice is a problem that needs to be addressed by reform efforts, and if so, how that should be done, is a major question. It should be answered based on empirical evidence.

In the access discourse, access is not a clearly defined concept, and neither is justice. That makes them viable for political discourse on aspirations and claims. For academic exploration, for instance quantifying and comparing levels and impacts, and for devising reform strategies, they are not immediately practical. Until recently, the debate was conducted without much of an evidence base. Now, however, empirical evidence on barriers to access is beginning to build up.

Evidence

This section provides a brief overview of the evidence that is emerging. The body of evidence for access to justice as a problem has started to accumulate only fairly recently. There were no reliable quantitative data about the needs, interests and experiences of those ostensibly lacking access (Genn p. 1). This gap is beginning to be filled by research on experience in solving justiciable problems. Starting in the 1970s, a body of knowledge on access to justice and its impediments gradually built up. Research on people using legal services was done in the 1970s in the United States by the ABA (Genn 1999 p. 6). A Dutch study also explored legal needs and the use of legal assistance (Schuyt 1976). In the United Kingdom, Paths to Justice (Genn 1999) examined what people do and think about "going to law", that is, using the legal system in England and Wales. The study was later repeated in Scotland (Genn 2001). Contrary to the U.S. studies, the methodology's object of study is the legal problems people face, not people using legal services. The Paths to Justice methodology was used for a study in the Netherlands by Van Velthoven and Ter Voert (Van Velthoven 2004). The report of their study is called the "Dispute Resolution Delta 2003." It was published in 2004. Both Paths to Justice and the Dispute Resolution Delta started out with screening surveys of a representative sample of the general population. Paths to Justice followed them up with interviews of all those individuals who reported having had a problem, about their justiciable problems and how they responded to them. Selected individuals were interviewed more in depth about their experience (Genn 1999 p. 15). The Delta conducted a second survey with those who reported having had a problem and conducted 17 interviews with selected individuals (Van Velthoven 2004 p. 39). Interviewees were questioned on the barriers they perceived, the motivation for taking action, the outcome of different strategies and their experiences and perceptions of legal proceedings, the courts, and the judiciary. The Dutch screening survey was done through an Internet panel. The Dispute Resolution Delta also provides information on the problems' time track and on explanations for patterns in legal aid. This research has produced a wealth of empirical evidence that helps us understand more about problems of access to justice and its institutions. Both studies will be used extensively in the discussion of information aspects of access to justice that is the main part of the second chapter.

Dilemmas

This section highlights two dilemmas that come up frequently in the justice reform debate about access to justice.

The first dilemma is the apparent choice between institutional reform and access to justice: Why bother getting people access to justice if the justice institutions are functioning poorly or not at all? To a certain degree, this is a chicken-and-egg kind of debate about what comes first. Access to justice and functioning justice institutions are interdependent; they need each other to exist. Some development programs and donors have chosen to concentrate on access to justice programs because institutional reform was not a viable option in the actual circumstances. This is likely to be the case in countries with more or less dysfunctional institutions, such as the ones in Michael Johnston's Oligarchs and Clans group and in the Official Moguls group (see the chapter on corruption, Johnston p. 155 and appendix B). Faundez has pointed out how corruption and inefficiency of ordinary state courts have given rise to non-state justice institutions in Latin America. He argues that the shortcomings of official courts can be understood better with a better understanding of non-state justice systems. Investigating non-state justice systems can yield a wealth of evidence with which to gauge the social and political needs of ordinary people, as well as their expectations and responses to law and legal institutions (Faundez 2006 p. 136). Ordinary people and their justiciable problems are the major focus in the next few chapters. Their experiences tell us a lot about information and knowledge barriers to access to justice, and about how their perception of courts helps or hinders the resolution of problems. That is valuable understanding of how courts and judiciaries can improve their role in the resolution of disputes. Is this apparent dilemma specific to developing countries, as the reference to the Oligarchs and Clans groups suggests? The research that is the basis for the next chapters was done in Western Europe. As we shall see, it shows that court improvement has a role to play in improving access to justice in highly developed justice systems too, and not just in developing countries.

The second dilemma is the choice between diversion and access: Is it better to keep people out-of-court by providing alternatives to court dispute resolution, or should access to courts be improved? As with the first theme, this is also partly a chicken-and-egg debate. The shadow function of the law, also known as the radiating effect of courts (Galanter 1983a) is an established fact: out of court problem solving and settlement are supported by courts fulfilling their role of setter and guardian of the norms. Alternative dispute resolution is more effective in a system where well functioning courts are a serious alternative. Genn says diversion and access as reform goals logically conflict: the more court access is enhanced, the less the public will be interested in wasting time in possibly fruitless self-help remedies or alternative dispute resolution processes (Genn 1999 p. 263). She also notes there is little empirical evidence for either choice. We will come back to this debate at the end of the second chapter.

Access to legal information

Legal information, be it to inform people about their rights, help them settle their disputes, or tell them how to bring a case to court, is relevant in all those situations: out-of-court settlement, diversion through alternative dispute resolution, dispute resolution by a court. Because of its capacity to disseminate legal information at low cost, information technology, and particularly the Internet, is regarded as an important means to improve access to justice. Moreover, the outcomes from the chapters on case delay suggest that for some groups of cases, communicating with the parties and access to legal information potentially help to lower the need for access to court (see Chapter 3.4). Access to information also potentially reduces the opportunity for corruption (see Chapter 5.3). These very general suggestions will be taken up and examined in more detail here.

Approach of these chapters

These chapters will attempt to answer some parts of the question how courts and judiciaries can contribute to better access with uses of information technology. In order to do that, this first chapter identifies barriers to access to justice in general. The second chapter then goes on to examine lack of information as a barrier. As observed before, the evidence base is only beginning to build up. There is some information on how people in a few countries deal with some of their justiciable problems. That information will be the starting point for the third chapter, which discusses how courts can contribute to improving access to justice using information technology. These chapters will focus mainly on those topics for which there is a sufficient evidence base.

These chapters will not look into:

- Information sources for judges, and those for lawyers and other legal professionals. Richard Susskind developed a vision for this sort of information in *The Future of Law* (Susskind 1996). The subject deserves a more empirically-based discussion. However, that would take up more space than it can be given here.

- The market for legal information that is available for sale, because the topic is too far removed from the discussion on judicial reform and information technology support for it. This exclusion includes most of the discussion of lawyers and other professional service providers.

The discussion concentrates on individual litigants. It is guided not by a general intuitive feeling or by any kind of program, but by the empirical evidence that is available. The overall approach in this discussion is as follows:

It starts with a discussion of the normative framework.

The next section describes the most commonly identified impediments to access to justice as well as some possible technological solutions.

The second chapter examines lack of knowledge and information as barriers to access to justice. It examines information and knowledge needs and deficits that keep people from resolving their problems. It uses empirical evidence on justiciable problems people face, from Paths to Justice and the Dispute Resolution Delta.

Then, the third chapter addresses those problems in the context of courts. It discusses forms of information technology than can be expected to support the remedies identified.

The normative framework for access to justice

International conventions guarantee access to a court: Everyone is entitled to a fair and public hearing by an independent tribunal - in the determination of their civil rights and obligations or of any criminal charge against them.[1]

This right to access is generally associated with equal opportunity to invoke protection of the law. A well functioning justice system should afford everyone the opportunity to protest violations of their rights. By performing this function well, it also should make the protests less necessary through its deterrent effects (Reiling 2007 p. 66). Allegedly realizing that their actions will be sanctioned, would-be violators would refrain from doing what the law prohibits or do what it mandates. This is the "shadow function" of the law. Court decisions have a shadow function of their own (Galanter 1983). This is the theory. The theory assumes that information about court decisions is readily available.

In practice, many factors affect whether violations and disputes ultimately end up in court or not. To be precise, we have to note a major distinction here in the factors that influence whether cases come to court. There are (1) barriers that prevent issues that should come to court from getting there, and (2) factors that make taking issues to court unnecessary because there is some other way of resolving them. There are also important lessons to be learned about the second group of factors. They will emerge in the course of the discussion.

These chapters focus on the barriers. The next section presents an overview of those factors impeding court access that have been identified in the research so far.

Impediments to access to justice

Before giving an overview of known barriers to access, this section looks at some methodological problems with identifying barriers to access.

In practice, the normative framework turns out to be less than solid for our purpose here. It does not provide us with clearly defined concepts that can be the object of academic study. Access to justice is not a straightforward concept, as observed above. Consequently, diagnosing whether it is deficient in a given context, and identifying the factors involved, are equally problematic. Increases in the numbers of court users or high and/or low litigation rates do not necessarily signify an improvement in access to justice. It is possible that there are alternatives to courts for resolving disputes. There may also simply be relatively few conflicts that could be solved through legal means or by way of court procedures. Another possibility is that the barriers to court are high. Establishing whether there is an objective need for access to courts is problematic. These issues are still very much in discussion, and far from resolved. Resolving them is, in any case, beyond the scope of this study.

I just note there are no established methodologies for:

- Comparing and quantifying levels of access within or across countries
- Developing means to assess and measure impacts, except on the immediate beneficiaries
- Developing integrated strategies that incorporate the variety of mechanisms that people may use to resolve their problems.

Consequently, there is much we do not yet know where access to justice is concerned.

The discussion in this section will concentrate on those issues about which we do know enough to examine them for the purpose of identifying solutions involving information technology.

Barriers to access

The first topic to address is that of the barriers to access. There are many approaches to this field of issues. The discussion here is confined to barriers for which there is potentially a solution in some form of information technology as defined in Part 1. From the literature, we derive the following major barriers to access:

Distance can be a factor impeding access to courts. In many countries, courts are concentrated in the main urban centers or in the capital. Furthermore, in large and/or sparsely populated countries, courts are simply far away or far apart. Examples of the latter are Brazil and Australia. Courts can also be out of reach when travel is difficult or costly (Dale p. 2). Generally speaking, distance is a fairly straightforward factor to diagnose. The geographical situation of large countries like Brazil and Australia evidently makes it difficult to cover the distance to courts for people living outside the few urban concentrations. Factors expressing the number of courts per capita can also indicate the presence of this factor. The judicial map, showing the locations of courts in a country, can show concentration of courts in a few areas. In Brazil, there has been an experiment with traveling courts to extend the reach of formal justice to populations in distant, sparsely populated regions. In this experiment, a boat traveled up and down parts of the Amazon basin. The experiment involved both judicial functions and civil register functions, such as marriages (Hammergren p. 136). In Australia, courts travel circuits to wide areas. They also experiment with forms of videoconferencing to extend the reach of the formal court system to outlying, partly aboriginal communities. Videoconferencing is used for a range of pretrial and administrative purposes, as well as in hearings. In large measure, its popularity is a product of both the enormous distances courts have to cover, particularly in the larger states, and the consequent costs associated with travel for witnesses, lawyers and the judiciary (Macdonald p. 652).

Language barriers are present when justice seekers use a language that is different from the language of the courts. They can be immigrants or people who are not familiar with the official language when a country uses one or more different languages for everyday use. The right to a fair trial in the international conventions usually includes the right to be informed of the accusation in a language one understands, at least in criminal law. An obvious remedy is to provide for translation of documents and interpretation of the spoken word. The most common form of interpretation is consecutive: every sentence or group of sentences is translated after it has been spoken. A more advanced form of interpretation is simultaneous interpretation, where what is spoken is translated (nearly) at the same time. Presumably, this form of translation can save time in a hearing. There is dedicated technology to facilitate simultaneous interpretation with microphones and earphones. Interpretation technology is used in all the international courts. It is not used on a large scale in most other courts. It involves installing technology in existing courtrooms that may not be suited to it. This may incur cost, while the benefit of time saved is not easy to quantify.

Physical challenges, like impaired sight and hearing and motor and cognitive impairments, as a barrier to access are an emerging topic in the debate on technology support in courts. On the one hand, electronic information can provide improved access with text to audio. On the other hand, electronic information is an additional challenge for people with impaired sight or hearing. Using electronic information sets new requirements for accessibility (Waters c.s.).

Cost, in many forms, has been identified as a factor affecting access to courts. The most common forms of cost are legal and court fees, and the costs of additional documents.[2] In order to be complete: costs can also involve speed, money and bribes. As observed before, cost is a complex phenomenon. It will not be discussed further here (see Chapter 1.2 for the reasons).

Lack of information and knowledge, lack of familiarity with the court process, complexity of legal and administrative systems and lack of access to legal information are commonly identified factors (Cotterrell p. 251, Hammergren p. 136). They are related because they all refer to the availability of information. Potentially, information on the Internet can provide some form of solution for these problems.

The first three factors in the list above have in common that they are relatively straightforward and do not strike at the heart of the legal process. For this reason, they do not merit further attention in this study. Cost, as explained in Chapter 1.2, is outside the study's scope.

The next chapter, therefore, will focus on access to legal information and knowledge. Lack of information and knowledge as a barrier to access to justice is the focus for discussion in the first few paragraphs. The rest of the chapter will identify information needs from empirical studies of justiciable problems and how they are handled.

Chapter 4.2 Access to Information

This chapter will examine access to legal information in more detail. In order to find a first, tentative answer to the larger question of how IT can support improving access to justice, it examines information needs and defects as an impediment to access to justice. It will study justiciable problems in order to identify related needs for information. Once those needs have been identified, the next chapter will move on to discuss how courts and judiciaries can play a role in enhancing access to justice by providing information.

In 1974, Marc Galanter pointed out the disadvantage in the legal field of those who come to court only incidentally over those who routinely use the courts as part of their business. His 1974 article "Why the Haves Come Out Ahead," challenged the idea that the principle of equality before the law brings parties on equal footing in litigation. One-shotters go to court perhaps once in their lifetime. Repeat players are engaged in many similar litigations over time. Some of the advantages for the repeat players in litigation are:

- Advance intelligence because of previous experience
- Ability to structure the next transaction and build a record
- Control over interaction with form contracts and security deposits
- They develop expertise and have ready access to specialists.

Repeat players are the claimants in most debt collection procedures: banks, insurance companies, and other institutional service providers. Administrative agencies dealing with social security and government agencies are also repeat players. In criminal matters, the prosecution service is the repeat player par excellence.[3] These repeat players are part of the legal information chains that also include the courts. In terms of the information and knowledge classification laid out in Part 1, the repeat players' advantage lies mainly in the previous experience that enables them to process the information generated in litigation, and act on it.

One-shotters do not have these advantages. According to Galanter (1974), they suffer a lack of knowledge and information that makes them come out behind. Not much was known about this apparent lack of knowledge and information until later.

Later empirical research challenged the idea that the most common method of dispute resolution is that disputes are resolved by courts after they have been brought there by the parties and their lawyers. One study by the ABA and the American Bar Foundation showed that lawyers were used only for problems of a specific nature (Genn p. 7). This suggests there were other problems that did not make it to legal advice, let alone to court. An ABA study of legal needs in 1994 confirmed this suggestion. It found that over the course of a calendar year, about half of the households surveyed faced one or more situations that could have been addressed by the civil justice system, that nearly three-quarters of those situations faced by low-income households, and two-thirds of those situations faced by moderate income households did not find their way into the system (Genn p. 7).[4]

In order to identify information needs to improve access to justice, we need to find out which information defects are at the root of these findings. We will first look into the problems as people experience them.

Next, we map the different ways in which people handle their justiciable problems. This will help us learn more about their need for information when resolving their problems.

Empirical evidence: Justiciable problems

If most disputes never come to court, what happens to them?

This section looks at the kinds of problems people face that could potentially end up in court. It draws on the results of the surveys on justiciable problems in England and Wales, and in the Netherlands. Genn defined a *justiciable event* as a (non-trivial) matter experienced by a respondent which raised legal issues (Genn p. 12) . This definition excludes problems that are not recognized as legally worthy of protection.

Van Velthoven defined *justiciable problem* as: those situations in which problems cause trouble or where parties strive for aims that are irreconcilable, and combat each other with certain means, as well as problem-charged situations in which legal aid was invoked (Van Velthoven 2004 p. 44). From this definition, it is unclear to what extent legal recognition of a problem is part of the definition. In any case, it seems correct to assume that problems that are not legally recognized as worthy of protection are not included in the surveys. Despite this apparent gap in meaning between both definitions, the results of both surveys are similar enough to lend themselves to careful comparison, and to some equally careful conclusions. We first look at the screening surveys of a representative sample of the general population for an overview of the problems that occur.

What justiciable problems occur?

The two screening surveys provided a lot of information about the kinds of justiciable problems people in England and Wales and the Netherlands experience. Table 16 compiles the results of the screening surveys, listing them by type of problem and relative share in England and Wales (E+W) and the Netherlands (NL). Some categories were combined to make comparison easier.

Table 16 *Incidence of Justiciable Problems*

	E+W	*Netherlands*	*Remarks*
Percentage of respondents with problem	40 %	67 %	
Faulty goods and services	11 %	21 %	
Work related	6 %	13 %	
Money problems	9 %	13 %	
Possessing real estate /owning residential property	8 %	12 %	
Renting accommodation/ living in rented accommodation	7 %	8 %	
Relationships and family, including divorce	10 %	6 %	6 % relationships, 4% family in Genn.
Health problems caused by third parties, including negligent medical treatment	10 %	4 %	Genn treats negligent medical treatment as a separate category; I have included it in health problems together to facilitate comparison
Children under 18	3 %	2 %	
Renting out real estate	-	2 %	

Sources: Genn 1999 p. 24 and Van Velthoven 2004 p. 68.

There are some noteworthy differences between the outcomes of the two studies. Relatively more respondents report justiciable problems in the Netherlands. More work and money related problems are reported in the Netherlands as well. More family and relationship problems and health problems are reported in England and Wales. The Delta, published four years after Paths to Justice, puts forward some candidate explanations for the difference in experiencing problems: greater population density resulting in more legal problems in the Netherlands; different composition of the population; a different, more service-oriented economy; and more extensive regulation. These differences and their explanations are outside the scope of the discussion here.

With regard to the incidence of types of justiciable problems, the results in the table are quite similar:

- Most problems have to do with faulty goods and services.
- Money problems come in second place.

- Work related problems come in third place in the Netherlands. In England and Wales, third place is held by health related problems.
- Eighty-nine percent of the problems reported in the Netherlands are civil justice matters; the remaining 11 percent are problems covered by administrative law (Van Velthoven 2004 p. 81).

The studies observe that income levels affect the type of problems people experience. Higher-income people have more problems with real estate; lower-income people have more problems with living in rented accommodations.

Another observation in both studies is that problems do not come by themselves: most people reported more than one problem, on average 3.7 problems per person (Van Velthoven 2004 p. 81). People who reported work problems were likely to also have health and/or money problems. Money problems correlate with problems concerning faulty goods and services. Divorce problems correlate with problems with children under 18, other family problems and money problems (Genn 1999, p. 31). Because problems do not come by themselves, information services should take into account the chance of underlying problems that need to be uncovered at the first request for help. Resolving only one problem may not take care of the entire complex. This is particularly true for courts. A particular court, legally charged with deciding particular types of cases, may be able to decide the divorce, but not the money problem or the other family problem.[5]

Dealing with problems

People with a justiciable problem have some choices when it comes to taking action:

- Lumping or resolving it[6]
- Resolving it themselves or seeking help
- Seeking help from friends, experts, or legal aid
- Starting a procedure.

Table 17 shows the most frequent actions for each problem category.

What does Table 17 tell us about people's choices for addressing their justiciable problems? Accurate comparison between the results of the two studies is difficult due to differences in the way they are presented. Some patterns emerge from both studies:

The top lumping categories are renting out real estate and family problems in the Netherlands and health problems in England and Wales.

Table 17 *Which Action for Which Problem?*

	E+W	*Netherlands*
Percentage of respondents with problem	40 %	67 %
Faulty goods and services	60 % self 73 % contacting other side 36 % advice	72 % contact with other party 35 % expert advice
Work related	78 % advice 20 % to court	49 % contact with other party, 36 % expert advice 6 % to court/tribunal
Money problems	50 % self help 41 % advice	63 % contact with other party 23 % expert advice
Possessing real estate / owning residential property	85 % advice	52 % contact with other party 41 % expert advice
Renting accommodation/ living in rented accommodation	49 % advice	54 % contact with other party 27 % expert advice 10 % court/tribunal procedure
Relationships and family, including divorce	92 % advice/legal aid	11 % lumpers 45 % advice from friends, 45 % expert advice 18 % court
Health problems caused by third parties, including negligent medical treatment	15 % lumpers 69 % advice	66 % expert advice
Children under 18	26 % court	63 % expert advice
Renting out real estate	n.a.	14 % lumpers 45 % contact with other party; 11% court procedure

Sources: Genn 1999 p. 105-133 and Van Velthoven 2004 p. 84.

For faulty goods and services and money problems, people mostly find solutions themselves, mainly by contacting the other party.

A need for expert advice is shown for problems with children under 18, health problems, relationship and family problems and possessing real estate.

Problems ending up in court or in some other formal procedure are family problems, renting out real estate and renting accommodation and work problems.

Problem solving differs per problem. Further research confirms that the type of action taken is determined largely by the type of problem (Genn p. 141, Van Velthoven 2004 p. 94).

This gives us an idea of what justiciable problems people have and how they address them. The next question is whether the problems are resolved, and how.

Outcomes

Table 18 provides some statistics on the way problems have ended.

Table 18 *Outcomes*

Outcome	*E+W*	*Netherlands*
Abandonment, unresolved, no agreement or adjudication	51%	46%
Agreement	35%	48%
Adjudication	14%	7%

Sources: Genn 1999 p. 147 and Van Velthoven 2004 p. 117, 127.

A very important finding in these studies is that about half of all members of the public who experience non-trivial justiciable problems fail to achieve any resolution to those problems, whether or not they seek advice. Legal advice and active assistance increase the likelihood that a case will end in an agreement, adjudication or court order. In the Netherlands, the agreement group is considerably larger than in England and Wales: nearly half as opposed to about a third of all outcomes. In the Netherlands, agreements are reached with third party assistance in a considerable proportion of the outcomes.

What clearly emerges is the very limited use made by the public of formal legal proceedings to resolve justiciable problems. The proportion is twice as high in England and Wales as it is in the Netherlands. Almost all cases that end up in a formal procedure got there after advice was obtained. People are reluctant to voluntarily become involved in legal proceedings. Involvement in legal proceedings is most common in cases concerning divorce and separation, education tribunal matters, ownership of residential property, employment disputes, and accidental injury.

Problem type is very important in the outcome of justiciable problems. Employment problems, neighbor problems and problems with landlords tend to have a generally low rate of resolution. Divorce and separation problems, money problems and consumer problems have a higher rate of resolution. Money remedies are easier to achieve than some change in behavior (Genn p. 176-178).

Success rate

In those cases where the problem was resolved, people's main aim was largely achieved, and they largely perceived the outcome as fair.

Table 19 *Aims Achieved, Perceptions and Effects*

	Main aim achieved, completely or partly	*Outcome fair*	*Compliance*	*Negative effects on personal life*
NL overall	73,2%	86%	89	
E+W overall	56%	76%		
NL agreement	90,2%	86%	91	Little
E+W agreement	86%	78%		
NL official decision	65,8%	58%	86	
E+W official decision	68%	71%		
NL lumpers	52%			Yes, work, stress, sleep problems, health

Sources: Genn 1999 p. 196, 200, Van Velthoven 2004 p. 158, 163

Agreements achieve better results than official decisions:
- The rates for aims achieved are higher.
- Perceived fairness is higher.
- Compliance is somewhat higher.
- Effects on personal and work life are less negative than for official decisions or for lumping (Van Velthoven 2004, p. 167).

People report they are pleased with having stood up for their rights and with having some control over their own situation.

Some of these effects may be explained by the nature of the problems that are resolved through agreement, and that of the counterparts:
- Most are consumer problems, and they are relatively easy to resolve.
- The problems are generally not as serious, making them easier to resolve.
- Most problems are with repeat players. Repeat players deal with problems in a more functional manner; they have more routine procedures for dealing with problems (Van Velthoven 2004 p. 153). This may also explain to a degree why problems with repeat players are resolved more easily than those with one-shotters.

Official decisions also achieve good results, but they cause much more stress. The majority of people whose problem ended with an official decision still report their main aim was achieved and the outcome was fair. Compliance is still quite high. People are pleased with having stood up for their rights. They report even more satisfaction than people who settled their dispute with an agreement. They also report significantly more stress, sleep and health problems than the agreement forgers. Their reported stress and health problem level is about the same as that of the lumpers (Van Velthoven 2004 p. 167).

When asked about their regrets, only 18 percent report any regret. When asked what they regret, most people mention regret about their own behavior:
- Not having taken action earlier
- Not having had the required tenacity
- Not being assertive enough.

Some of those whose problem ended with a decision also feel they should have found themselves a lawyer or other adviser (Van Velthoven 2004 p. 166).

Family and relationship cases are relatively costly.

Problems are still going on: 14 percent, 22 percent in official procedures, 6 percent in agreement and 25 percent in lumpers.

People report they do not appeal official decisions because they experience a sense of powerlessness (Van Velthoven 2004 p. 163).

The next question regards the role of information in the choices people make in addressing their justiciable problems. How does it play a role in half the problems not being resolved?

Information and knowledge needs

This section identifies some information and knowledge needs and deficits from the findings of the two studies.

When making choices about their justiciable problems, people are presumably affected by what they know and the information they can obtain. How does this affect whether they ignore their problem, settle it with the other party, find advice and expert help, or take their case to court?

Lumping the problem

The first choice people make is between lumping a problem and taking action. How often do the lumpers cite lack of information and knowledge as a reason for doing so?

In the Delta, on average 8 percent of those experiencing justiciable problems take no action to address them. On average, 35 percent of them give "I did not think anything could be done about it" as the main reason for doing so. The number of people giving this reason differs greatly depending on the problem. It is the reason most cited by lumpers for their decision. If we also include the group saying "I did not know who could help," the average percentage goes up to 44. In England and Wales, only about 5 percent took no action about their justiciable problem (Genn p. 69). Within this group, about 20 percent said they took this course of non-action because nothing could be done about it. Genn observes that this judgment is made without the benefit of any kind of advice.

This analysis leads to the conclusion that nearly 4 percent (the Netherlands) and 1 percent (England and Wales) of those experiencing justiciable problems take no action for lack of knowledge and information. The study on the Netherlands does not identify the problem of lumping for lack of information as a problem of access. This raises the question why it is not considered a problem.

Seeking advice

Whether advice is sought is largely determined by problem type. Problems (a) involving issues that are relatively complex and (b) with issues that are difficult to resolve by means of self-help strategies are likely to lead to advice seeking. The highest scoring on these points are those problems that involve a relationship: employment, family matters, and neighbor problems. Advice is sought in a very high proportion of cases with divorce and separation problems. In England and Wales, it is well over 90 percent, in NL it is 60 percent (Van Velthoven 2004 p. 93-94, Genn p. 140-142).

Factors determining the need for advice:
- The competence/resources of the party
- The importance of the problem
- The intransigence of the opponent.

A competent, resourceful party may still need advice for an important problem or when the opponent is difficult to deal with (Genn p. 143).

What advice?

If people go looking for advice, what kind of advice are they looking for?

Table 20 *What Kind of Advice Do People Look For?*

Advice on	*E+W*	*Netherlands*
Ways to solve the problem	68 %	46 %
Rights and duties	47 %	45 %
Financial aspects	20 %	23 %
Legal procedures	15 %	34 %

Sources: Genn 1999 p. 95 and Van Velthoven 2004 p. 109.

First and foremost, people want advice on ways to solve their problem.

Next is information on rights and duties. In the Netherlands, the next most important subject is information on legal procedures, a need that is not as prominent in England and Wales. Finally, there is a sizable need for information on financial aspects.

On the whole, the advice received was considered largely useful.

What people need when they go for advice is determined by the type of problem and by their own personal competencies, such as confidence, verbal skills and literacy (Genn p. 99).

Whose advice?

When people sought expert advice, their first port of call was the following:

In the Netherlands, they went – in order of frequency - to:

- Trade unions and specialist associations
- Lawyers
- The police
- Legal aid bureaus
- Legal assistance insurance (Van Velthoven 2004 p. 102).

In England and Wales, the most visited providers of expert advice were:

- Solicitors
- Citizens' advice bureaus
- Local councils
- Police (Genn p. 83).

The specialist associations in the Netherlands include such organizations as home owners' associations and consumer associations. It is interesting that the police are a resource for many people.

Advice or assistance?

Sometimes advice is not enough to resolve the problem at hand and people need active assistance. Genn reports that in many cases where people went looking for help, they needed more positive assistance than what was offered by the provider of advice (Genn p.103). People had a need for active assistance and credible threats to be made.

Active help and assistance are needed most for:

- Approaching the other party (26 percent),
- Taking legal steps (17 percent)
- Approaching a different adviser (12 percent).

In the Netherlands, 11 percent of those seeking advice needed legal representation (Van Velthoven 2004 p.109).

The need for assistance is higher for problems that involve dealing with bureaucratic and legalized bodies, like government institutions (Van Velthoven 2004 p. 105). A possible explanation is that there is less room for informal solutions when dealing with the government, according to the Delta.

What assistance?
What assistance did people actually get? Providers helped them with the following (in order of frequency from Genn p.97):
- Contacting the other party (30 percent)
- Negotiating with the other party (24 percent)
- Helping to file complaint/petition (13 percent)

In the Netherlands, assistance with helping to contact the other party occurred in 11 percent of all instances of assistance (Van Velthoven 2004 p. 110).

This information enables us to draw conclusions on the knowledge needs and information barriers in the concluding paragraphs of this chapter.

Conclusions for this Chapter

This chapter explored information needs as impediments to access to justice. The analysis brought up some questions that need to be addressed before we can move on to a discussion on the contribution courts can make to improving access to justice:
- Whether the identified information needs can be met using the Internet
- Whether diversion or access to courts needs to be improved
- Whether routines help or hinder problem resolution.

These will be discussed below.

The main focus of this chapter was on the information needs of individuals when they encounter justiciable problems. Empirical evidence of people and their justiciable problems in England and Wales and the Netherlands points to some information needs and deficiencies.

Knowledge and information barriers to access to justice
The main aim of this chapter was to identify information defects as impediments to access to justice. An important finding is that around half of all justiciable problems are not resolved at all. Analysis of empirical evidence, on individuals and their justiciable problems, produced the following findings with regard to information and knowledge barriers:
- Inaction in the face of a justiciable problem because of lack of information and knowledge occurs in a small percentage of cases.
- Unavailability of advice negatively affects dispute resolution outcomes. It lowers the resolution rate. Cases where people went to find advice were resolved with a higher rate of success than those of the self-helpers.

- Inability to find advice. If people go looking for advice, the barriers to finding it have more to do with their own competencies, such as confidence, emotional fortitude and literacy skills, than with the availability of the advice.[7]
- Incompetence in implementing the information received. Different competence levels will affect what can be done with information and advice. Competencies in implementing the information received include, for example, skills such as working out what the problem is, what result is wanted, how to find help, simple case recording skills, managing correspondence, confidence and assertiveness, and negotiating skills (Advicenow 2005).[8] Some people do not want to be empowered by having information available. They want assistance, or even someone to take over dealing with their problem. People with low levels of competence in terms of education, income, confidence, verbal skill, literacy skill, and emotional fortitude are likely to need some help in resolving justiciable problems.
- Ignorance about legal rights exists across most social groups. Genn notes people are not educated about their legal rights (Genn p. 102).
- People lack confidence in the legal system and the courts, and have negative feelings about the justice system. Genn observes that people do not want to become voluntarily involved with the courts. They associate courts with criminal justice. People's image of the courts is formed by media stories about high profile criminal cases (Genn p. 247). This issue is related to the public image of courts, as well as to the wider role of courts as setters of norms. It will be discussed in more detail in the next chapter.

One-shotters and the access to justice crisis

Galanter's model of repeat players and one-shotters raises the question how one-shotters can achieve justice, while at the same time they will never become repeat players with all the knowledge advantages that brings.

The discovery that one-shotters are at a disadvantage when it comes to the administration of justice has caused a major shift in thinking. Now, it is no longer considered acceptable that parts of the population do not actually enjoy the legal protection they are awarded by law. From the empirical evidence discussed in this chapter, we have learned that the availability of advice and assistance, as well as information on resolving disputes and on rules and regulations, improves the chance that problems will be resolved and justice achieved. Thus, the one-shotters' disadvantage is, to a degree, compensated for by information, advice and assistance. Chapter 4.3 examines some ways in which this compensation can work.

Use of the Internet

This section is a first exploration of the potential of the Internet as an answer to those information needs. We have learned that levels of competence are a major factor in the resolution of justiciable disputes. They are going up as more people get a better education. That enables them to act on information. What we do not yet know is whether people use the Internet as a resource for resolving their justiciable problems. What about Internet competence? In the studies, we have not found evidence whether people used the Internet to find information to help them with resolving their justiciable problems. Both studies were done some years ago. The data for Paths to Justice were collected before 1999, and those for the Dispute Resolution Delta before 2003. In both the United Kingdom and the Netherlands, Internet use has increased considerably since then. Between 2000 and 2008, Internet use grew in the United Kingdom by 171 percent and in the Netherlands by 284 percent.[9] The level of Internet skills has also been going up, according to European Union statistics. In 2007, there were more people with Internet skills overall than in 2005. In the Netherlands in 2005, 80 percent of the general population had at least one Internet skill. In 2007 the rate had gone up to 84 percent. For the United Kingdom, the 2005 figure is not available but the 2007 level was 71 percent.[10] In an online poll in August 2008, users of Advicenow, a U.K. resource for legal information, were asked where they would go for advice when they have a problem: 19 percent went to their mother, 5 percent went to the local advice agency, 8 percent reported they wait for divine inspiration and 68 percent said they went to the Internet or a help line.[11]

It looks as if the Internet could be an adequate channel to provide people with justiciable problems with information on resolving them. Chapter 4.3 explores some examples of information and advice on legal issues on the Internet.

Routines or bureaucracy?

A noteworthy finding is that problems with firms or organizations are relatively easily resolved as opposed to problems with other individuals ((Van Velthoven 2004 p. 153). The reason put forward is that firms and organizations have routine procedures for dealing with problems. At the same time, there is the finding that people needed more assistance in dealing with government institutions because these institutions have bureaucratic and legalized ways of working (Van Velthoven 2004 p. 105). These two findings seem to conflict. What is the difference between routines and bureaucracy? Is bureaucracy bad routines?

This is an issue we should keep in mind, because it comes back in many instances when we talk about court procedures. Developing routines is discussed extensively in the chapters on case delay. In terms of information management, routines have to do with structured as opposed to form-free information exchange. In the next chapter, there is a discussion of online forms as a way of communicating with individual litigants. We will take up this issue in that context again.

Diversion or access, empowerment or court improvement?

The debate about the objective of legal policy has been going on for some time. It discusses which is preferable or which should come first, diversion, access, empowerment, or court improvement. The choices are to:

- Enhance access to legal forums for the resolution of dispute
- Prevent problems and disputes from arising
- Equip as many members of the public as possible to solve problems when they do arise without recourse to legal action
- Divert cases away from the courts into private dispute resolution forums.

According to Genn, it is not an answer to say that diversion and access should be the twin objectives of policy, because they logically conflict. On the strength of Genn's own empirical material and that of the Delta, I would like to submit some possible lines of reasoning for a way out of this apparent dilemma.

The first line of reasoning is based on the higher degree of satisfaction people reported at having resolved their own problem and in the stress they experience over having to go to court. The outcomes of court cases are often uncertain.[12] Consequently, there will always be a degree of stress involved in going to court. Reducing that stress by more realistic, positive images of the court will not take it away entirely. Hence, ensuring that as few cases as possible come to court is preferable, since it reduces uncertainty and increases satisfaction with the outcome.

The second line of reasoning is based on the finding that resolutions are to a large degree problem specific. Could it be that the way out of the dilemma is also problem specific by strengthening the itinerary the resolutions take? This would mean, for instance, that specialist organizations that make it their business to provide specific information, advice and assistance should enhance their role. There is an empirical base for this in Paths to Justice and the Dispute Resolution Delta. Goods and services cases are largely resolved through self-help, out of court settlement and ADR, but they still come to court. Devising ways to help informal problem solving and diverting them to other dispute resolution mechanisms can still keep more of them out of court. Even in matters for which a court decision is compulsory, like divorce, there are ways of sorting out the disputes before the case needs to be filed.

Comparison between England and Wales and the Netherlands with regard to dispute outcome (Table 18) shows the following: The Netherlands has fewer unresolved disputes, more disputes resolved by agreement and the rate of resolution by adjudication is half that of England and Wales. It looks as if there is more capacity for resolving justiciable problems in Dutch society than there is in society in England and Wales. Apart from the legacy of the justice system that Voltaire described, many factors may be at work in the Netherlands to produce a higher level of problem solving capacity. One probable factor is the level of education and the related competence levels for dealing with problems and the legal framework. The functional illiteracy rate is only half that in the United Kingdom. Another factor may be a propensity to settle differences by reducing the complexity through policies and routines.

User statistics from MCOL and the labor compensation caseload in Chapter 2.3 do not suggest that changes in procedure facilitating access in themselves lead to higher caseloads. Changes observed in the caseloads are attributable to market forces in both cases.

All this should not keep us from making going to court when necessary less stressful. Information can help reduce people's stress and it improves their chances of achieving justice. The next chapter, on courts and how they communicate with individual litigants, will take this finding up again.

Information needs for resolving justiciable problems

The other aim of this chapter was to identify access-related needs for information and knowledge. Using the way people deal with their justiciable problems as a guide, we can pinpoint those needs. The evidence tells us that the most frequently occurring justiciable problems are those with goods and services. People will resolve simple, easy to solve justiciable problems themselves. They are mostly resolved satisfactorily by self-help, or with advice from specialist organizations. As the importance of the problem grows and the problem becomes more complex, people will find more expert help. The most difficult to resolve are problems that involve a relationship. Any of the problems discussed in this section may lead to a court procedure. However, the problems that are the toughest to resolve are also the ones that most frequently come to court.

When people go looking for information, they first and foremost go looking for information on how to solve the problem. People in the Netherlands primarily get their information from specialized organizations, and from legal advice providers in second place. In England and Wales, solicitors are the first port of call, followed by the Citizens' Advice Bureaux. In both countries, the police is a significant source of information on justiciable problems. This is especially remarkable because the problems researched were not criminal justice issues.

If people require legal information, they primarily need straightforward information about rules and regulations. Next, they look for information about ways to settle and handle disputes once they arise. Information about court procedures is a separate category that becomes relevant only in case people need to go to court.

For taking their case to court, people need information on how to resolve problems, on rights and duties, and on taking a case to court. The justiciable problems that normally come to court tend to be difficult for people themselves to resolve. They are also experienced as serious. Many of them involve long-term relationships: family, employment, neighbors. Therefore, people will tend to go looking for advice. Some of them may need assistance. Most people seek and receive some kind of advice before they come to court.

The next chapter on access to justice focuses on the role of courts and judiciaries in providing information to support access to justice. It will explore the ways in which information technology, particularly the Internet, can support courts in performing this role. People's competence and their confidence in the courts are important issues to be kept in mind.

Chapter 4.3 Access to Court

This chapter examines how information technology can support the role of the courts in providing access to justice. After examining what information needs people have when they experience justiciable problems in the last chapter, we now look at the implications of those findings for the courts.

Some conclusions from the previous chapter relate to the role of courts in resolving justiciable problems:

- The most complex justiciable problems are the most difficult to resolve.
- On the most complex problems, people need help (information, advice, assistance, ADR) most.
- These problems are also the most likely to become court cases.
- Going to court is stressful.
- People associate courts with criminal justice.

More specifically, this chapter examines what courts can do with information technology to meet the information needs that one-shotters have when it comes to resolving their justiciable problems. In order to answer that question, this chapter analyzes:

- The cases for which one-shotters come to court
- Their related information needs
- How information technology can help to meet those needs.

The information needs are primarily individual information needs, related to the problem in the case. However, there are also more general or collective information needs. They are related to the shadow function of the law and to the image people have of courts. The need related to the shadow function of the law is discussed first, in the section on keeping cases out of court. The specific information need related to the image people have of courts, and how that affects the resolution of their justiciable problems, is discussed in a special section.

Which cases come to court?

This section analyzes which cases come to court with one-shotters as litigants. To that end, we first go back to Galanter's framework on party configurations in litigation between one-shotters and repeat players (those who are engaged in many similar procedures over time, repeat players). Galanter has constructed a model in the shape of a matrix showing the litigation configurations of repeat players and one-shotters. Next, we integrate this configuration into the matrix from the case processing chapter.

Figure 5 shows the types of cases that may come to court, by type of claimant and defendant. Galanter theorizes about the configurations:

Quadrant I: One-shotter vs. One-shotter: Most cases in this group are family cases.

Quadrant II: Repeat player vs. One-shotter: Repeat players use the courts for routine processing of claims against one-shotters. The great bulk of litigation is in this quadrant. The litigation can be characterized as routine mass processing. Even greater numbers of cases are settled, and settlements are shaped by possible litigation outcomes.

Quadrant III: One-shotter vs. Repeat player: Such cases come to court only infrequently except for personal injury cases. In auto injury claims, litigation is routinized and settlement is closely geared to possible litigation outcomes.

Quadrant IV: Repeat player vs. Repeat player: Cases between repeat players do not generally come to court. Repeat players will try and establish mutually beneficial relationships. For any dispute resolution,

Figure 5 *Matrix of a Taxonomy of Litigation by Strategic Configuration of Parties*

Defendant/ claimant	One-shotter	Repeat player
One-shotter	I OS vs. OS Parent vs parent (custody) Spouse v. spouse (divorce) Family v. family member (insanity commitment) Family v. family (inheritance) Neighbor v. neighbor Partner v. partner	II RP vs. OS Prosecutor v.accused Financeco. v. debtor Landlord v.tenant I.R.S. v. taxpayer Condemnor v.propertyowner
Repeat player	III OS vs. RP Welfare client v. agency Auto dealer v.manufacturer Injury victim v.insurance company Tenant v. landlord Bankruptconsumer v. creditors Defamed v.publisher	IV RP vs. RP Union v. company Movie distributor v.censorship board Developer v. suburbanmunicipality Purchaser v.supplier Regulatoryagency v.firms of regulatedindustry

they will rely on arbitration or other less official third parties. Finally, the government is a repeat player (Galanter 1974 p. 14-15).

To take up the conclusions from the case processing chapters on different groups of cases again in the context of access to justice, we go back to the case matrix developed in the case processing chapter. Figure 6 translates Galanter's party configurations to the case matrix from the case processing chapters.

Figure 6 shows the most common party configurations in the case processing matrix. The matrix classifies cases according to the level of unpredictability of the outcome, and the level of cooperation between the parties affecting that outcome. The win-win cases lend themselves to forms of settlement, whereas the zero-sum cases are adjudicated more or less predictably.

Title group claimants are mostly repeat players. They have a routine way of handling claims, and taking cases to court is part of that routine. Most one-shotters in this group will be potential respondents who choose not to contest the claim. They may well be helped with informa-

Figure 6 *Matrix of Party Configurations*

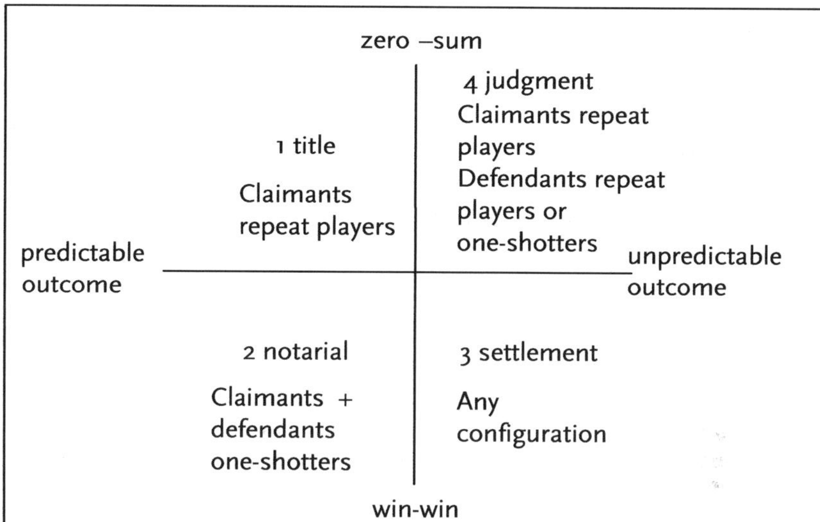

Source: Chapter 3.2.

tion on how they can settle to keep their case out of court. One-shotters who may have a defense will be helped with information on how to defend themselves or on finding help with it. If they decide to file a defense, the case moves to the judgment group or, in case of settlement, to the settlement group. Early user statistics for Money Claim On Line show a quick rise in individual organizations that file claims after MCOL first went live in early 2003 (MCOL 2004). This could mean there is a latent demand in the group of one-shotters who are potential claimants.

The notarial group comprises what Galanter calls pseudo-litigation. There is no real dispute between the parties. They mostly involve family and labor matters between one-shotters. Even a large part of the employers in the labor matters are one-shotters, individuals with small businesses. Courts are addressed ad hoc. Parties come to court because the law requires a judicial decision.[13] In the family cases, both the initiators and the respondents are likely to be one-shotters: spouses requesting a divorce because they have agreed to end their marriage, family members who request a provision for parental authority, an authorization for forced medical treatment, an insanity declaration. Some cases may require representation by a lawyer.

Cases involving relationships can be difficult to resolve. If there is a real dispute between the parties, the case moves to the right in the matrix, to the settlement group if it is settled during the life of the court procedure, and to the judgment group if it ends in a judgment after adversarial proceedings.

Settlement group matters can be any party configuration. They may come to court because negotiations between the parties have stalled because of a legal point, or because of something else that was insurmountable for one of the parties. It could be they need help on a legal point, after which they can settle. Court help with settlement may well be most needed in unequal party configurations. This will prevent these matters from becoming group 4 cases.

The judgment group's party configurations are similar to those of the title group, but now with a defendant. The most frequently occurring configuration will be with repeat players as claimants/initiators, and mostly one-shotters as defendants/respondents. Occasionally, defendants will be repeat players. Information needs in this group will, therefore, be diverse. One-shotters are likely to need help on how to bring a case to court as well as on the rules and regulations regarding their dispute.

Information needs for litigation

Next, we look at the information needs of one-shotters in the different groups. What do we know about their need for information, and how can courts help them to:

- Settle and stay out of court
- Bring their case to court well prepared so their case can be resolved in the best manner possible.

Keeping cases out of court

This section looks at information needs related to resolving cases without bringing them to court. The problem resolution process can be pictured as a continuum: Self-help first, then guidance for problem resolution, with or without assistance, for a settlement that needs to be ratified by the court or not. A small percentage of justiciable problems will come to court. They come to court because the problem cannot be resolved otherwise and it is serious enough to be taken to court. However, some problems come to court even though they could be resolved without it, because a court decision is a legal requirement.

In the last chapter, we learned the following:

- For the kind of justiciable problems that as a rule come to court, people always need advice.
- For those problems, they usually seek and find information.
- They need information on how to resolve problems, on rights and duties, on taking a case to court.

- To find information on resolving problems, they mostly go to specialized organizations in the Netherlands, and to legal aid organizations in the United Kingdom.

If guidance about court jurisprudence and policies should play a role in resolving problems, information on the policies needs to be available to those organizations as well as to individual information seekers. In practice, specialist organizations, such as the consumer associations or home owner associations communities build up their own knowledge bases. Those repositories are sometimes made available in their publications and on their web sites. Depending on the organization's web site's business model, the information may be available to the general public in part, or as a whole. Nowadays, there are examples of specialized organizations to deal with damages suffered by large groups of one-shotters through one specific cause or event, like risky investment products or an accident, set up around a web site.

People may also need assistance with resolving their problem. The assistance can range from contacting the other party, to helping with a settlement, to forms of ADR. There is potential for settling a considerable number of cases that come to court. One-shotters tend to have little experience in resolving disputes. In the chapter on court case processes, we concluded that cooperation between the parties can produce a win-win outcome. One-shotters may need help with resolving their differences so they can bring a ready settlement to court. The example of labor contract dissolution in the notarial group illustrates how that can work. In Dutch court practice on labor contract termination, the employer generally initiates the termination procedure by filing the request containing the agreement the parties have worked out beforehand. These requests make up the bulk of notarial group cases in the local courts (Van Velthoven 2005 p. 22).[14] About half of the employers initiating a procedure are individuals; the other half are legal bodies (Van Velthoven 2005 p. 29). We do not know what proportion of those legal bodies could be regarded as one-shotters. The policy developed by the local courts is public information; it is known in labor unions; and it is publicly available on the web sites of many organizations specializing in providing information and support for either employers or employees. In this win-win group, this example illustrates how information about norms that are applied by the court can help the parties.

This discussion of notarial group cases draws a picture of a landscape of settling justiciable problems in different phases of their development, aided by court jurisprudence and policies. This kind of information rings of what Richard Susskind called the golden legal nuggets: punchy, jargon-free practical points, rather than detailed legal analysis (Susskind p. xlviii). Their basis may be no more than tendencies in decisions by lower courts, but also established case law or jurisprudence. In the case of the justiciable problems for which the legal golden nuggets are not available, generating information on general trends is an option, possibly with technological support.

Some of the information to support out-of-court settlement can be laid down in policies, which in turn can be contained in court decision support systems. Court decision support systems help judges and courts to reach decisions. Van den Hoogen, referring to the requirement of public, transparent administration of justice in the European Convention on Human Rights, advocates making decision support systems public (Van den Hoogen p. 105). If they are public, they can also guide out-of-court solutions. However, making judicial decision support systems public may well change their character. It seems likely they will be regarded as norms or standards (Oskamp 2008). Legal and problem solving cultures may be more geared toward informal dispute resolution in some countries than in others. An indication could be that in the Netherlands, 7 percent of justiciable disputes end in an official decision; it is more than 14 percent in England and Wales. Such a difference may signify more or less receptivity to the type of information service discussed in this chapter.

Bringing cases to court

This section will look into ways in which information technology can help one-shotters who need to take their case to court. There are a number of reasons why this question is relevant.

The first one is that correct, adequate information can enhance the procedural position of the court users, thereby giving one-shotters a better chance of a just and fair outcome of their case.

Second, a modern government organization can be expected to inform the public clearly about its procedures. That holds for courts too.

The third reason needs a little more introduction. From the results of the Delta and Paths to Justice, we know that so far, almost no one-shotters come to court without having first received advice and/or assistance. They hardly ever come by themselves. At the same time, compulsory representation by a lawyer is gradually being reduced, at least in the Dutch system. The value amount for which claims can be filed in the local courts has been raised several times in the past ten years (Eshuis 1999 p. 9). It now stands at € 5,000. More than 74 percent of all civil cases were disposed in the local courts in 2007. There are plans to raise the amount to € 25,000 in 2011. Consequently, the proportion of civil cases handled in the local courts will grow. In the local courts, representation by a lawyer is not compulsory. As a result, in more and more cases parties can come to court, either without assistance or assisted by someone other than a lawyer.[15] In other areas, we see disintermediation: intermediaries disappearing or being bypassed by communication on the Internet. The most striking are online banking and the travel business: instead of physically going to their bank for transactions, many people now manage their finances online. They also book flights, hotel rooms and theater tickets by themselves, bypassing travel agents. It is likely that court users will increasingly come to expect a similar level of service too.

Therefore, it is timely and useful to explore how these developments and expectations can be met. There is some indication of how some court users in the Netherlands experience the present information service provided by the courts. In 2007, a study commissioned by the Netherlands Council for the Judiciary evaluated existing communication services and outlined improvement of information services for court users (Mein 2008). The study examined, among other things:

- To what extent are court users provided with information about the business and the course of things in court?
- How do they rate the information obtained, and how do their wishes compare with the actual situation?

The study interviewed approximately 250 court users before and/or after their hearing. The interviews were spread as much as possible over all sectors: criminal, administrative, local court, and civil (juveniles and estate division). Five court users were interviewed more in depth. The team also analyzed information materials and correspondence. They interviewed legal aid providers as well. The sample of users is very small, so the findings are indicative only. The findings indicate that information services for court users in the Netherlands are not very effective.

Most users do not actively seek and find information in preparation for their court case. There is a latent demand for information about the procedure, but users are unable to articulate their demand for legal advice and assistance. Hence, they cannot seek and find information to prepare for their case. If users do go looking for information actively, lawyers are their most common source. That makes information service a fairly random process. Users have a passive attitude, partly due to feelings of guilt and shame. The users want to be informed by a clearly written letter from the court. They are not interested in modern media.

People are altogether relatively satisfied about their court experience. This positive evaluation is caused mainly by the attitude they encounter from the judge in court.

The information provided by the courts in letters and leaflets focuses on the sender of the information and the sender's needs. Legal correctness and procedural functionality are the main criteria. The information is not geared to answering questions; it does not take the recipient of the information into account.

Users get their information from other sources as well: lawyers, legal kiosks, bailiffs, the prosecution. Bailiffs, legal service providers, clerks and ushers all give information. This information is neither coherent nor coordinated.

The study concludes that "paradigmatic change" is needed. It makes some recommendations. The style of the information service needs to be reconsidered. A more proactive, demand oriented and differentiated information service deserves recommendation. This also involves a reconsideration of the implications of the rule that courts do not give legal advice. The study has not given a more detailed recommendation with regard to this rule. I feel the rule itself should not be reconsidered, but the implications need to be looked into. The implication of the rule is now interpreted, at least by district courts, to mean that people with a question are, as a rule, referred to a lawyer. Local court staff, who are more used to dealing with self-representing parties, tend to be more forthcoming with help. The study also recommends setting up a dedicated web site for informing court users about coming to court. They recommend it should be a new web site dedicated to practical information for court users per type of (frequently occurring) procedure. The language level needs to be simple; the site must be easy to navigate. A project is under way to implement these recommendations in a new web site.

I would submit that the paradigm in question needs a few more new features:

- Multi-channel information: In the letter inviting parties to court, there should at least be a reference to information on the web site.
- Information coordination with the other sources.
- Unified and simplified court access.

The next section will explore some of the features of the change that would be needed, by looking into experience from the United States and the United Kingdom where information technology has been a tool for courts for a longer period of time. This section will look first at experiments with more advanced forms of information technology for court access.

Online court access: First experiences

This section looks at IT functionality for providing online access to courts. Courts in the United States have experimented with Internet technology for helping self-representing litigants navigate their way to and through court. The pilots, presented regularly at the bi-annual Court Technology Conferences of the National Center for State Courts in the United States, are a response to what has been called the access to justice crisis: the realization that many people, particularly those with low income, do not get the help that would make their legal problems go away (Hough 2007). The philosophy of the access to justice pilots is that courts, as a justice institution, should ensure decisions are not made on defaults or lack of knowledge, that decisions are followed because litigants understand how to comply, and people have a right to their day in court. Information technology can provide different functionalities to achieve these goals.

As outlined in Chapter 2.1, courts' external communication occurs with very different counterparts:

- Non-users and users
- Lawyers and other regular professional court users
- Non-professional court users.

Looking at the level of the interaction, the approach below follows the four-stage model for benchmarking e-government projects in the European Union (EU Benchmarking p. 16):

Stage 1: Information online about public services
Stage 2: Communication/interaction: Downloading of forms
Stage 3: Communication/two-way interaction: Processing of forms (including authentication)
Stage 4: Transaction: Case handling, decision and delivery (payment).

Below is an analysis of the ways in which those functionalities have been mobilized to provide access to justice. The examples range from one-sided information service to increasingly interactive forms of communication:

- Web sites and information
- Forms and document assembly
- Videoconferencing
- Customer friendly e-filing
- Case management systems
- Chat models
- Records access.

Some of these functionalities are still experimental. They are discussed in the final sections. First, the next section discusses and analyzes functionality for providing information. This is the activity with the largest body of experience available of all the functionalities discussed here.

Providing Information

This section looks at experience with providing information on the Internet. It first lists some requirements for this type of information service. Next, it compares some web sites providing information on divorce. The information is analyzed for web readability and effectiveness. The section closes with some specific conclusions for court information services.

Providing information is generally regarded as a one-sided activity. Information is "pushed" to the recipient. This does not mean the receiver of the information is irrelevant. For information to be effective, it needs to meet four major requirements:

- The recipient can understand it.
- The recipient can act on it and will know what to do next.
- The recipient feels confident that the actions he or she undertakes will achieve the result envisaged.
- The information must, of course, be correct. This criterion is not examined further in this context.

The general problem with any professional communication is that it tends to presume a professional, post-graduate level of understanding. Information for members of the general public needs to be specifically targeted.

For legal information service on the Internet to be effective, the first requirement means that people with limited knowledge of the law or even limited education in general must be able to understand it. The second requirement is that they must also be able to follow up on it.

Testing legal resources on the Internet

To examine some of the implications of these requirements, a number of Internet resources were tested on those two requirements. The first test is for readability. The second test checks if the information points the reader toward what to do next, and whether the reader can, if the steps are followed, expect the desired result. I compared web information on divorce in the United Kingdom and in the Netherlands. I chose divorce because it is a type of court case that belongs in the notarial group in the matrix. For this group, information service to support dispute resolution by people themselves was identified as an opportunity for using IT to improve court performance. Moreover, this choice follows up on the studies on justiciable problems in those two countries in the previous chapter. From those studies, we know that divorce, is a problem for which people will most likely look for advice. In order to obtain a divorce, they will also need to go to court. In the United Kingdom, a simple divorce can be requested by the parties without a lawyer representing them. In the Netherlands, all divorce requests need to be filed by a lawyer. Divorce is a complex issue. It involves procedures and rules, and it has a strong emotional component. That makes explaining the legal situation and its implications no easy task. The sites listed below were tested, first for web readability, and then for effectiveness. The details of both tests are explained below.

The sites tested were the instances figuring in Paths to Justice (Genn) and the Dispute Resolution Delta (Van Velthoven 2004), their successors or their offspring, and the official web sites of the ministries of justice and the judiciaries and courts. Screen dumps of the web pages are collected in Appendix A. These sites, listed here in alphabetical order, were tested in September 2008:

CAB: Citizens' Advice Bureaux, the United Kingdom's network of advice agencies. For online advice, visitors to the CAB web site http://www.citizensadvice.org.uk/cabdir.ihtml are referred to the site of adviceguide.org. Once there, five clicks, through to family matters and to ending a relationship bring the visitor to: http://www.adviceguide.org.uk/index/family_parent/family/ending_a_marriage.htm#divorce

HMCS: Her Majesty's Court Service: the United Kingdom's national office for the courts. There is a link on the home page for divorce proceedings. The divorce proceeding page lists six choices. I have chosen "I want a divorce – What do I do?" (leaflet D184):
http://www.hmcourts-service.gov.uk/courtfinder/forms/d184.pdf

Advicenow: a cooperative web site of a number of advice providers in the United Kingdom. On the home page, there is a quick search link for divorce. There is a list of search results for divorce from different sources: a guide to help with splitting up, a survival toolkit, and pages that discuss mediation and conciliation. Clicking through on information about divorce leads to another page with search results. Clicking on the survival toolkit, which promises information on the divorce process, leads to an introductory page that discusses the feelings the reader may have and offers help in the process. Another click brings the reader to the page that explains how divorce law works.
http://advicenow.org.uk/advicenow-guides/family/divorce. The page addresses the mental picture people may have of divorce from the media, and also their anxieties about being involved with courts. Advicenow is a winner of the 2006 Plain English Web Award, for the clear language, design and organization of the site.

Juridisch loket (Legal kiosk) is the web site for the Netherlands' network of legal advice providers. There is a link for family matters on the home page. On the next page, there is a link to everything you need to know about divorce. http://www.hetjl.nl/hetjl

Minjus is the web site of the Ministry of Justice of the Netherlands. On the home page, there is a link for the theme of family. On the family page, there is a link for divorce and alimony. On the divorce page,

there is a link to "you are going to divorce." This leads to a pdf of a paper leaflet.
http://bestel.postbus51.nl/content/pdf/06BR2006G015-2006523-123436.pdf-2006523-123436.pdf

Rechtspraak.nl is the (also award-winning) web site of the Netherlands first and second instance courts in the Netherlands.[16] There is no pointer to general information about getting and filing a divorce on the home page. I have randomly selected two court web sites. The information provided there is presented under the heading: "for lawyers." The text on the first one turns out to be a general text addressed to an indefinite audience.
http://www.rechtspraak.nl/Gerechten/Rechtbanken/Utrecht/Over+de+rechtbank/Rechtsgebieden/Handels-+en+familierecht/Familierecht.htm.

The other court web site presents information specifically for lawyers.
http://www.rechtspraak.nl/Gerechten/Rechtbanken/Roermond/Voor+juristen/Rechtsgebieden/Civielrecht+familie/Echtscheiding.htm.

Jeugdsite (Youth Site) is the dedicated space on Rechtspraak.nl to inform young people about the law and the courts.
http://www.rechtvoorjou.nl/#/ik_moet_naar_de_rechter/ik_word_gehoord_want_mijn_ouders_gaan_scheiden

Readability

To test for readability, I used a common online web readability test (Table 21).[17] The test is an automated tool that works with conventional readability tests. It was designed to help web designers test their pages for readability. Copied text can be entered into a field, after which it is processed and the results are reported right away. The tests were designed for use with English. A similar test for Dutch is not readily available. English is a more compact language than Dutch. That probably puts the Dutch language sites at a slight disadvantage in this test, which was designed for English language text. In my experience, that does not affect the outcome of the test for the purpose of this discussion.

Table 21 *Divorce 1 - Readability of Web Site Information*

	Know what to do?	*Expected result?*
Advicenow	No	Yes
HMCS what do I do leaflet D184	Yes	No
Rechtspraak.nl jeugdsite	No	No
CAB	Yes	Yes
Juridisch loket	Yes	Yes
Minjus	Yes	No
Rechtspraak.nl Rechtbank – for the lawyers	No	No
Rechtspraak.nl Rechtbank – for the general public	No	n.a.

a Some observations on web readability

Only two web pages meet the web readability standards on all three tests: Advicenow and leaflet D184 of HMCS. The CAB scores come very close to the standard. The Juridisch loket and the jeugdsite also approximate the standards. All these pages were clearly written with a non-legal audience in mind.

The Minjus page, judging from its content, was written for the general public, but its scores do not come close to the web readability standards.

The first Dutch court web page was written with lawyers in mind. As such, its scores are adequate.

The second Dutch court web page contains only general information. Judging from its content, it is clearly not intended for lawyers. The score for reading ease is 19, with a web readability reading ease standard between 60 and 80. The grade level score is 15.1, against a standard of 6 or 7. These scores show it is far too difficult for a general audience.

Effectiveness

The second test is for effectiveness. Does the reader know what to do, and is the reader confident that the desired result will be achieved? I have not rated the sites for legal correctness. The aim of the test is to illustrate the implications of the web information service, not to judge the sites concerned.

Table 22 displays the results of testing two other major requirements: the reader should, after reading the page, know what to do next. The reader should also feel confident that the required action will produce the desired result.

First, a brief description of the contents of each page:

The page on Advicenow does not tell the reader what to do, but there is a menu on the page directing the reader to sections of the site that

Table 22 *Divorce 2 – What to Do?*

	Know what to do?	*Expected result?*
Advicenow	No	Yes
HMCS what do I do leaflet D184	Yes	No
Rechtspraak.nl jeugdsite	No	No
CAB	Yes	Yes
Juridisch loket	Yes	Yes
Minjus	Yes	No
Rechtspraak.nl Rechtbank – for the lawyers	No	No
Rechtspraak.nl Rechtbank – for the general public	No	n.a.

do tell the reader what to do. The page addresses preconceptions about courts, the law and divorce, and corrects them by explaining how things work in reality. In this sense, it has learned from the lessons in Paths to Justice about people facing justiciable problems: they only know courts from TV and the media, they associate courts with criminal law, they are going through a stressful process, and divorce is expensive.

The HMCS D184 pdf leaflet provides the reader with factual information about the process. For example, how forms are exchanged between the party and the court: The initiator files form D8 (divorce petition), he or she gets form D9H (notice of issue of petition) back from the court, and next form D10 (acknowledgement of service), and so on. It describes the technical, formal side of filing a divorce, up to the acknowledgement of service. For the next steps, the reader is referred to another leaflet.

The Rechtspraak.nl jeugdsite, a dedicated space explaining courts and the law to young people, explains divorce from the perspective of the child in a marriage. It explains what happens. There is a reference to legal aid for children on another page.

The CAB page explains that in order to get a divorce, the reader can apply to any county court. It also explains that the court will grant a decree nisi and a decree absolute that will formally end the marriage.

Juridisch Loket explains to the reader that he or she can make arrangements with his or her spouse. It recommends getting the help of a mediator. The reader can take the agreement to a lawyer who can file the request. It also explains that the divorce will be final only after, at the request of the lawyer, the court decision is entered in the civil register.

Minjus is a pdf of a paper leaflet. It says the reader can file the request, by way of his or her lawyer. The reader will have the decision sent to him or her by way of his or her lawyer.[18]

Table 23 *Total Web Site Score*

Site tested	*Readability*	*Clicks*	*Ranking readability*	*Ranking effectiveness*	*Ranking overall*
HMCS what do I do leaflet D184	23	4	27	4	31
Advicenow	22	2	24	4	28
CAB	16	4	20	8	28
Juridisch loket	15	4	19	8	27
Rechtspraak,.nl jeugdsite	15	3	18	0	18
Minjus	9	3	12	4	16
Rechtspraak.nl Rechtbank – for the general public	5	3	8	0	8
Rechtspraak.nl Rechtbank – for lawyers	4	3	7	0	7

Both the Rechtspraak.nl web pages do not tell the user what to do or what the expected result will be.

Table 23 presents the ranking of the sites on readability and effectiveness. Each site was ranked between 8 and 0 on each of the three readability counts, 8 being the highest possible score and making 24 the highest possible total for readability. The ranking on the number of clicks was 4 for the lowest, and 1 for the highest number of clicks. A site also scored 4 points for an affirmative answer on each of the two effectiveness scores. Maximum possible score was 36.

The HMCS leaflet D184 ranks best overall. The scores are quite consistent on all aspects tested. The Dutch Rechtspraak.nl sites were being overhauled at the time of writing.

Box 10 What Is a Decree Nisi?

What is a *decree nisi*?
I was particularly struck by the use of Latin terminology in communication with the general public on the HMCS web site. It explains the divorce procedure. The *decree nisi* comes up in two instances:
Leaflet D186 explains that a *decree nisi* is the first of two decrees you must have before you are finally divorced and free to re-marry.
Leaflet D187 (I have a *decree nisi* - what must I do next?) will tell you how to get your final decree (called a "decree absolute").
Nowhere does the site tell you what a *decree nisi* actually is. A legal scholar, but not educated in the United Kingdom, even I had to look it up:
The *Oxford Dictionary of Law* told me the following: decree nisi: A conditional decree of divorce, nullity, or presumption of death. For most purposes the parties to the marriage are still married until the decree is made absolute. During the period between decree nisi and

decree absolute the Queen's Proctor or any member of the public may intervene to prevent the decree being made absolute and the decree may be rescinded if obtained by fraud.

Help is also at hand in the Advicenow divorce jargon buster:
Decree nisi
For a married couple, this is the first stage of the divorce. You are not finally divorced by this.
Decree absolute
For a married couple, this is the final stage of divorce. At this point you stop, legally, being husband and wife.

a Some observations on effectiveness

The differences between the sites allow for some observations:

Information should be geared toward the general, most common picture. If most divorces are non-contested, paper-based procedures with no court hearing, this is what needs to be explained first. Lawyers' approaches tend to be geared toward exceptions. That is a different orientation that is inadequate for providing general information to the general public.

The pdf's examined here are electronic copies of paper leaflets. They are practical and cheap to produce, but their usefulness is limited because they are static. They do not make much use of the capabilities of web technology for providing targeted, custom information. They do not, for instance, contain live links to other sources of information or clickable menus. If another paper leaflet is referred to, it takes at least three clicks to open it. Repurposing informational materials for use on the Web can make communication much more effective by taking advantage of web functionality.

Advicenow starts by addressing the emotions surrounding divorce and the preconceptions people may have about the process. The preconceptions include negative images of the law and the courts. It begins by correcting those preconceptions, as they may stand in the way of effectively handling the problem at hand. This approach looks like it was inspired by the findings in Paths to Justice. It can be expected to help the reader become more receptive to the more factual, formal and legal information about divorce.

If representation by a lawyer is compulsory, courts do not need to communicate with the public directly. Therefore, they do not feel the need to take the recipient into consideration. This affects their communication, as can be seen from the content of the Dutch Rechtspraak page intended for the general public. The change required, referred to earlier, is that toward communicating directly with litigants who are not legally trained.

Without legal representation, the process as explained by the HMCS leaflets becomes predominantly bureaucratic. This process of standard, routine processing resembles that of the standardized processes of repeat players and government agencies.

The United Kingdom, like the Netherlands, has a petition, not a summons system. However, in the United Kingdom the court administrations themselves have to deal with sending the petition to the respondent. In the Dutch system, there is a compulsory system of legal representation in court. Comparing the U.K. and Dutch practices leads to some conclusions about paperwork. Where representation by a lawyer is compulsory, the lawyer also takes care of the court paperwork. Self-representing litigants need to take care of the paperwork themselves. In simple uncontested cases, that may be fairly straightforward. But as issues become more complicated, the explanations on the HMCS web site make it look quite daunting.

Courts are usually barred from giving legal advice. Legal advice in this context means making a judgment on facts presented, counseling on steps to be taken and taking a measure of responsibility for the result. This is radically different from presenting one's audience, be they litigants or members of the general public, with facts about the steps needed when taking a case to court, about what result can be expected, and including links to credible resources. These activities are not covered by the rule on legal advice.

If courts choose to provide information on facts about taking cases to court through a web site for the entire legal system, this information needs to be consistent for the whole of the legal system, usually the country, in question. This means the information from one single source needs to be correct for all courts. This has two implications: (1) the court practices need to be the same, and (2) the information service needs to be vested in a central agency. These far reaching implications will be examined further later.

The preconceptions people have about courts will also be addressed below, when we discuss their image of the courts and how that affects them.

In summary, this section examined web site use for the purpose of providing information to individual litigants. It tested two aspects: readability and adequacy of the information. The majority of the pages tested did not meet all the readability requirements. Information was judged adequate if it told the reader what to do, and conferred confidence with regard to the required result. The majority of the web sites also did not pass the effectiveness tests on all counts. The U.K. sites ranked higher on all counts. Differences in practice, like compulsory legal representation, affect what information is required. They also affect courts' attitudes to information services. As there appears to be a movement towards broadening the scope for self-representation, it is prudent to be prepared for a growing need for direct access to information. This will imply centralizing the information service as well as unifying some court practices. It will also involve providing information on more than one channel by referring to web site information in correspondence with parties. Information coordination with other information sources, such as bailiffs and legal aid organizations, will ensure better consistency of the information provided.

A larger scope for self-representation will also result in an increasing demand for digital access to courts. This is the topic of the next section.

Beyond information push: developing digital access to courts

This section examines the functionality that enables digital court access for self-representing litigants. There are many different forms of communication between courts and self-representing litigants. Experience with any of them is limited in most judiciaries. However, there is a growing body of experience with - increasingly interactive - communication with self-representing litigants in the United States. Some of this experience, from pilots in different parts of the United States and presented at CTC10, is listed below. The examples can be divided into two groups: online processing and human help. There will always be a need for human help for people for whom information is not enough. Therefore, there should always be some form of human help as back-up, in case someone does not manage the tasks required independently.

Recalling the EU benchmark for e-government projects (Chapter 2.1, EU Benchmarking p. 16), the next section looks at interaction:

Stage 2: Communication/interaction: downloading of forms

Stage 3: Communication/two-way interaction: Processing of forms (including authentication)

Stage 4: Transaction: Case handling, decision and delivery (payment).

Digital access and online processing

Online processing facilitates the filing of cases by self-representing litigants. There are different ways of doing so, and they are being piloted in some courts in the United States. They are discussed here in ascending order: from simple to more complex and sophisticated forms.

Forms and document assembly

The simplest functionality is that of online forms. Forms provide a streamlined channel of communication: the recipient of the information, in this case the court, specifies what they need to know; the sender of the information, the court user, can be sure that a completely filled out form will produce the required outcome. It can be a court order of some sort, or a decree formalizing a divorce or a decision granting a money claim. We have seen examples of the use of forms in the uncontested divorce procedure in the United Kingdom. Including forms on a web site can be the next step in developing digital access, after pushing information. The simplest form of digital access can be downloadable forms that have to be printed, filled out by hand, signed and returned by mail or fax (stage 2). They fit into the paper-based process most courts still have. More sophisticated types of forms can be filled out electronically (stage 3). They may have a help function, they can have embedded calculation functions and analytic tools, and some can even be filed electronically. Even more developed forms provide the function of interactive, for instance question-based, document assembly. These forms can fit into electronic file processing, but they can still be printed out and processed through a paper based process. For this type of digital access service, full electronic processing in court is not a necessity.

Experiments with more interactive access

Beyond forms and document assembly, there are experiments with a few more functionalities. They also require more developed electronic case processing systems in the courts. I list them here for completeness. There is not much documented experience with them yet.

Customer friendly e-filing

Beyond forms and document assembly, this modality allows for electronic filing. It replaces coming to court to fill out paper forms to file a case. It is expected to free up court staff for other tasks.

Case management systems:

Functionality in the systems can capture data on self-represented litigants, for instance from previous cases. It can connect cases, especially in family law to avoid conflicting orders. It allows courts to provide orders to litigants after the procedure.

Records access

This provides self-representing litigants, but also legal service organizations that give them advice and assistance, access to their court records.

For people who find problems difficult to deal with on their own, human support should be available.

Providing human help

From the research on justiciable problems, we have learned that there are always some people who need human help. In all the functionalities listed here, there is a human help backup function. Here are some examples of providing such human help using technology:

Videoconferencing

In the United States , videoconferencing is used to give self-representing litigants legal counseling over distance using existing court video networks, normally used for court hearings over distance. The existing court video networks are used to give people access to lawyers over distance, to allow them to consult those lawyers in order to be better prepared to present their case. This facility allows for multi-lingual service and specialized forms of legal counseling.

Chat functionality

Online chat functionality can assist users to find information and resources and assist users of automated forms. It ensures that users can find and understand the information. As a backup facility, it presents an opportunity to learn more about user needs as well.

Digital access: Some indicative conclusions

This part has explored of different forms of online access to courts that have been tried, but not yet widely implemented . The more advanced forms of online access are still experimental. However, for judiciaries wanting to expand their services for self-representing litigants, it is quite possible to provide simple forms of access without having a sophisticated system for receiving electronic information directly. Full e-filing capability in courts, like electronic filing, case management and electronic case files, is not an absolute condition for providing more digital access. An important lesson from the previous chapter was that human help should always be available in case a user cannot manage the instruction provided independently. The examples of experimental IT-supported human help given here are not necessarily limited to cases that come to court. They are also useful for information and advice services.

A special information need

This section discusses a special problem with regard to people's attitudes toward courts. This problem is discussed in this chapter because (1) it affects access to justice, and (2) it involves the communication of courts and judiciaries with the outside world, be it users or the general public.

Genn reports that people's expectations of courts are largely formed by what they see in the media. People associate courts with criminal justice. Without personal experience, their beliefs and stereotypes have been formed by televised representations, newspaper stories and sometimes stories from friends (Genn p. 225-232). The Dutch study on communicating with court users indicates that people did not prepare themselves well because they were paralyzed by guilt and shame (Mein p. 45). The Delta reports that the majority of people in general feel the courts and judges do their jobs well (Van Velthoven 2004 p. 174). However, those with experience in a court have a more negative opinion than those without any court experience (Van Velthoven 2004 p. 176). Interestingly, Dekker observed that people who rate their court experience positively also have a higher degree of trust in the judiciary (Dekker p. 95). Paths to Justice results indicate that respondents were generally positive about their experience in court (Genn 1999 p. 221-222). The Dutch study on court users also indicates that people are positive about their experience in court (Mein p. 45). Mostly, this is because their expectation of the court experience is more negative than the treatment they encounter from the judge in reality. Those who were well prepared for what happens in court rated the experience more positively than the small number of respondents who described their court experience as traumatic.

Paths to Justice and the Dispute Resolution Delta both signal how people's attitudes toward courts and the justice system are crucial for successful problem resolution. How people feel about courts affects their willingness to come to court, their experience when they get there, and their perception of the outcome of their case. This finding indicates one more information need in the context of access to justice. This need for a fact-based realistic understanding of their processes and roles also constitutes an important requirement for court and judiciary information services: judiciaries and court systems, if they want to improve access to justice, should ensure that their information service helps people to have a realistic understanding of their processes. They can also provide litigants with practical, correct and complete information on what they can expect when they come to court, and how they can prepare for their case. This will improve access to justice for people who need a court decision only occasionally in their lifetime. Because this information can enhance public trust in the judiciary, it cannot be left to others and is the responsibility of the judiciaries themselves.

Conclusions for Part 4

How courts and judiciaries can improve access to justice using forms of information technology was the main question of these chapters on access to justice. These conclusions summarize the main findings.

The first chapter identified barriers to access. It concluded that access to legal information is an important area to be explored further, for two reasons. The first reason is because of the role of information in access to justice. Access to information can support fairer administration of justice by providing information for people to act adequately when confronted with problems with a potentially legal solution. It can compensate, to some extent, for the disadvantage one-shotters experience in litigation, thereby increasing their chance of a fair decision. The second reason is because the Internet provides a channel for legal information service, but experience with it is limited in most judiciaries.

The second chapter examined the information needs that arise when people experience problems with a potentially legal solution. Information needs turn out to be problem-specific. Most problems are resolved by people themselves, sometimes with the help of information, or help in the form of advice or assistance. The help is provided by many different organizations, but mostly by specialized organizations or providers of legal aid and alternative dispute resolution.

The third chapter examined the implications of those findings for the role of courts in improving access to justice using information on the Internet and digital access to courts. Two strains on the role of information in access to justice run through this theme: information to keep disputes out of court, and information on taking disputes to court.

Information to keep disputes out of court

An almost implicit understanding is that parties with information on the "rules of thumb" of how courts deal with types of disputes will settle their differences more easily and keep them out of court. This supports settlement in the shadow of the law. Most of this type of settlement will be done with the support of legal or specialist organizations. In the pre-litigation stage, information about general approaches judges and courts have to specific types of problems can help the informal resolution of those problems. This will require that information about the way courts deal with those types of problems becomes available. Some of the ways in which courts deal with specific issues are laid down in policies. Moreover, judicial decision making is supported by decision support systems reflecting policies. In order to help out-of-court settlement, policies and decision support systems need to be available publicly.

This study generally supports the idea that access to justice can be effectively improved with information services. The information services identified here should serve the purpose of getting justice done. They should not keep people from getting the justice they deserve by preventing them from taking a justified concern to court.

Information on taking disputes to court

If a dispute needs to come to court, information can reduce the disadvantage one-shotters have in dealing with the court and with legal issues. Access to information for individual, self-representing litigants increases their chance of a just, fair decision. Litigants need information on how to take their case to court. Such an information service requires a proactive, demand-oriented attitude from courts and judiciaries. Multi-channel information services, such as a letter from the court with reference to information on the court's or judiciary's web site, can meet people's information needs. Beyond information push, increasingly interactive forms of information technology can provide access to court. Not all of them require full-scale implementation of electronic case management and electronic files. In order to be effective for everyone, the information services discussed will require human help backup. There are also technologies to provide this, but they may still not be sufficient for everyone. The information services discussed here, in order to be effective, will require a central agency for the entire legal system.

Public trust

A final finding is the importance of public trust in the courts for access to justice. Judiciaries can actively contribute to improved access to justice in this field by ensuring correct information about their processes. The requirement of public trust becomes a more urgent issue where court users complain about corruption in the judiciary and in the courts. This issue, and how information technology can support reducing corruption and improve impartiality and integrity in the courts, is the subject of the next part of this thesis.

Notes

1 article 14 ICCPR, article 6 ECHR.

2 With its comparison of estimated court costs (discussed in the chapter on case delay), the DB database provides a means of getting an indication of costs for one particular type of civil procedure.
3 Galanter remarks that the top-scoring repeat player is the alcoholic derelict. But that was in 1974. By 2008, due to changes in culture and law enforcement, others may have taken over this place.
4 This is commonly referred to as the Access to Justice Crisis.
5 I remember a case where a dispute between owners of parts of a building had its root in the official document that split the ownership of the building between them. The problem with the document could only be resolved by a public notary. We, the court, could decide that one of the owners should cease renovation activities, but were not allowed to deal with the problem in the document that was at the root of the problem.
6 The words "lumping" and "lumpers" are used by Genn to denote the category of people who remain inactive in the face of their justiciable problems.
7 In the United Kingdom, about 20 percent of the population is so poor at reading and writing that they cannot cope with the demands of modern life. (http://www.literacytrust.org.uk/database). In the Netherlands, the percentage of similarly low literacy is estimated at about 10 percent (http://www.lezenenschrijven.nl/nl/analfabetisme).
8 Advicenow.org.uk – ISB Self Help Project Final Report March 2005, on www.advicenow.org.uk.
9 http://www.internetworldstats.com/stats4.htm
10 Source: www.eurostat.eu
11 Polls Archive - Home - Advicenow
12 Even if the outcomes are not objectively uncertain, as was argued in the chapters on case delay, they may still be perceived as uncertain by the litigants.
13 This requirement was recently abolished for termination of labor contracts. At the time of writing, in 2008, it is too early to tell the effect this change in the law will have. See the chapter on case delay (Chapter 3), p. 10-16.
14 There are also labor cases in group 4 (or 3). In the majority of those cases, there is no agreement on termination, or the relationship was terminated but the final accounting has developed into a dispute.
15 It will enable special interest organizations to extend their services to litigation support.
16 A project is under way to overhaul the website.
17 http://www.addedbytes.com/readability. I have learned a lot from this site about ways to make writing more understandable: using shorter words and breaking up sentences, for instance.
18 In October 2008, the page tested turned out to have been taken off the site. It has been replaced by a page providing a link to a downloadable pdf brochure.

Part 5 Impartiality, Integrity and Corruption

The next three chapters examine how information technology can support reducing corruption and improving impartiality and integrity in courts and judiciaries.

Corruption in the judiciary and in the courts is a common complaint in many parts of the world. During my time at the World Bank, I was told time and again that the only way to ensure a favorable judicial decision is to bribe the judge. This impression is difficult to test, because corruption is extremely difficult to verify empirically. In 33 of the 62 countries polled for TI's Global Corruption Barometer, a majority of respondents describe their judiciary/legal system as corrupt. This group includes all countries in Africa and Latin America except South Africa and Colombia. In the United States, the percentage of respondents describing their judiciary/legal system as corrupt is about 55, and it is 33 percent in Canada. In Asia, the percentage for India is well over 70, and for Pakistan it is around 55. However, for Singapore, Malaysia, Hong Kong and Thailand the percentages are lower than 25. Eight of the ten countries with the lowest percentages are in Western Europe. In all former communist countries, 45 percent or more people described their judiciary/legal system as corrupt (TI 2007).

From Part 4, we have learned how important public trust in the courts is for peaceful dispute resolution and for the administration of justice. Part 5 examines the role of information, and consequently information technology, in engendering public trust, ensuring impartiality and integrity, and reducing corruption in courts and judiciaries.

Relevance

Corruption in the judiciary and the courts is relevant in more ways than one. First, corruption in society is commonly believed to impede economic growth and disproportionately affect the poor (Lambsdorff 1999 p. 5). The judiciary, part of the larger justice system, is an important instrument in combating corruption. If corrupt practices in society in general should be punished, they must be prosecuted, tried in court and sanctioned. The justice sector institutions serve to prosecute and judge such corrupt practices. In the shadow of effective prosecution and trial, people may refrain from corrupt practices for fear of being prosecuted themselves. Therefore, justice sector institutions are indispensable in combating corruption in society. There is some empirical evidence of a correlation between the quality of the judiciary and the incidence of corruption in society: The 1997 *World Development Report* found a significant correlation between corruption and the predictability of the judiciary in 59 countries, while controlling for other explanatory variables (World Bank 1997 p. 104). Lambsdorff questions the direction of the correlation (Lambsdorff 1999 p. 6). Therefore, whether judicial independence reduces corruption, or reducing corruption increases judicial impartiality, or whether they just go together is uncertain. Feld and Voigt conclude that de facto (actual, practical) judicial independence[1] positively influences gross domestic product (Feld p. 23). Therefore, it is probable that well working judiciaries, low levels of corruption and economic growth go together. We do not know enough to understand the causal relations between them. However, we do know, in summary, that a well working judiciary is an essential institution in reducing corruption.

The second reason why corruption in the judiciary is relevant is that corruption in the judiciary will undermine the legal system and the confidence people have in it. As a peaceful means of conflict resolution, judicial dispute resolution relies largely on voluntary compliance. Where public trust in the judiciary is harmed by corruption, confidence in the legal system and voluntary compliance with it are at risk.

The third reason is in the international conventions, discussed in Part 1: everyone has a right to independent, impartial judges and courts.[2] In the context of this study, independence is regarded as an institutional condition to safeguard impartiality. Independence is understood as a part of the framework of conditions that make impartiality possible. For this reason, impartiality, not independence, is discussed here as the primary norm for the judiciary in the context of the discussion on corruption. If courts and judiciaries perform the task set out in the conventions effectively, there is less incentive for corruption to collect debts, protect property rights and for other private enforcement.

The role of information technology

Introducing and using information technology is often believed to reduce corruption in courts and judiciaries because it is expected to introduce more impersonal ways of working. In most countries where I advised World Bank judicial reform projects, people told me they believed corruption would go down after the introduction of computers. However, it was difficult for them to explain why. Possibly, they were saying it just because they expected that would induce the World Bank to give them funding for computers. Another possibility is that they expect the introduction of computers to make their problems go away without much effort on their part. I do believe they are right in that introducing computers and IT can help reduce corruption in the courts. Making that happen, however, will require more than just money or introducing IT. It will require targeted effort, based on understanding what the problems are, how they can be resolved effectively and what information technology can realistically contribute. These chapters set out to provide some answers to those questions.

Plan for these chapters

These chapters examine corruption, in general and more particularly in judiciaries and courts, in order to find out how IT can realistically be expected to contribute to reducing corruption in the judiciary and the courts. The first two chapters are dedicated to a better understanding of the problems of corruption. Chapter 5.1 is concerned with theory. Chapter 5.2 presents empirical material. Chapter 5.3 discusses remedies and their effectiveness, and then goes on to examine the role of information and its consequences for information technology support for reducing corruption.

For those purposes, the following areas will be covered:

Theoretical framework
Chapter 5.1 will set up a theoretical framework that can serve to examine corruption based on empirical evidence, and explore possible remedies. It discusses the normative, legal framework, some definitions of corruption from different perspectives, some of the leading theories about causes of corruption and a comparative, cross-country approach.

Empirical evidence of corruption in courts and judiciaries
Chapter 5.2 examines empirical evidence of corruption in courts and judiciaries. Using the theoretical framework form Chapter 5.1, it will conduct case studies of empirical evidence on the incidence of corruption in the judiciary and the courts in Slovakia, Bulgaria, Georgia, Nigeria and the United States.

Possible remedies: Corruption in courts and judiciaries as an information problem
Chapter 5.3 analyzes the information-related aspects of the findings. The resulting insights are used to draw conclusions on ways in which forms of IT can be used to combat corruption in courts and judiciaries.

Chapter 5.1 Corruption - Theory

This chapter introduces theoretical approaches that will help us to understand corruption in courts and judiciaries. It discusses the normative framework for courts and judiciaries with regard to corruption, how corruption is usually categorized, some ways in which it is defined, and the most current theory about its causes.

Normative framework

This section highlights the specific normative international framework for the topic of impartiality and corruption in courts and the judiciary. The Universal Declaration of Human Rights of 1948[3] states that everyone is entitled in full equality to a fair and public hearing by an independent and impartial tribunal, in the determination of his rights and obligations and of any criminal charge against him. Article 14 of the International Covenant on Civil and Political Rights,[4] by stating that everyone is entitled to a fair and public hearing by a competent, independent and impartial tribunal established by law, affirms this statement, as do the regional human rights conventions. All these conventions award everyone the right to impartial judges and courts. Since the vast majority of countries are party to one or more of the conventions mentioned above, the normative framework as described binds those countries and the judiciaries and courts in them, directly or indirectly.

The United Nations Convention against Corruption (UNCAC)[5] aims to promote and strengthen measures to prevent and combat corruption and promote international cooperation and technical assistance in the prevention of and fight against corruption, and promote integrity, accountability and proper management of public affairs and public property. The Organisation for Economic Cooperation and Development has also produced an anti-bribery convention aiming to prevent international bribery and corruption.

UNODC – Bangalore Principles of Judicial Conduct

Conventions need implementation in order to be effective. The United Nations Office of Drugs and Crime (UNODC) supports implementation of the international anti-corruption agreements with its Global Programme against Corruption. The Programme builds capacity by providing a knowledge base and conducting training and education. Because a corrupt judiciary is a serious impediment to the success of any anti-corruption strategy, the Programme also examines judicial corruption, and is seeking to identify means of addressing it. To this end, it supports a Judicial Group on Strengthening Judicial Integrity (JIG).

The JIG, active since 2000, consists of chief justices from Africa and Asia. Among the outputs of this group are the Bangalore Principles of Judicial Conduct.[6] The Bangalore Principles are based on principles found in the majority of judicial codes of conduct around the world. They intend to provide a code against which the conduct of judicial officers may be measured. They list six principles of judicial conduct: independence, impartiality, integrity, propriety, equality, and competence and diligence, followed by guidance on the application of each principle. In the context of this chapter, only the first two principles will be discussed because they are the two principles that are central to focusing on what constitutes judicial corruption .

The first principle in the Bangalore Principles is independence. From the text of Principle 1 and its application, it is clear that it attempts to combine different understandings of independence. Independence of courts and judges has been the subject of much, sometimes ideologically flavored, debate. For example: lawyers from country X argue that there would be less corruption in the courts of country Y if only those courts were more independent. Evidently, independence is understood differently in different contexts (Carothers p. 90). Arrangements guarding judicial independence are the outcome of complex political processes in a given context, and therefore they, and their understanding, are specific to that particular context. In itself, this does not constitute a problem in the context of this study. If we look at what court users object to as corruption in courts, it is unfair court processes and decisions. In this study, independence is regarded as a condition, an arrangement enabling impartial, fair decisions by judges and courts.

Impartiality is JIG's Principle 2. Impartiality means performing judicial duties without favor, bias or prejudice, with regard to the decision itself but also to the process by which the decision is made. In the famous adage, justice must not only be done, it must also be seen to be done.[7] Impartiality requires the existence of actual impartiality as well as the appearance of impartiality as seen through the eyes of the reasonable observer. That is why perception is important. In the section on empirical evidence, we will see how the impartiality of court decisions is perceived, how important appearance is, and what is important about independence as a condition for impartiality.

Council of Europe – GRECO

Another modality in anti-corruption implementation is the Group of States against Corruption (GRECO), established in 1999 by the Council of Europe to monitor states' compliance with the organization's anti-corruption standards. GRECO monitoring comprises a horizontal evaluation procedure evaluating all members, and leading to recommendations for reform, and a compliance procedure to assess the measures taken to implement the recommendations. To date, GRECO has conducted three evaluation rounds. GRECO has 46 members, 45 European states and the United States. Most GRECO reports are public.[8]

Definitions and categorizations of corruption

This section examines some commonly used definitions and categorizations.

Corruption is a term that is used in many different ways. A commonly accepted way of tackling this conceptual variety is to introduce a definition. Definitions do not capture the full reality of a complex phenomenon like corruption. The approach taken in this section does it only limited justice. This treatment of the definitions attempts to limit the scope and provide some focus to the discussion. The comparative perspective introduced later on will paint a more nuanced picture.

Abuse of public roles for private benefit is the most commonly used definition of corruption. A more precise and elaborate definition is: Behavior that deviates from the formal rules of conduct governing the actions of someone in a position of public authority because of private-regarding motives such as wealth, power or status (Mustaq Khan 1996 p. 12, quoted in Andvig, p.12).

Most definitions of corruption focus on its economic aspects, but corruption can also consist of a social or cultural exchange. Likewise, most definitions of corruption will focus on the state-society relationship because public sector corruption is believed to be a more fundamental problem than private sector corruption, and because controlling public sector corruption is considered a prerequisite for controlling private sector corruption.

A frequently used categorization of corruption is the following (Andvig p. 18, Anderson 2006 p. 7):

- *Administrative or bureaucratic corruption,* "petty," low level forms of bribery in connection with the *implementation* of laws, rules, and regulations.
- *Political corruption, or state capture,* high level corruption in the lawmaking process, firms shaping and affecting *formulation of laws and regulations* through private payments or other means of influence to public officials and politicians.

When applied to judiciaries and courts, this grouping distinguishes corruption in:

(1) Bureaucratic corruption: influencing routine implementation of laws and regulations: case handling and everyday, common judicial decisions in first instance courts.

(2) Political, high level corruption: influencing judicial decisions that are relevant on a higher level, for instance regarding election results, judicial control of the executive by the high instance court, high profile criminal cases, or decisions shaping jurisprudence, and influencing judicial appointments.

Forms of corruption include bribery, extortion, cronyism, nepotism, patronage, graft, and embezzlement; they are described in the *Oxford English Dictionary* as follows:

- Bribery means to dishonestly persuade [someone] to act in one's favor by paying them or giving other inducement.
- Graft includes bribery and other corrupt measures pursued for gain in politics or business.
- Extortion is to obtain something by force, threats, or other unfair means.
- Nepotism is favoritism shown to relatives or friends, especially by giving them jobs.
- Cronyism is the improper appointment of friends and associates to positions of authority.
- Patronage means support given by a patron, as well as the power to control appointments to office or the right to privileges.

Patronage apart, the descriptions all include an explicit morally negative qualification of the activity in question: dishonestly, corrupt, unfair, improper, implying that the activity in question crosses the dividing line between proper and improper behavior. Paying someone to act in one's favor as such is not bribery. What makes it bribery is that it is done against the rules and standards. The standards are stricter for public officials than they are in the private sector. Paying a member of parliament to act on one's behalf is improper, but paying a lobbyist to try and influence that same parliamentarian on one's behalf is not.[9] Helping one's relatives in itself is alright; it becomes favoritism when it crosses the line between proper and improper help, for instance when a job is given bypassing the usual procedures for hiring staff, where a family member is given priority in case handling. What also makes it improper is the purpose of private gain. Impropriety therefore has two components: violation of a standard, and private gain.

Nepotism, cronyism and patronage influence *who* takes a decision, rather than what its content is. With regard to judiciaries and courts, the question of who takes a certain decision involves several levels of the organization. It has to do with assigning individual cases and groups of cases, as well as with judicial appointments. In both cases, that can involve both administrative and political corruption. It can also involve bodies and persons inside or outside the judiciary. And ultimately, the content of the decisions is the purpose of the influence.

That leads to the conclusion that, for the purpose of discussing corruption in courts and judiciaries, using a somewhat elaborate definition emphasizing the improper elements will sharpen our focus. Here is the definition that suits that purpose: *Corruption in courts and judiciaries thus means an improper use of judicial power for private gain, resulting in decisions that are not impartial.*

A legally-oriented understanding of the term corruption generally relates it to the violation of a rule of a national law. This implies that judgments over the legality of various practices will also vary with different national legislation (Andvig p. 66). This is also valid in a wider sense. What is considered proper or improper depends on the context. Consequently, a solely legal understanding of corruption is insufficient for the purpose of finding ways to combat it, in judiciaries or elsewhere. However, where the international conventions say judges and courts have to be fair and impartial, that should provide something of a normative framework for the discussion as to what is proper and improper for courts and judiciaries.

Some theories about causes of corruption

This section examines some of the leading academic approaches to causes of corruption in order to gain insight into ways of limiting corruption in courts and judiciaries. The leading academic approaches to corruption and its causes are mostly American. I chose them for inclusion here because they are helpful for my analysis, which targets organizational aspects of the issues courts and judiciaries face.

The first approach focuses on power and checks on that power. It identifies three factors:

- The exclusive power of the decision-maker
- His or her discretion
- The lack of accountability for abuses of this power and discretion.

Framed in a formula, the relationships between the factors look like this:

*Corruption = monopoly + discretion – accountability (*Klitgaard 1988 p. 75). Applied to judges and courts, Klitgaard's formula means that judges would be far more likely to be corruptible and corrupted if they have:

(1) A monopoly over legal dispute resolution, for example where there are no viable alternatives such as arbitration or mediation
(2) Broad discretion, for example, where they are independent from review
(3) Limited accountability, for example, in non-oral processes, non-public venues, non-continuous trials, non-participatory dispute resolution, or unpublished decisions.

Judges and courts ultimately do have a monopoly over sanctioning state force in dispute resolution. Referring to the second factor, judges seldom have very broad discretion; their discretion is generally limited by the provisions of the law.[10] Judicial decisions are often subject to appeal or review. Finally, where processes are dealt with in public and decisions are published, abuse of judicial power can be expected to be limited. When applied to the judiciary, each factor entails risks. It also suggests arrangements to mitigate those risks. Higher levels of monopoly can be offset with reduced discretion, or more accountability, or both.

The focus on power explains the conditions under which that power may be abused. It does not explain why people actually do abuse their power, in general or in the judicial processes.

The second approach focuses on motivations and incentives for people to actually abuse power. Corrupt behavior, in this analysis, is mainly determined by:

- The level of available benefits
- The riskiness of corrupt deals
- The relative bargaining power of the briber and the bribee (Rose-Ackerman 1999 p. 225).

These basic factors can be applied to judges and courts. Low salaries, poor working conditions and scarce resources can all be obvious incentives for judges and court staff to take bribes for the benefits they entail. They may abuse their power especially where the risk of detection is low, or where detection does not lead to sanctions. Here, independence can be a risk factor in itself: where the only mechanism for discipline is internal because judges themselves judge accusations of abuse of judicial power, the risk of prosecution and sanction can be relatively low. Another factor affecting the level of risk is the effectiveness of the organization. If information on the workings of the organization is not available or opaque, that will facilitate corrupt behavior because it lowers the risk of detection.

The relative bargaining power of the judge or court staff member and competing litigants is mainly determined by the degree of financial need, resources, and competition. These factors all affect the level of corrupt practices. The relative bargaining power of the judge or court staff member will be affected by the existence of a monopoly, the degree of discretion and the level of accountability.

This approach examines motivations; it does not focus primarily on the conditions that give rise to these incentives. Both approaches look at the behavior of individuals; they do not primarily study differences in the level of economic or political development of a national system that may explain variations in corruption.

If corruption should be limited by increasing the riskiness of corrupt deals and raising accountability, the most obvious remedy that may come to mind is that of strong repressive measures. These can take the form of anti-corruption campaigns and prosecution. Many of those campaigns have not led to a sustainable reduction of corruption.

So far, we have implicitly assumed corruption is the same phenomenon all over the world. The next section examines a comparative approach that may provide some explanation for the failure of those campaigns.

A comparative approach: Syndromes of corruption

The first thing that is striking in the comparative perspective is that there is apparently less corruption in richer, more developed countries. The World Bank's World Governance Indicators have shown a clear correlation between the level of economic development and corruption: corruption tends to be lower in richer countries. Likewise, judges with higher salaries are less corrupt. Almost half, 46 percent, of the variation in judicial corruption is "explained" by the variables per capita income and openness of the economy, although the openness of the economy is not significant (Voigt in TI GCR 2007 p. 298). Higher judicial salaries and lower levels of corruption are strongly correlated. However, raising judges' salaries as an isolated measure does not significantly affect the level of corruption The significant factor here is not the level of the individual judge's salary; it is the overall level of development.

The third approach in this section on theory relates levels of development and levels of perceived corruption. It compares patterns of corruption across countries and identifies cross-country patterns of corruption (Johnston 2005). The level of development and the level of perceived corruption were the main factors used to group countries into syndromes of corruption. Ninety-eight countries were sorted into four corresponding groupings by applying widely used indicators of participation and institutions (Appendix B). The main indicators used are the World Bank's World Governance Indicators, the United Nations Development Programme's Human Development Index and Transparency International's Corruption Perception Index, valid for 2001. They are all publicly available.[11]

The syndromes are about systemic corruption, not individual cases of corrupt behavior. The approach identified four syndromes of corruption, reflecting frequently encountered combinations of stronger or weaker political participation and stronger or weaker institutions:

The *Influence Markets* syndrome has fully developed, functioning democratic institutions, but it is weak on the participation side. Voter turnout is low, and party financing is a critical issue. Corruption has been checked by legalizing the political role of wealth, yet policies favor moneyed interests. Those policies may well be seen as the result of unfair or corrupt influence International firms participate in corrupt practices in developing countries, where strong public institutions make influence well worth buying or renting, and strong economic institutions (such as banks, currencies) make these societies safe havens for corrupt takings amassed elsewhere.

In the *Elite Cartels* syndrome, top figures collude behind a façade of political competition and colonize both the state apparatus and sections of the economy. Elections are fraudulent, indecisive, or uncompetitive. Institutions are moderately weak. Political and economic opportunities are often expanding at least somewhat, however, making the elite cartel a way of staving off potential competitors in both spheres.

In the *Oligarchs and Clans* syndrome state, political and social institutions are very weak and ineffective, and participation is risky. Politically and economically ambitious elites are insecure. They build bases of personal support from which they exploit both the state and the economy. Corruption of this type is unpredictable and a powerful source of injustice. Courts, the police and the bureaucracy are hijacked as well.

In the *Official Moguls* syndrome, there is official impunity. Institutions are very weak, popular participation in government is feeble and orchestrated from above, and corrupt leaders and their personal favorites exploit society and the economy, including aid and investment, rather than developing it.

This approach provides a nuanced understanding of the various forms of corruption and the interaction of public sector institutions with the surrounding societies. The syndromes approach includes all countries, not just developing countries. It suggests starting points for reform in societies at all different stages of development. Consequently, it is relevant for identifying remedies for corruption. Tailoring reform to the particular syndrome will increase its chance of success. For instance, reform requiring strong political resolve will be difficult to carry out where institutions are very weak. The potential consequences of this approach for reform will be examined more closely in Chapter 5.3, on remedies. First, in Chapter 5.2, country cases of corruption in the judiciary will be introduced to provide some understanding of the phenomena.

Conclusions for this chapter

This chapter set the theoretical framework for studying corruption in courts and judiciaries. Corruption in the context of judiciaries and courts means behavior by judges or court staff that is improper because - for private gain - it deviates from the rules of conduct derived from the provisions in the international conventions concerning judicial impartiality. It can be facilitated by arrangements that go with independence, for example internal disciplinary mechanisms that lower the risk of detection or sanction. Weak institutional development also facilitates corruption in courts and judiciaries. Low pay and lack of resources can raise the benefits of corruption. Corruption is likely where judges have the following:

- A monopoly on decision, therefore no competition
- Wide discretion, for instance when there is no or limited possibility of review or appeal
- Low accountability, because there is no public scrutiny or the risk of detection or sanction of corrupt behavior is low.

A low detection risk points to institutional weakness. The level and form of institutional weakness are important determinants for corruption. The actual level and form the corruption takes in a given situation are related to the level of development and they depend on the applicable corruption syndrome. Both the level and form of institutional weakness determine where the starting points for reform are. This framework provides some focus for an examination of the incidence of corruption, in general and in judiciaries and courts, in the next section. It will help us to gain some understanding of the starting points for reform to reduce corruption in courts and judiciaries in countries in different syndromes. This will provide a foundation for identifying how, in each case, forms of information technology can support reducing court corruption.

Chapter 5.2 Court Corruption - Empirical Evidence

This chapter examines the incidence of corruption in judiciaries and courts, and the forms it takes in real life in different contexts. The chapter starts by discussing methodological issues with empirical evidence of corruption. Next, it analyzes those issues with regard to evidence of corruption in courts and judiciaries.

The chapter then examines well-documented examples of both administrative and high level corruption in countries from all the different corruption syndromes. Empirical evidence of corruption will come from different sources. Some of the evidence comes from surveys;

most of it is derived from case studies. The case studies serve as illustrations. This empirical information, about the incidence of corruption and the actual forms it takes, is given a fairly lengthy treatment. The reason for this is that the information is of particular importance for those members of the audience with a Western, developed country background. It has been my experience that understanding what that corruption actually looks like is problematic because their experience with systemic public sector corruption is limited.

Finally, the chapter offers some conclusions on causes of judicial and court corruption, and some tentative indications of remedies.

Methodological issues

This section discusses some methodological issues related to empirical research into judicial and court corruption. It discusses the strengths and weaknesses of survey methodologies and of various indicators that affect the research.

Empirical evidence of corruption in general, and of corruption in courts and judiciaries in particular, is scarce. This is especially true for case studies. As a consequence, a relatively large part of the empirical evidence comes from surveys. However, what we can learn from surveys has its limits.

We need to distinguish surveys reporting on *experience* with corruption, and surveys on corruption *perception*. Both types entail their own risks. Actual *experience* may not always be truthfully reported. Respondents may be reluctant to admit having paid a bribe. Justice officials may be reluctant to report corruption in their own profession or peer group due to a sense of loyalty to the group. The *perception* of corrupt practices in the justice system may be caused by actual corrupt practices but also by delays or incompetence from other causes. It can also be caused by a general feeling that all public servants are corrupt. Perception of judicial and court corruption in the general public tends to be higher than perception of corruption by court users, those who have actual court experience (TI GCR 2007 p. 14). Perception of corruption may also go up when governments actually begin to tackle corruption, and the subject gets more attention in the press. A case in point is the Czech Republic; its score in the Transparency International Corruption Perception Index went down from 3.9 to 3.7 between 2001 and 2002, as the Czech Republic prepared to join the European Union (TI CPI 2001 and 2002).

Hence, both experience and perception surveys need to be treated with care, particularly in the context of diagnosing problems. However, they can serve to provide a sense of the incidence of corruption, thus helping to identify directions for further enquiry and examination. For diagnostic purposes, they need to be supplemented with information from more qualitative studies, and case studies in particular.

A worldwide view of corruption in courts

As a first step in examining the empirical evidence of corruption in courts and judiciaries, Transparency International's Global Corruption Barometer provides a worldwide impression. It surveys the form and extent of corruption from the view of people around the world. The most recent Barometer is from 2006. There is interesting information about corruption in courts: worldwide, 29 percent of all respondents believe the courts are corrupt. Twenty-four percent agree with the proposition that, in order to be sure that a court passes a fair judgment, you need to bribe someone. Of that 24 percent, 51 percent believe you have to bribe a judge. Of those respondents who had used the legal system and the courts in the previous 12 months, 11.5 percent report they or a member of their family have paid a bribe (TI GCR 2007 p.11). Thus, while 24 percent believe bribes are a necessity, only 11.5 percent of court users report they actually paid a bribe.

Syndromes of corruption

This section also takes a world view of corruption, but with more detail. Table 24 illustrates the comparative approach of corruption syndromes from the theoretical framework. Here, the methodology is applied to compare a number of countries based on their level of development and corruption, grouping them into syndromes. Their rankings in the major indexes discussed in Chapter 1.3 are included as well.

Table 24 shows the rankings and scores from the various sources. For each country, its corruption syndrome grouping is in column 1. The country name is in the second column. Column 3 gives the 2008 Transparency International Corruption perception index score out of a possible maximum of 10; column 4, the Human Development Index, out of a possible maximum score of 1.0 (2005 is the most recent index available); column 5: the 2008 ranking in the TI CPI with 1 being the score for the lowest corruption perception; column 6, the Doing Business Database time in calendar days for contract enforcement from the first step up until and including enforcement; column 7, the time in calendar days for only trial and judgment; and column 8, the Worldwide Governance Indicators percentile ranking scores for Rule of Law.

The countries were selected because they figure in this study, and/or because their ranking is illustrative of the syndromes approach. The table gives a general sense of worldwide trends in levels of development,

Table 24 *Corruption and Rule of Law in Selected Countries*

1 group by syndrome	*2 country*	*3 TI CPI 2008*	*4 HDI 2005*	*5 TI CPI 08 rank*	*6 DB time in days 2007*	*7 DB trial and judgment*	*8 WGI RoL 06*
1	New Zealand	9.3	0.943	2	216	152	97.6
1	Singapore	9.2	0.922	4	120	88	95.2
1	Netherlands	8.9	0.953	7	514	442	93.8
1	United Kingdom	7.7	0.946	16	404	313	93.3
1	Costa Rica	5.1	0.846	47	877	547	64.8
2	Belgium	7.3	0.946	18	505	400	91
2	South Korea	5.6	0.921	40	230	90	72.9
2	Slovakia	5.0	0.863	52	565	365	61.4
2	Paraguay	2.4	0.755	138	591	466	18.1
3	Sri Lanka	3.2	0.743	92	1318	1000	54.3
3	Romania	3.8	0.813	70	537	365	50.5
3	Bulgaria	3.6	0.824	72	564	334	50
3	Nepal	2.7	0.534	121	735	365	29
3	Nicaragua	2.5	0.710	134	540	331	25.7
4	Macedonia	3.6	0.801	72	385	280	43.8
4	Georgia	3.9	0.754	67	285	100	32.9
4	Egypt	2.8	0.708	115	1010	720	53.8
4	Morocco	3.5	0.646	80	615	365	53.3
4	Benin	3.1	0.437	96	720	375	36.7
4	Kenya	2.1	0.521	147	465	365	15.7
4	Nigeria	2.7	0.470	121	457	273	8.1
4	Gambia	1.9	0.502	158	434	302	47.6

Sources: TI CPI, HDI, DB, World Bank 2008a, WGI.

governance effectiveness, levels of corruption and the quality of judicial systems. On the whole, a high level human development ranking (column 4) goes together with a low level of corruption (TP CPI, columns 3 and 5). Johnston's syndrome ranking was based on figures for 2001. With the 2008 figures, some of the results would probably have come out differently.

Generally, a high score on rule of law also comes with a high level of development, but these results are less directly correlated. That also holds for the two DB scores on the number of days needed to process a contract enforcement claim. Clearly, for a realistic assessment, a more in-depth, qualitative study is necessary. Such an approach is presented in the next section.

The Judicial Integrity Group's indicators

The Judicial Integrity Group, supported by UNODC, has drawn up a list of indicators derived from empirical studies on judicial and court corruption (UNODC 2001). The JIG commissioned a number of assessments of the status quo of the justice sector in Indonesia, Nigeria,

South Africa, and Sri Lanka. The assessment methodologies include desk reviews, surveys and focus groups. All stakeholders were interviewed about - among other things - their experiences and perceptions of corruption in the judiciary and the courts.

In its 2001 publication on Strengthening Judicial Integrity Against Corruption, the JIG has listed 16 indicators for corruption. These indicators are not indicators in the sense described above. They are facts or circumstances that may indicate the presence of corruption in a judicial system. This is their list (UNODC 2001 p. 6):

Indicators of corruption, *as perceived by the public*, include:

- Delay in the execution of court orders
- Unjustifiable issuance of summons and granting of bails
- Prisoners not being brought to court
- Lack of public access to records of court proceedings
- Disappearance of files
- Unusual variations in sentencing
- Delays in delivery of judgments
- High acquittal rates
- Conflict of interest
- Prejudices for or against a party, witness or lawyer (individually or as member of a particular group)
- Prolonged service in a particular judicial station
- High rates of decisions in favor of the executive
- Appointments perceived as resulting from political patronage
- Preferential or hostile treatment by the executive or legislature
- Frequent socializing with particular members of the legal profession, executive or legislature (with litigants or potential litigants)
- Post-retirement placements.

The JIG indicators do not differentiate between symptoms, such as inconsistent decisions and prejudices, and facilitating circumstances, like lack of access to records of court proceedings and prolonged service in a particular judicial station. They use criteria such as "unusual" variations in sentencing and "high" acquittal rates. To be useful, those criteria should be elaborated in the specific context, less relative and also less subjective. Even a concept such as delay needs some standard to establish whether a decision is overdue, in the sense that it should have been delivered but has not been.

In order to be useful for the analysis of both incidence of corruption and potential remedies in a judiciary, court or court system, these indicators need to be divided into meaningful groups. I have categorized them as follows.

a Deficiencies in the execution of court work

- Delays in the execution of court orders

- Delays in delivery of judgments
- Disappearance of files

Delays are, as explained in Chapter 3.1, understood to be "things that should have been done within a certain time frame, but have not been": overdue judgment, execution that has been put off. In that sense, there is a normative component to delays. Therefore, in order to decide whether there is a delay, it is necessary to have a standard against which to gauge it.[12] Besides, delays are different from backlogs. A backlog is "something that has not been done yet." With regard to the disappearance of files, the JIG report gives the example of files that were made to disappear only to reappear after a payment. These indicators will mostly point to administrative corruption in courts.

b Inequalities in the administration of justice

- Unjustifiable issuance of summons and granting of bail
- Unusual variations in sentencing
- High acquittal rates
- High rates of decisions in favor of the executive
- Prejudices for or against a party, witness or lawyer - individually or as a member of a particular group.

These indicators are all about outcomes of the judicial process. There may also be some indicators that have to do with entry points, such as leave for appeal. Inequalities, just like inefficiencies, need to be measured against a standard. Case file analysis is the most frequently used methodology to establish whether these inequalities have in fact occurred. In this methodology, concrete case files are sampled or randomly drawn. They are examined by legal experts who are sufficiently familiar with jurisprudence in the given legal system. Inequalities may point to either administrative or political corruption, or both. The inequalities may have been caused by factors other than corruption, like ignorance of the standards due to lack of education and training.

c Status and career of judges

- Conflict of interest
- Appointments perceived as resulting from political patronage
- Preferential or hostile treatment by the executive or legislature
- Frequent socializing with particular members of the legal profession, executive or legislature (with litigants or potential litigants)
- Prolonged service in a particular judicial station
- Postretirement placements.

The presence of any of the first three factors in this list may point to deficiencies in judicial career management. The deficiencies can be either the cause or a symptom of political corruption. Where political patronage is systemic, for instance in group 3 or 4 syndrome countries, it is likely that patronage prevails over the norm of impartiality. In order to underpin impartial judicial decisions, judicial career management should be governed by the need for independence. Frequent socializing and prolonged service may be risk factors for either administrative or political corruption. Especially in this group, it becomes clear that differentiation according to the country is needed in order to draw valid and useful conclusions. Prolonged service in a particular judicial station, for example, would not in itself be regarded as an indicator of, or a facilitating circumstance for, judicial corruption in most influence market (syndrome 1) countries. Moreover, other factors need to be taken into account to explain why there is corruption in some systems, and less corruption in others. Indicators in this category will need to be addressed in countries where corruption is perceived as a problem.

d Other things to look for

The last group comprises some other circumstances that may indicate corrupt practices, notably prisoners not being brought to court and lack of public access to records of court proceedings.

Prisoners not being brought to court may, but does not necessarily, point to corruption in the judiciary or the courts. It can also be due to other factors, such as either political or administrative corruption in the prosecution or the police. It may show up in statistics about the length of pre-trial detention, but it will most probably have to be examined in the local context. Lack of public access to records of court proceedings indicates low accountability, a factor we already encountered in the theoretical framework.

Each of the JIG indicators may be a manifestation of the possibility of corruption in a judiciary or a court. That makes them useful for diagnostic purposes, but they are not, in themselves, a solid basis for a plan for introducing remedies. They do not tell us why the corruption is there; they can be proxies for causes of corruption, but they are not in themselves causes as discussed in the theoretical framework. In order to diagnose judicial and court corruption, we need to know, for each country context:

- Whether judicial and court corruption is perceived as a problem
- Its manifestations
- The causes and incentives .

This diagnosis is the basis for analyzing the possible viable remedies . For identifying opportunities for using IT as a remedy, we also need to establish what the information aspects related to the corruption are – both in general terms and in each specific case. The next section examines some examples, using the approach described here.

Administrative corruption – bribe paying surveys

This section examines examples of bribe paying in the context of administrative corruption. Our main source for the first part of this discussion is a World Bank experience survey of bribe paying by businesses in the Eastern European and Central Asian region. The reason for choosing this source is that the survey in question provides such a well-detailed picture of corruption experience. Part of the survey asks businesses whether they have paid bribes to courts. The 2006 survey notes that, on the whole, firms report that both bribe paying and state capture have gone down in most countries in Eastern Europe. However, in contrast to taxes and customs services, judicial systems have not reduced corruption. Businesses report having paid more bribes to courts (Anderson 2006 p. 54).

The case of Slovakia
Slovakia's TI CPI score for 2008 is 5.0; for 2001, it was 3.7. It joined the European Union in 2004. It is an elite cartels (syndrome 2) country. For courts and judiciaries, this could mean that judges are partners in elite networks, using their powers to aid cartel partners and sharing the corrupt proceeds.

The World Bank conducted a special study of corruption in Slovakia, published in 2002 (Anderson 2002). It provides an example of how, in many ways, identifying the problem of corruption is easier than identifying both its causes and incentives and its remedies. In Slovakia, corruption in the educational system is centered mostly around universities. There is also a widespread perception that one cannot gain admittance to law or medical schools without paying bribes. Both the justice system and the health sector are reported to have widespread corruption. Possibly, students who have bought their way into university education carry those practices with them when they enter the legal and medical professions.

The study also reports how the courts were identified by the three sample groups - households, enterprises and public officials - as slow and largely corrupt:

- "Slowness of courts" was selected by 80 percent of enterprises as one of the three most serious obstacles of all the obstacles that enterprises face in their business development.
- Seventy-five percent of enterprises indicated "low executability of justice"[13] to be a major problem. Among enterprises that had been involved in a recent court case, nearly 19 percent indicated that they had encountered bribery.

- The average bribe was more than 25,000 SKK, and the median was more than 11,000 SKK, more than any of the other 20 governmental bodies covered by the enterprise survey.[14]
- Courts received a dismal quality rating, among the worst in the survey. Only one in nine enterprises that were involved in court cases gave favorable ratings for quality.

Of the 13 percent of households that were involved in court trials, 25 percent gave something "special" to a court employee, judge, or attorney. The rate was highest among those who were the accusing parties in civil trials, such as divorces, property disputes, etc. Thirty-two percent made such unofficial payments.

Thirty-five percent of enterprises evaluated their experiences with the courts as unfair or biased, and 30 percent felt is was corrupt. Less than 17 percent felt the process was fast and without unnecessary delays.

Between 2002 and 2005, the frequency of bribery in the courts went down from approximately 12 percent to approximately 5 percent of firms indicating that bribes related to courts are frequent (Anderson 2006 p. 55). The Slovak Republic introduced merit-based selection of judges and strengthened the capacity to prosecute cases of judicial corruption. Court case disposition time, as reported in Time in Days for the Doing Business court case, decreased from 655 to 565 days.

The case of Bulgaria

Bulgaria, an Eastern European country formerly in the Soviet bloc, joined the European Union in 2007. Bulgaria's TI CPI score for 2008 was 3.6; for 2001 it was 3.9. Bulgaria is an oligarchs and clans (syndrome 3) country. This can mean that judges are part of competing oligarchs' personal followings, in effect "retained" to perform legal services (issuing writs, filing/dismissing charges, etc.) from the bench. In 1999, the World Bank's Bulgaria justice sector assessment examined the courts and the national governance structure for the judiciary. The assessment includes a description of some of the circumstances that facilitate corruption.

"The lack of sufficient national record-keeping and administrative follow-up also contributes to corruption. The Supreme Judicial Council does not have staff to handle either statistical information or administrative supervision, and the MOJ does not collect data which would permit reviews of job performance or actions/delays in specific cases, nor does it have supervisory authority over the judicial branch. The presiding judges of the courts systems have a variety of administrative duties, as well as their own caseload, and also have no administrative staff to support a thorough review of the caseloads of the other judges. Nor is there any modern docketing system for case files. The result is a lack of systemic administrative support of supervision of the judicial branch. One consequence of this situation is that judges, prosecutors and investigators who decide to resolve cases corruptly can do so with the high probability that their actions well be neither reviewed nor questioned. According to strong anecdotal information, this kind of corruption is more common than the resolution of cases on the basis of the facts and applicable law." (World Bank 1999, p. 13)

Between 2002 and 2005, the frequency of bribery in the courts in Bulgaria stayed almost constant at a level of approximately 18 percent of firms indicating that bribes related to courts are frequent (Anderson 2006 p. 55). The case disposition time as reported in Doing Business did not change.

The case of Georgia

Georgia's TI CPI score for 2008 was 3.9. Its earliest measured score was 2.4 for 2002. Based on the 2002 score, Georgia would most probably be an official moguls (syndrome 4) country.[15] This could mean that judges are personal clients of top regime figures, performing political as well as legal functions at the behest of a dictator or ruling circle.

Since the Rose Revolution in November 2003, under the leadership of President Michael Saakashvili, Georgia has gone through rapid changes. The 2008 scores indicate it could now also be an oligarchs and clans (syndrome 3) country, discussed above. During my World Bank mission to Georgia in 2004, I interviewed a number of leaders in the judiciary at the time.[16] Some of them have since left the judiciary, voluntarily or otherwise.

During one of my court visits, case handling was explained to me. This is what I understood of how case handling worked, at least at the time of my visit:

A case is filed, which means someone brings one or more documents to the court building. The file is taken by the clerk. The clerk gives the file a case jacket. The file in its jacket is then passed to the judge, who keeps it in his or her cabinet throughout the life of the case. The judge then needs to determine the court fee. This should be done by estimating the work the court will have with this case, judging from the nature of the dispute and the content of the file. There is no established fee structure. No one but the judge handles the case file. The judge writes a notice to the filing party asking for the estimated court fee.

When asked what the most important short-term issue in the Georgia judiciary is, the majority of my counterparts mentioned eliminating corruption in the judiciary. There is no reliable estimate of the extent of corruption in the judiciary. The following circumstances were put forward as facilitating corruption:

- Judges do not know what to do with the cases for lack of training
- Lack of (professional) court management
- Lack of consistent management of resources
- Low salaries
- Integrity is, so far, not a criteria for the selection of judges
- Many *rayon* (small, sub-district) courts consist of only one judge.

In 2005, in a World Bank survey, firms report that both administrative corruption and political corruption in the form of state capture have fallen markedly and that corruption is far less of a problem for business. Bribery in the courts has decreased from about 15 percent to about 10 percent of firms indicating that bribes related to courts are frequent (Anderson 2006 p. 55). Georgia has – as one of the first countries in the region - introduced entry examinations for judges. It has also restructured the internal judicial discipline mechanism by including outside stakeholders on the panel. The single judge courts in distant mountain areas were integrated into larger courts in regional centers.

The case of Nigeria

Nigeria's TI CPI score for 2008 was 2.7. Its 2001 score was 1.0. Nigeria is an official moguls (syndrome 4) country. This could mean the judges, as personal clients of top regime figures, perform political as well as legal functions at the behest of a dictator or ruling circle.

In Nigeria, the JIG study confirmed the strong relation between delays and bribe paying in courts. Court users reported how the payment of bribes occurred in connection with applications for bail, institution of proceedings, issuing of summons to the defendant, interrogatories, delivery of judgments and obtaining certified copies of proceedings. People who had to return to court several times for the same case were the ones who were asked to pay bribes more frequently. Delays are a compelling incentive for court users to accelerate the procedure by paying bribes. Delays are often in fact an implicit request for a bribe in exchange for an unanticipated service. Procedural complexity may also facilitate corruption. This also suggests that the likelihood of incidence of corruption relates directly to the overall duration of the case (UNODC 2006 p. 140).

The case of Benin

Benin's TI CPI score for 2008 was 3.1. Its earliest recorded score was 2.9 for 2004. Benin is also a group 4 syndrome country. Here, too, judges may be personal clients of top regime figures, performing political as well as legal functions at the behest of the ruler.

Benin's justice sector was diagnosed in 1999-2000 as part of the process toward a justice reform program supported by the World Bank. The report calculated that in 2008, there would be no judges left in Benin unless the conditions were drastically improved. All the old judges would have retired, and no new judges were forthcoming because of the low status and pay of the profession. One example of the low level corruption this may induce is illustrated by a case I encountered during my visit in 2004. Some judges had tampered with the checks they had received to reimburse their travel costs, by adding one or more zeros to the number on the checks. The official in charge of bookkeeping had received part of the proceeds. While I was in Benin, some of the judges were serving jail sentences. The judges were slated to be dismissed after having served their sentences.[17]

The case of the Netherlands

The Netherlands' TI CPI score for 2008 was 8.9. Its score for 2001 was 8.8. It is an influence markets (syndrome 1) country. Generally speaking, syndrome 1 countries have fully developed, functioning democratic institutions, but the systems are weak on the participation side. Voter turnout is low, and party financing is a critical issue. Corruption has been checked by legalizing the political role of wealth. Policies favor moneyed interests; those policies may well be seen as the result of unfair or corrupt influence. For the courts and judiciaries, this may generally mean that judges are bribed or practice extortion in connection with specific cases. The Netherlands ranked third in TI's Bribe Payers' index for 2008 with a score of 8.7 out of 10 (TI BPI 2008). I have not found sufficiently documented cases of administrative corruption in the courts of the Netherlands. The user satisfaction surveys (Prisma) show that people were not pleased with the disposition times and the waiting times in their cases, but there is no indication that they were displeased because of unequal treatment. Another source of information in this context could be reporting on complaints to the court. However, there is no public record of complaints to courts boards or how they were handled. From my own memory, I recall a case where courtroom ushers were bribed by lawyers to let defendants go first in a criminal court in Groningen in the 1980s. The case was prosecuted and tried, and the defendants were convicted.

Conclusions about administrative corruption: corruption as a problem of information

The Nigeria case illustrates how procedural complexity and longer duration create opportunities for bribery. The extreme weakness of the institution means there is little risk of detection. In Georgia, candidate causes offered by stakeholders in the judiciary included lack of training and education, deficient court management and very small courts. The Georgia case handling story shows there was no case administration to speak of in this example: no administration, no clear, unambiguous procedure for setting court fees. The judge in the case had a monopoly as the only case handler, wide discretion with regard to the court fee, and a very low risk of detection of a possible unfair decision. Georgia, with its improved TI CPI score, also shows that measures to address corruption can have an effect.

Institutional weakness, consisting of a lack of systemic administrative support for supervision of the judicial branch, is described vividly in the Bulgaria assessment. In Slovakia, the most significant factors are the quality of internal administration, information flow, and the existence of meritocracy. Such deficiencies, occurring with more or less severity depending on the level of development of the country in question, show up as opportunities for unchecked administrative corruption. This is a starting point for thinking about information, and access to information, as a remedy against corruption. Unfair decisions and procedures will be more difficult to carry out when:

- Information flows within the organization are clear
- Decisions are public
- Internal administration is done on the basis of clear, unambiguous predefined procedures
- Careers are managed on the basis of competence and merit.

Clear procedures and public accountability will limit the scope of discretion. All improvements to information flow will raise the risk of detection as well as accountability.

High level political corruption: Influencing decisions and appointments

High level corruption is generally understood as influencing decisions in the law-making process, such as firms shaping and affecting the formulation of laws and regulations through private payments to public officials and politicians. What is called high level corruption would, for the courts and the judiciary, mean influencing two things: (1) judicial decisions, and (2) judicial appointments. The judicial decisions in this group are usually the decisions of higher courts with political impact, such as decisions about the legality and correctness of election results, decisions regarding the legality of executive action, or high profile criminal cases involving the powerful. It is very difficult to find examples of judicial decisions that are not impartial because they were influenced. It is even more difficult to document them properly.

The appointment of judges can be a politically sensitive process. Generally speaking, legislation regulating judicial appointments is done in a way that safeguards the judiciary's independence, if followed.

In Germany, for example, judges in the ordinary courts are - mostly - appointed by parliamentary committees after a post-academic training program. In other systems, judges are appointed by the head of state on the recommendation of another state body. Some countries distinguish lower and higher level judicial appointments. In these countries, lower level, first instance judges are appointed by a body within the judiciary, for instance, a judicial service commission. Members of the Supreme Court or the appellate courts are appointed by the head of state after a recommendation by one or more other state bodies. The involvement of different state powers is intended to ensure the judiciary's independence. Both the internal and high level appointments run the risk of being influenced by patronage systems where these are strong and where institutional weakness is such that no countervailing policies are strong enough to curb it.

The case of Sri Lanka

Sri Lanka's TI CPI score for 2008 was 3.2. Its TI CPI score for 2001 was 3.2. Sri Lanka is an oligarchs and clans (syndrome 3) country. This could mean that judges are part of competing oligarchs' personal followings, and in effect "retained" to perform legal services (issuing writs, filing/dismissing charges, etc.) from the bench.

In Sri Lanka, there was great public dissatisfaction with the integrity of the judiciary following the last appointment of a president of the Supreme Court of Sri Lanka. The President of Sri Lanka appointed him as chief justice in 1999 from the position of attorney general. This was a breach of the usual convention of appointing the most senior judge on the supreme court to the chief justice position. The most senior judge at the time was well regarded internationally and noted for delivering judgments that went against executive and legislative abuse of power. He was bypassed - allegedly for those judgments - by the President of Sri Lanka (TI GCR 2007 p. 275-278). Under the Constitution, the Judicial Service Commission (JSC) exercises the powers of appointment, promotion, dismissal and disciplinary control of the judges of the lower courts. However, there are no disclosed criteria. The International Bar Association Report of 2001 gives examples of instances where original court judges were arbitrarily disciplined and even dismissed by the JSC headed by this chief justice. The IBA Report concluded that the perception of a lack of independence of the judiciary was in danger of becoming widespread and that it was extremely harmful to ordinary citizens' respect for the rule of law. It was "concerned that not only is there a perception that the judiciary is not independent, there may indeed be some basis in fact for the existence of such a viewpoint in relation to a minority of the judiciary" (IBA 2001 p. 33). There were also serious concerns expressed about the discipline, retirement, appointment, transfer and promotion of judges under the auspices of the Judicial Services Commission (IBA 2001 p. 38). In his April 2003 report to the UN Commission on Human Rights, the United Nations Special Rapporteur on the Independence of the Judiciary wrote that he "continues to be concerned over the allegations of misconduct on the part of the Chief Justice Sarath Silva, the latest being the proceedings filed against him and the Judicial Service Commission in the Supreme Court by two district judges [in 2003]."[18] In 2006, the other two members of the JSC besides the chief justice resigned for "reasons of conscience" (IBA 2006).

On the presumption that all judges are somehow equal, the principle of seniority is a very common criterion for selecting presiding judges. This is particularly true when managerial capabilities are not considered a key competence for the presiding judge. Potentially, bypassing the seniority criterion is a way of invading the judiciary with a patronage network. Lower court judges are appointed by the Sri Lanka JSC. There are no disclosed criteria for the careers of judges in the lower courts. The absence of those criteria is an institutional weakness that leaves room for developing a patronage network. This example also shows the importance of external agencies, in this case the International Bar Association and the UN Special Rapporteur on the Independence of the Judiciary, for observing what goes on in a country and debating it publicly.

The case of Texas

The TI CPI score for the United States for 2008 was 7.3. The TI CPI score for the United States for 2001 was 7.6. The United States, of which Texas is a part, is an influence markets (syndrome 1) country. Generally speaking, syndrome 1 countries have fully developed, functioning democratic institutions, but the systems are weak on the participation side. Voter turnout is low, and party financing is a critical issue. Corruption has been checked by legalizing the political role of wealth. Policies favor moneyed interests; those policies may well be seen as the result of unfair or corrupt influence. For the courts and judiciaries, this may mean that judges are bribed or practice extortion in connection with specific cases.

In the United States, judges in state courts are mostly elected. In most states, the elections are non-partisan. In Texas and seven other states, judges are elected in party elections. Once elected, they are allowed to contribute to others' election funds. Parties with cases pending in court are allowed to contribute to the election or re-election funds of the judges concerned. In 2003, former Chief Justice of Texas Tom Phillips said: "Our partisan, high-dollar judicial selection system has diminished public confidence in our courts, damaged our reputation throughout the country and around the world, and discouraged able lawyers from pursuing a judicial career."[19] This example shows how partisan elections may endanger judicial impartiality. From discussions with many judicial colleagues and other lawyers in the United States, I understand that partisan elections of judges are widely considered a serious flaw in the system.

The case of Nepal

The TI CPI score for Nepal for 2008 was 2.7. The TI CPI score for Nepal for 2004 (earliest score available) was 2.8. Nepal has recently gone through major constitutional changes, after years of unrest. Nepal is an oligarchs and clans (syndrome 3) country. Nepal has a number of specialized tribunals, some of which have been set up to circumvent alleged corruption in the ordinary courts. During my mission in 2004, the following case became headline news: A British citizen was arrested in Kathmandu's Tribhuvan Airport with heroin in his luggage and in one of his shoes. He admitted having the drug in his possession. The special court for drug cases convicted him to 17 years in prison and a hefty fine. The case was heard on appeal by the appeal instance for the special court. This appeal court is a panel of two members of the Supreme Court. The panel acquitted the defendant. The reasons that made it into the public press were twofold. Apparently, the police report was unclear as to whether the heroin was in his right or his left shoe. He also had allegedly not had the service of an interpreter while being questioned by the police. The press voiced the suspicion of corruption, saying that no member of the organized drugs mafia had so far remained in custody. The Bar Association studied the decision. Its conclusion was that the decision was completely against established jurisprudence. The Bar and the Attorney General demanded an investigation by the Judicial Council. The two judges went on leave. A three-member panel reported to the Council, or at least to the Chief Justice. The official procedure for dismissal of Supreme Court judges is that they have to be impeached before Parliament, which can depose them with a two-thirds majority. At the time, there was no Parliament. One judge resigned after having been advised to do so. The other judge decided to resist the advice to resign[20].

This case, about influencing a high level judicial decision, is an example of the role of public scrutiny and external pressure. The institutional weakness of an absent parliament to decide whether to dismiss the judges in this case created a problematic situation.

The case of the Netherlands

For the sake of completeness, here are the data on the Netherlands from the previous section again: The Netherlands' TI CPI score for

2008 was 8.9. Its score for 2001 was 8.8. It is an influence markets (syndrome 1) country. Generally speaking, syndrome 1 countries have fully developed, functioning democratic institutions, but the systems are weak on the participation side. Voter turnout is low, and party financing is a critical issue. Corruption has been checked by legalizing the political role of wealth. Policies favor moneyed interests; those policies may well be seen as the result of unfair or corrupt influence. For the courts and judiciaries, this may generally mean that judges are bribed or practice extortion in connection with specific cases. A public source on misconduct by judges is the annual report of the procurator general. The procurator general is in charge of requesting the dismissal of judges, for misconduct or other reasons. In the published annual reports, I have found two investigations regarding judicial impartiality (Hoge Raad p. 142-143). Both are ex officio investigations into reports raising doubts about a judge's impartiality. In the first case, a party to a case and her lawyer accused a judge of lack of impartiality because of ties in the past between him and the director of the other party; among other things, the judge was said to have bought a piece of land below market value from this director. Investigation showed this had not been the case, nor were there other grounds for conflict of interest or partiality. The other case concerned a statement made by a judge in a newspaper interview; the subject matter of this case is completely outside the scope of this study. Complaints, generally, should be made to the court where the alleged impartiality has taken place. Until now, reporting on those complaints is not public. However, there is a public register showing each judge's official activities outside court on the Internet. Provided an interested party knows the name of the judge in his or her case, the data on this judge's activities are publicly available.[21]

Institutional weakness in high level judicial corruption

Obviously, in high level judicial corruption public scrutiny is important. Without it, I would not have been able to report these cases.

The Nepal example shows the institutional weakness of not having Parliament in place to deal with the dismissal of Supreme Court justices. The partisan elections in Texas do not reflect syndrome 1, but rather syndrome 2: elite cartels with party allegiance as a factor impeding impartiality. The Sri Lanka example illustrates the patronage networks syndrome eloquently: no publicly disclosed career management for judges, leaving them at the discretion of the leadership of the judiciary. The case of the Netherlands illustrates how a fully developed institution displays little sign of high level corruption. Unfortunately, this may also be caused by the lack of accountability, since reporting is largely not public.

Conclusions for this chapter

The quality of internal administration, procedural complexity, and career management based on merit and the actions of external watchdog agencies such as the press, the private bar, and civil society groups are factors influencing the incidence of corruption.

The illustrations and the research discussed above strongly suggest that the underlying cause of corruption is mainly institutional weakness. The weaknesses uncovered include absence of clear information flows and poor internal administration. They result in poor accountability and low risk of detection. Poor or absent career management goes together with clientelism and political intervention in appointments and promotions.

With regard to the role of information, some observations can be made:

- Internal administration is mostly a matter of information about ongoing work. More transparent internal administration increases detection risk.
- Excessive procedural complexity is related to sub-optimal internal administration. Simplification of procedures will reduce the number of opportunities for bribe-taking.
- A career based on merit presupposes that the knowledge and information required are available. This means that knowledge and information on standards, as well as training and education, need to be available.
- The actions of external watchdog agencies, and public accountability more in general, are evidently mostly about information.[22] Increased transparency will enhance public scrutiny and thereby pressure for, ultimately, more impartial judicial decision making.

That makes information an important tool against corruption in courts and judiciaries. Consequently, technology that deals with information can be an instrument against corruption as well. This can be technology providing information about internal processes and technology supporting communication with external parties. Searching for potential remedies that can be supported by information technology in order to combat corruption and improve impartial decision making is, therefore, the next step.

As observed before, the level of corruption and the form it takes are influenced by the level and form of institutional weakness, which strongly correlates with the level of development of the country in question. This last observation needs to be taken into account when identifying starting points for reform that point to effective remedies.

Chapter 5.3 Court Corruption - Remedies

This chapter examines ways in which IT can support reducing corruption in judiciaries and courts. Building on the theoretical insights from the first chapter on corruption and the findings from the empirical chapter, it focuses on potential remedies. Therefore, it first identifies information aspects of the problem of corruption. It then goes on to identify starting points for remedies. The syndromes approach suggests options for reform in each syndrome. Although those suggestions do not apply specifically to judiciaries or courts, they offer some guidance for remedies that will be examined later. The chapter ends by drawing conclusions about some of the ways to use IT for corruption reduction in courts and judiciaries.

Distinguishing clearly between identifying the problem of corruption in the judiciary and identifying its source, solutions or remedies is of the essence in the process of figuring out how corruption can be reduced. For each country or system, a thorough diagnosis is needed to gain insights into the proximate and underlying causes (Reiling 2007, throughout). This diagnosis can serve as a basis to identify starting points for remedies. The scope of this study, into ways in which IT can support reducing corruption in courts and judiciaries, is more limited. However, there are some general observations about remedies to be made from the empirical evidence above, in combination with the theoretical insights in the first sections of this chapter.

Remedies for judicial and court corruption

This section looks at remedies in relation to the level of corruption and development in different countries, and in their judicial systems.

If corruption is wrong, the first remedy that may come to mind in a legal setting is that corrupt behavior should be punished. Repression, sanctioning corrupt behavior after it has happened by means of prosecution and/or by firing the perpetrator from his or her job, is one type of remedy. It has a value in that it sets a norm; it expresses that corruption is wrong. However, repression does not address the causes of corruption. In the case of judicial corruption, prosecution faces particular difficulties because the perpetrators would have to be judged by their colleagues. Preventing corruption before it can happen is another possible remedy. From the above, we know that corruption is caused by a poorly functioning system. The Nigeria example shows how administrative corruption is facilitated by delays, complex procedures and a high incidence of court appearances. The weaker the court management, the more this corruption can go unchecked. Improvements to the system may reduce opportunities for corruption and thereby prevent corruption from occurring. If, as in the Slovakia example, students have to bribe their way into a legal university education, the culture of corruption in education is easily perpetuated in the court system. Understanding those fundamental factors is needed for an effective reform program. Here, we will try and understand how a poorly functioning system can be made to function better in order to prevent corruption from happening.

This conclusion is confirmed by the theoretical approaches to the causes discussed above. The power-oriented analysis suggests balancing discretion and monopoly with relatively high transparency and accountability. Monopoly can be reduced by introducing checks and balances like appeal and review. Discretion can be reduced, for instance, by forms of policy. Increasing accountability with public hearings, public decisions and reporting on performance also constitute forms of institutional improvement. The incentives approach suggests lowering available benefits, raising the risk of detection and influencing the relative bargaining power of the parties. This last point again confirms the suggestions from the power approach: reducing bargaining power can be done by reducing either a monopoly or discretion. When procedures are improved and transparency increased, the risk of detection will be higher too.

Institutions can be more, or less, dysfunctional. This is what we learn from the syndromes approach: official mogul countries have practically no functioning institutions; in influence market countries institutions are fully functional.[23] Hence, the best place to start our search for remedies to the dysfunctionality underlying corruption is within the framework of the syndromes of corruption. This approach does justice to the fact that, due to the different levels of institutional functionality, countries have different starting points for reform. For reform in each syndrome, there are some suggestions for the role of the judiciary function in reforming society. Those suggestions are strategic in nature, quite general and not very detailed. For example, for syndrome 3, credible criminal law enforcement is suggested as a general starting point. This will most probably involve improving the effectiveness of criminal courts and their internal administration too, but the syndromes study does not go into that level of detail. This study, however, is looking for remedies at that level as well.

Here is how we will address this question: Judiciaries in each syndrome have different levels of functionality and, consequently, starting points as well. In this sense, they are the same as other institutions. In order to find remedies for corruption in the judiciary, the more general recommendations for institutional change and reform in each syndrome will be taken up. They will then be extrapolated for their meaning for the judiciary as an institution by analogy. For reform in each syndrome, there are specific risks, things to avoid and things to put off until later. This discussion is relevant for the judiciary too. It should produce some criteria to select and prioritize the remedies that may work in each specific syndrome.

The next section will draw up inventories of possible starting points, risks and opportunities for reform in the judiciary for each particular syndrome. Such an inventory can serve as a first step toward a reform program. However, it cannot be stressed enough that a reform program for a specific country or system needs to be tailored to the circumstances found in that particular country.

After having done all that, we will come back to the role of information in the remedies identified.

Corruption in syndromes

The purpose of this section is to identify starting points for reform to reduce corruption. It will discuss, for each syndrome, the characteristics of the political system in general and the role of the judiciary in it. The possible starting points for reform in each syndrome will be identified in order to find the remedies that can be effective. In each case, we will also examine risks and opportunities for that syndrome. By analogy, we will identify possible starting points, risks and opportunities for reform in the judiciary in each of those syndromes in question. Finally, we will look at the role of information in the remedies identified. That will help us uncover opportunities for introducing and implementing forms of information technology.

a Influence markets syndrome (1)

In this syndrome, institutions are fully functional and independent. The system suffers from declining political trust and popular dissatisfaction with political choices. Outright corruption in society in general is rare in this group. There is likely to be popular distrust of institutions. This distrust can take the form of perception of corruption.

The system has strong, independent professional judiciaries. The judiciaries are capable of running their own business.[24] Corruption in the judiciary is incidental. Popular distrust in institutions includes the judiciaries. This distrust can take the form of perception of corruption. In the United States, more than 50 percent of the respondents in the Global Corruption Barometer survey included in the Gallup Voice of the People survey for 2006 described their judiciary/legal system as corrupt (TI GCR 2007 p.13). In the Netherlands, the percentage was 25. In the United Kingdom, it was almost 40 percent (TI GCR 2007 p.13). Consequently, it is useful to discuss it here. Professional organizations have risks of their own. Partly, this is the problem of the ivory tower: a strong professional orientation in the courts and the judiciary may weaken the orientation toward the needs of court users. It may mean a lack of awareness of the needs of the court users. Professional norms may override societal needs. There is evidence that this is the perception of considerable parts of the public. In the United Kingdom, the public believes that the courts are important, but also that the courts serve the interests of the wealthy and that the judiciary is remote and out of touch (Genn p. 246). In the United States, perceptions that courts are too costly, too slow, unfair in the treatment of racial and ethnic minorities, out of touch with the public, and negatively influenced by political considerations are widely held (Rottman 2000 p. 1). Approximately 80 percent of the respondents in the 1999 National Survey on How the Public Views the State Courts indicate that they agree that "judges' decisions are influenced by political considerations" and "elected judges are influenced by having to raise campaign funds" (Rottman 1999 p. 28). Dispute resolution in court may not resolve the disputes at all. Genn's study on what people do and think about going to the law in the United Kingdom reports that of those whose problem was resolved on the basis of a court or ombudsman's decision, about one in three said that they had not achieved their main objective (Genn p. 199). In a similar study in the Netherlands, of the respondents who opted for agreement, 90 percent indicated that they had achieved their objective compared with 66 percent of the respondents who went to court (Van Velthoven 2004 p. 199).

The professional orientation may also involve a strong orientation toward the lawyers, the Bar, and/or the prosecutors. The JIG mentions the public perception of frequent socializing between lawyers and judges as an indicator of perceived corruption. In the United Kingdom, judicial appointments were limited to barristers and they were opened up for solicitors only recently. In the Netherlands, a web site of a discontented group has a list of lawyers and judges – under the name of Jurikaste, which translates as lawyer's caste – and their affiliations, in order to demonstrate how "partiality, prejudgment, conflict of interest and corruption spoil our legal system" thus explicitly displaying their disbelief in judicial independence.[25] More seriously, there was a complaint against the Netherlands to the U.N. Human Rights Committee concerning a possible conflict of interest of members of the Supreme Court. The complaint was dismissed, but the Committee expressed "some doubts about the propriety of a system that allows judges to sit on a supervisory board established by a business association"[26] (Langbroek 2007 p. 124-125). In addition, there was an informal alert to the Netherlands from the Council of Europe's office on efficiency of justice (CEPEJ) regarding the availability of data on disciplinary proceedings in the Netherlands judiciary. Those data are not public, and therefore they were not reported to the Council of Europe. Hence, there is no way of knowing whether complaints against judges were filed, and how complaints, if any, were dealt with.

To deal with such objections, and also to avoid any semblance of partiality, well enforced ethics and conflict of interest rules that are transparently enforced are a necessity. More generally, in order to improve public trust, the judiciary will need to become more transparent. It will need to develop its presence in the public debate. Public reporting about the enforcement of ethics as well as about the way the courts are run, using court and judiciary web sites, can be an effective remedy against public distrust. Public reporting is more than a communication issue; it is also an incentive for the organization to comply with the norms. Another remedy for public distrust is to publish court decisions and make them available without charge on the Internet, since that will provide a measure of control for the public to check decisions for partiality and corrupt decision making. Judicial decisions can be expected to be of better quality when they are published.

The starting point for the reform of judiciaries and courts in this syndrome is lack of public trust.

In terms of information, the main focus of the remedies discovered in this syndrome is that of transparent external communication, and communication of proper, correct practices at that. The obvious vehicle for doing this is the Internet.

b Elite cartels syndrome (2)

This syndrome has a closed, collusive, politicized economy with moderately weak institutions, sometimes colonized by political parties. For this syndrome, Johnston suggests underlining the value of an independent judiciary, free press and long-term efforts to shore up administrative autonomy and professionalism. Improved public management and enhanced transparency, functional independence through enhanced, transparent funding, and stronger civil society must be sustained by a wide range of incentives for a long time; emerging civil society groups will be better sustained by advocating their own interests. *Pantouflage*, that is, elite employment transitions back and forth between the public and private sectors, must be controlled as well as lobbying. There need to be checks on conflicts of interest. The interpenetration of political processes, the economy, elite networks and bureaucracy must be discouraged. An example of the kind of problem some systems in this group have to contend with is the following. Under the former socialist regimes in Eastern Europe, the judiciary function was not very well developed. The judicial function was part and parcel of the centralized party organization. Directives from the Central Committee were more important than the facts in the case, the legal provisions governing them, and a fair interpretation of both. Judges had low status and their role can be characterized as administrative, rather than judicial.

Creating a strong, independent judiciary can be a strategic objective. A striking instance of what an independent judiciary can achieve is the example of the mani pulite (clean hands) judges in Italy, who in effect "decimated an entire political class and their networks of corruption" (Johnston p. 98-100). The Italian judiciary was given strong and strictly regulated independence after WWII. This has effectively insulated the judges from the corrupt networks that affected politics. Another example from Italy is that of a 1999 decision of the Corte di Cassazione, the civil division. This decision changed jurisprudence on liability for damages to private parties by illegitimate acts of the public administration.[27] Before the decision, administrative judges could only void decisions by the public administration, but there was no legal recourse for compensation of damages caused by such acts. The Corte di Cassazione decision extended liability for damages to acts of the administration. Di Vita, who brought up this decision, maintains that "regarding the corruption phenomenon as a whole, using the indicators of Transparency International, we may affirm that corruption has declined in Italy starting from 2000." Whether this is a direct consequence of the decision needs more research, Di Vita remarks (Di Vita 2006). The TI CPI scores for Italy have gone from 4.7 in 1999 to 5.5 in 2001, 5.2 in 2007, and 4.8 in 2008. It seems reasonable to assume that damage claims addressed to the administration will raise the risk of detection for civil servants who abuse their power. This discussion of Italy shows that an independent judiciary can be an important factor in raising the level of institutional integrity in another government institution.

Creating such judicial independence will, in general, involve raising the level of professionalism of the judiciary and of the courts: well developed conflict of interest rules that are transparently enforced, high levels of bureaucratic professionalism, a corresponding level of pay and of status. Case assignment procedures can be an important issue in improving bureaucratic performance. Output-based budgeting, where funding is based on results, also increases a judiciary's independence.

Information-intensive measures, such as output-based budgeting, require that basic bureaucracy is in place. Information on output, and on the workings and performance of the organization, is needed before funding can be allocated based on output, and the risks this entails can be controlled. Then, information systems can be a basis for more transparent funding in order to increase functional independence. Functional independence is an aspect of how constitutional independence works in practice, with budgeting and accountability based on service delivery. Moreover, a funding system that rewards expedient case handling, and thereby reduced processing time, will also help to reduce opportunities for administrative corruption. Similar to the first syndrome, public trust and transparency can be enhanced with communication over the Internet about the ethics system, case assignment methodologies, reporting on enforcement of the ethics codes and other aspects of the courts' systems for effective dispute resolution and administering justice.

c Oligarchs and clans syndrome (3)

In the countries in this syndrome, institutions are very weak and participation is risky. Consequently, there is much insecurity and injustice. Liberalization may make things worse by adding to insecurity. Other activities that increase insecurity may prove counterproductive. Formally, constitutions declare the courts independent, but the reality is not that straightforward. The judiciary is itself part of the network of personal relations. That makes any attempt at increasing independence a hazardous exercise. The Sri Lanka appointment example illustrates how independence can be hazardous, and also how the network of personal relations may work. In Romania, the independence of the judiciary was introduced very soon after the fall of the Ceausescu regime in 1989. A code of ethics was introduced only in 2001. Without a corresponding level of accountability, independence became an instrument of judges' own oligarchies and clans (TI GCR p 269). A specific risk in this group is that anti-corruption initiatives may become weapons for rival oligarchs, so that tackling corruption head-on would worsen the rivalry and insecurity (Kaufmann 2005 p. 88). The courts may well be instruments in, or party to, such rivalry. There are some remedies that can be effective in this syndrome. Instead of confronting corruption directly in the crime prevention mode, reducing its most threatening forms indirectly by easing insecurity can be an effective way of dealing with it. Professionalizing the courts may help to reduce insecurity and promote credible law enforcement. Effective criminal law enforcement is a very important way of increasing basic security. Institution building and improvements in public management are urgent needs but lack political backing. Basic improvements in the judiciary and law enforcement are top priorities. More effective markets, courts and guarantees of property rights can discourage raids on other oligarchs' holdings. Thus, the recommendation is to build a framework of institutions by political means. The dynamics of oligarchs and clans are rooted in history, in long-standing family networks. Outside influence and assistance can be crucial. Judicious conditionality and rewards for progress can be development strategies, Michael Johnston observes.

The courts most probably share the fate of other public sector institutions in this syndrome. They can be expected to be very weak institutionally. Hence, in this group professionalizing the courts involves reviewing court processes, setting up basic administrative and case handling frameworks where they do not yet exist, and training and education. Reviews of court processes should examine whether simplifying procedures and speeding them up are viable. This will reduce the number of opportunities for corruption both in terms of steps and in terms of time.

Introducing computers and basic office automation can be a starting point for basic steps in professionalization. In themselves, these actions will not reduce processing times. That is why the procedures will need to be reviewed in order to uncover opportunities for simplification. Simple electronic case management systems can be set up. Introducing sound systems in courtrooms is another simple measure to improve transparency and thereby induce more professional behavior.[28] Making current legislation available online will help to reduce the uncertainty about what the law says, for those within the courts as well as for the general public and those seeking justice. The same holds for publishing court decisions. There is quite a bit of catalytic effect to be had in this group. This will be discussed in greater detail, in the context of both access to justice and case handling, in the respective chapters.

d Official moguls syndrome (4)

Official moguls are the people in power or their protégés who plunder an economy with impunity. In countries with this syndrome, the institutions are extremely weak. Corruption is a symptom of problems so fundamental that specific reforms will accomplish little. Because the institutions are so frail, there is practically no potential for improvement. Nor is there much chance that any change wrought can be sustained over the longer term. However, the implications of unchallenged power depend on the agendas of those who hold it, as demonstrated by the example of Singapore's successful anti-corruption and development agendas. Since 1959, the Government of Singapore has consistently worked to develop the economy and combat corruption. It is now in the influencing markets syndrome group.[29] Singapore ranks first in the Doing Business overall ranking for 2007 (DB). Its TI CPI score for 2008 was 9.2 (TI CPI 2008). Hong Kong has also combated corruption since the 1970s (Klitgaard p.100). Its TI CPI score for 2008 was 8.1. Giving groups in society a small measure of autonomy through more secure property rights and micro-credit, enhanced communications and press freedom is a step forward. Building a stronger and more active civil society will be a gradual process requiring basic political change. Civil society groups will be more sustainable if they are animated by self-interest, rather than by international development agendas. External pressures and resources will be critical. The Internet is an effective resource for supporting self-interest groups from outside. Transparency International has national chapters in most countries, and so does Amnesty International. Most national Transparency International chapters have their own web sites.[30] A factor of influence here will be the computer literacy of the nation in question.

The observation about institutional weakness applies to the institutions of countries in this group generally. It also applies to judiciaries and courts. This means that, in the syndrome 4 group of countries, there is not much opportunity for reform within the judicial institution. In Egypt, large amounts of aid have been poured into the courts for case management systems for a long time. Still, the so-called "family guilds" are actively protected by the Supreme Judicial Council. Family influence and gratuities are significant elements in the assignment process. The Ministry of Justice and the Judges Clubs are institutional mechanisms for accessing scarce government resources – apartments in Cairo, villas, automobile loans, free medical care in Europe or America for a judge or a judge's family member (Blackton, Egypt Country Report for USAID, p. 6-8, unpublished, quoted in Carothers, p. 120). It goes without saying that each country and its justice system and courts need to be assessed individually for opportunities, keeping in mind the restrictions inherent in the syndrome. Self-interest groups (Bar associations, business and professional groups) may be able to develop an atmosphere in which the judiciary is held more accountable for its role in administering justice. An example is the associations of women lawyers in Africa. The Zimbabwe Association of Women Lawyers set up mobile legal aid clinics around Harare in 2001. It also offers training for women on how to represent themselves in court.[31]

Sanctioning money laundering, as a measure against corruption from abroad, will ultimately require prosecution. Therefore, court intervention will be needed at some point. This may prove to be problematic in this group if the courts are very weak institutions. There is some confirmation of this observation in assessments of anti-money-laundering frameworks in group 4 countries. For Mauritania, for example, a World Bank assessment of the AML framework finds the courts wanting, and recommends training, education, funding and the setting up of procedures (World Bank 2005a).

There is growing interest in the role of non-state bodies in dispute resolution, particularly in this group. This possibly comes from the notion that non-state dispute resolution can provide competition for the state courts, or maybe also because this is where most people have their disputes resolved. Non-state institutions are outside the scope of this study. The results of ongoing research into non-state dispute resolution may provide us with more insight, but it is uncertain whether the results will produce clear ways forward with regard to reducing corruption in courts and judiciaries.

Another observation that needs to be made at this point is that there does not seem to be much opportunity for introducing IT in courts. If the institutions are largely non-functional, introducing technology is problematic. It is difficult to envisage introducing technology into an organization without processes to build on or an infrastructure to keep the technology working.

e Conclusions: Building judicial institutions from the bottom up

The corruption syndromes approach is helpful in uncovering effective starting points for remedies. The approach provides a nuanced understanding of the forces at work in each syndrome, the risks and opportunities, and possible starting points for reform. Therefore, it is for those starting points that we use it in this context. The starting point for judicial reform to reduce corruption is, as the case may be, improving public trust, institutional independence, basic administrative processes or external pressure.

Reform to reduce corruption in judiciaries and courts needs to start by building basic administrative structures and then building on this foundation. When we look for the information aspect of this development process, case registration and access to information are the two themes that emerge. The way cases are handled can be improved in all the syndromes. What needs to be done first depends on the starting point: Where there is none, basic case administration will have to be set up. This constitutes an opportunity for creating procedures and management systems that will provide increased transparency, and thereby discourage corruption. Existing systems for case handling can be examined for ways to simplify to reduce opportunities for corruption. With regard to access to information, nowadays the Internet is a relevant presence everywhere. Hence, the general public will increasingly come to expect transparency from public institutions, including courts and judiciaries. Courts and judiciaries in all syndrome groups have web sites. They also all have a need for improving public trust, though some more than others.

Comparing systems and their forms of corruption has led - tentatively - to some elements for an incremental model for opportunities to reduce corruption. In the next step, this study explores which remedies have proven to be successful in reducing corruption in courts and judiciaries.

Which remedies have proven to be effective?
There is a consensus that remedies are more effective when they can be combined and work together. No single remedy will be successful in isolation. The experience in Latin America has been that court systems that worked on their court processes were also more successful in combating corruption (TI GCR 2007 p. 144-5, Hammergren p. 282).

A similar conclusion can be drawn from the following quantitative comparison: simultaneous changes in a number of judicial institutions promise to have a more significant effect than isolated measures. The question of when judges are likely to be corrupt is examined with a quantitative, comparative approach, based on 63 countries, by Stephan Voigt (TI GCR 2007, p. 296-301). Which factors are most strongly correlated with the level of corruption in the judiciary? This is another approach that can help in selecting possible remedies. If changes in a factor do not influence the level of corruption, that factor may not be the first thing to focus on when looking for effective remedies. For instance, the income of judges and prosecutors is found to be highly – negatively -correlated with corruption: the higher the salary, the lower the judicial corruption. However, raising the salary as an isolated measure has only minimal influence on the incidence of corruption. Judges with higher salaries are not necessarily less corrupt because of it (TI GCR 2007, p. 296-301). According to the same source, there is a clear association between procedural formalism and the time needed to get a court decision, and judicial corruption. Three other factors were found to be insignificant: the obligation to publish court decisions, the level of checks and balances and the existence of anti-corruption commissions. Finally, the absence of a monopoly to prosecute leads to less corruption.[32] Increasing remuneration together with reducing procedural formalism, and reducing the time needed to arrive at judicial decisions are the relevant lines of action if corruption in a judiciary or a court should be reduced, according to these findings.

From what we already know, reducing incentives by improving processes and increasing accountability by deliberately working on raising public trust can be done in most syndromes, but from different starting points. An issue like low pay will have to be dealt with in order to make the other improvements work, but only in conjunction with other measures. Raising salaries as an isolated measure will do little or nothing to reduce judicial corruption (Klitgaard p. 77). In developing remedies, it will also be important to identify sources of support and resistance as a means of selecting entry points. This is why administrative corruption is sometimes easiest to attack first because it largely benefits low-level players who have relatively little bargaining power. As we have seen from the discussion on syndromes, institutional independence is a starting point in syndrome 2 countries. Increasing judicial independence in syndrome 4 or 3 countries can be counterproductive because it has the potential to create moguls or oligarchs who will start clans, empires and patronage systems of their own (Carothers p. 121). In moguls syndrome countries, the institutions are so weak that there is practically no potential for institutional improvement from inside the institutions, and not much chance that those changes will last. That is why the discussion of institutional improvement starts with the oligarchs and clans syndrome.

a Steps to improve case handling

In oligarchs and clans syndrome (3) country, the starting point is the weakness of the basic administrative structures. Therefore, addressing that weakness can help to reduce opportunities for administrative corruption. Reform starts with setting up a basic case handling system. The introduction of a basic automated case handling system can be an opportunity to review case handling procedures to reduce the opportunity for bribery:

- Remove unnecessary formalities and steps – and thus also reduce case processing time
- Divide responsibilities to reduce monopoly
- Reduce discretion by developing standard routines, like tariffs for court fees.

These are all activities that can be supported with an electronic case registration system. JIG refers to the experience in Karnataka, India as an example of what can be achieved. The Karnataka experience is described by Justice G.C. Bharuka, now chair of the India judiciary IT committee. He recounts how backlogs were reduced with the use of a database on cases: in some pilot courts, the backlog was reduced by 90 percent in three years (Bharuka p. 138-9). The information on case handling from an automated case management system will support what can be done, and it will also track changes in case handling. It can also help to detect unusual case handling that may indicate corruption (Klitgaard p. 82). What exactly needs to be done will depend also on whether there is no case management system at all, or whether a paper based case management system is already in place. Computerization of court files is another recommendation by the JIG (UNODC 2001 p. 10). It is expected to "reduce immensely the workload of the single judge and speed up the administration of justice but also helps to reduce the reality of appearance of court files being lost, and then requiring fees for retrieving them." The most minimal version of computerization of files is probably to set up a database of case files to track where they are. More sophisticated versions include bar-coding the files when they move, or even imaging them and storing the images in a database. The most comprehensive way of computerizing case files is to have fully electronic files on the court's file server. Worldwide, very few courts used only fully electronic case files at the time of writing this chapter in the last part of 2008. Using electronic files requires a high level of sophistication of the organization. As long as files can be made to disappear for a fee without detection, and maybe even reappear for another one, the court and case management in question is so ineffective that using electronic court files is not a realistic option.

Introducing basic office technology is a good way of training staff in the new way of working. The next step can be a simple, straightforward case registration and management system. Developing a case management system will require some expertise with computerized processes, so some experience with office technology will be a necessity. Electronic court management is a requirement for more professional ways of working. It may be expected to reduce opportunities for the embezzlement of court goods. However, that is not the topic of this study.

Using information systems to distribute legal resources, texts and jurisprudence will help to make judges and court staff understand what a correct legal judicial decision is. If those decisions, or at least more of them, are published, there is a chance that the possibility of public scrutiny will raise the quality of the decisions themselves, and their written record as well.

The starting point for elite cartels syndrome (2) countries is mainly insufficient institutional independence. Information management should be high on the agenda here: improving management and enhancing transparency, increasing functional independence through enhanced, transparent funding, and communicating with a stronger civil society. This will mean raising the level of professionalism of the judiciary and of the courts: well developed conflict of interest rules, and greater bureaucratic professionalism, pay, and status.

Who gets to decide which case, and who gets to decide that, can be an important source of concern for corruption. This concern is important for both the first instance and the appeal courts. It has become most apparent in elite cartels and influence markets syndrome countries. This concern is present in the other syndromes as well, but it can be more difficult to address in a situation where basic case management processes are weak or absent. For syndromes 1 and 2, a transparent and publicly known system for assigning cases, publicly known on the court Internet site, can be an effective means of addressing concern about collusion. Introducing an impartial, equitable, credible case assignment system can be undertaken on its own, but it should most certainly be part of any automated case management system. Professionalizing internal processes is discussed in more detail in Part 3 on internal case processing.

b Increasing access to information

The starting point for syndrome 1 countries in this context is primarily the lack of public trust. A remedy for this distrust could be to increase accountability to offset the monopoly and discretion awarded independent judiciaries in this syndrome. Increasing accountability by reporting about the way the judiciary in question safeguards its integrity can also enhance public trust:

- Transparent procedures and merit based systems for judicial appointments and careers, appointment, and promotion. Merit based recruitment and career management presuppose that knowledge, education and training are available.
- Methodologies for judicial case handling
- The ethics framework, codes of conduct and their enforcement
- Asset declaration: The Judicial Integrity Group advocates that all judicial officers should be required to declare their assets, and those of their parents, spouse, children and other close relatives.

Accountability can also be increased by publishing court decisions, or publishing more court decisions than before. Publishing court decisions also has different modalities: publishing the leading decisions of higher courts will help judges in lower courts understand the jurisprudence of the land. Publishing all court decisions on the Internet in order to increase transparency has not been achieved anywhere, as far as can be established. The debate about publishing decisions on undefended money claims and other decisions that are uninteresting from a jurisprudential point of view has not been resolved. We do know that public access to courts for the public and the media usually leads to better judicial performance. Likewise, public access to judicial decisions improves their quality. If decisions are published on an Internet site, the information will need to be more correct than when it stays out of the public eye (Blume p. 328).

The increasing penetration of the Internet will mean that the public will become accustomed to information being available. Hence, there will be increasing pressure for information, as listed above.

Implementing information technology

From this discussion, the strategic importance of information, access to it and how it is used becomes evident. Information is a crucial tool in reducing corruption in judiciaries and courts. That means there is also potential in introducing information technology. Both case handling and access to information can be improved and developed. Introducing and implementing information technology brings new issues and questions.

Introducing computers is a popular measure. Everybody wants computers. They are sometimes regarded as a status symbol. In patronage systems, they are used as rewards. The "top people" all get computers; this can even be a strategy to involve them in the improvement projects. In Nepal, I observed how IT was distributed very unevenly over the tiers of the court system. According to the data on 2003/4 in the Nepal judiciary's strategic plan, two of the 75 District Courts had 1 computer, none had a fax or a photocopy machine. Four of the 16 Appeal Courts had 1 computer each, all Appeal Courts had a photocopy machine and three had a fax. In the Supreme Court, there are 56 computers, 5 photocopy machines and 4 faxes (World Bank 2005b p. 30). The experience is that the computers are sometimes left unused. This is, or has been, one of the major difficulties of organizations implementing forms of IT: the leadership, for lack of experience, could not envisage its potential. Technology, in the context of these chapters, is primarily regarded as something with functionality that can support remedies against corruption. The mere introduction of computers and modern office technology already presents an occasion for improving basic bureaucracy. The experience is that the introduction of modern information technology has almost autonomous effects on an organization. Some changes need to be made in decision making, in relationships, in the types of disputes to be decided in court (see Chapter 2.1). Other changes occur almost unnoticed, for example more disciplined behavior with regard to documents and information. Moreover, because routines have to be changed and new ones invented, the way things are done in an organization is subjected to review. This is the catalytic function of information technology (Reiling 2006 p. 190): technology and its introduction affect the way people work together, governance, and the way budgets are managed. Introducing office technology, word processing, and databases for case management all require new skills that were not needed before. They also require new forms of support. After computers have been introduced, there will have to be a framework for managing and maintaining the hardware and for replacing it when it becomes obsolete or out of date. Experience has shown that, in an organization where no one else understands much of what they do, the people in charge of managing the information systems can become disproportionately powerful. They have a virtual monopoly on an essential resource, and if their discretion goes relatively unchecked, they may be likely to make use of that opportunity. The chair of the India judiciary IT committee told me his biggest problem was IT people who think they are in charge.[33] This creates an imbalance in the governance structure of courts and judiciaries. In the context of the corruption discussion in this chapter, it is prudent to point to this effect because it may present an opportunity for corruption in its own right. This new powerhouse, a new source of privileges and services, may become a new vehicle for corrupt practices, unless the risks are managed carefully by a proper governance structure.

Conclusions for Part 5

These chapters examined reducing corruption and improving the impartiality and integrity of courts and judiciaries with the support of information technology. Understanding what can be done has involved a long journey. The journey went from exploring existing theoretical and empirical knowledge about corruption and possible remedies to the role of information in those remedies.

If corruption in judiciaries and courts is to be combated effectively, accurate diagnostics are a prerequisite. Diagnostics are the first step in corruption reduction, in order to identify the problems and locate possible remedies. General comparative and theoretical insights help us to understand what to look for. Comparative and general insights on causes and possible remedies will have to be fitted to the specific situations. In each country, proper diagnostics should also identify the corruption syndrome that can serve as the starting point, the possible stakeholders and the level of ownership for judicial reform. The reform strategy needs to fit the syndrome that is applicable in the given context. Applied in the wrong syndrome, presumed remedies can turn into instruments of corruption.

Improving information handling in a broad sense can be the purpose of reform programs. The way information is handled is of strategic importance in the reduction of corruption. Developing basic bureaucracy is the first possible step. The findings suggest the institutions in question must be able to absorb and sustain change. This means it is not a viable remedy for existing institutions in syndrome 4 countries.

This improvement also involves access to information and knowledge: training, education and some measure of self-regulation and self-discipline. Targeted training, in how to deal with cases and disputes as well as in ethics, can be the starting point, even in situations where this is the only starting point available. That makes it a possible point of departure in syndrome 4 countries.

Introducing basic office technology can support the basic processes needed to process cases in an orderly, transparent manner. This is usually a good starting point for syndrome 3 countries. Case registration systems can support more automated, improved case handling. They provide a tool to reduce case disposition times. Reducing both processing time and the number of steps needed to reach a judicial decision will reduce the opportunity for bribery. Case registration systems, if properly set up and used, will also increase the risk of detection and thereby reduce incentives for bribe taking and for manipulating files and cases. As a tool for reporting, they can support increasing institutional independence, which is of particular importance for syndrome 2 countries.

Network technology can support increasing public trust by providing an effective means of communication between courts and their users and the general public. This is a primary point of attention for syndrome 1 countries. It can help make the arrangements supporting impartiality and independence visible.

Judicial and court integrity can be supported with information technology, provided it is implemented with these guidelines in mind.

Notes

1 There is a discussion on the concepts of de iure and de facto independence in Chapter 1.2.

2 For a legally oriented body like a judiciary, a legal norm is usually a more compelling reason for action than a fairly weak and hardly conclusive statistical correlation.

3 Adopted by General Assembly resolution 217 A (III) of December 10, 1948.

4 Adopted by General Assembly resolution 2200A (XXI) of December 16, 1966. The Convention entered into force on March 23, 1976.

5 Adopted by General Assembly resolution 58/4 of October 31, 2003. The Convention entered into force on December 14, 2005.

6 The Bangalore Draft Code of Judicial Conduct 2001 adopted by the Judicial Group on Strengthening Judicial Integrity, as revised at the Round Table meeting of Chief Justices, held at the Peace Palace, the Hague, November 25-26, 2002. It was submitted to the United Nations Commission on Human Rights at its 59th session in 2003. It is available on line at https://www.unodc.org/pdf/crime/gpacpublications/cicp10.pdf.

7 *Rex v. Sussex Justices, Ex parte McCarthy* ([1924] 1 KB 256, [1923] All ER 233) In a landmark and far-reaching judgment, Chief Justice Lord Hewart CJ said *justice should not only be done, but should manifestly and undoubtedly be seen to be done.*

8 http://www.coe.int/t/dghl/monitoring/greco/general/about_en.asp

9 Thanks to Michael Johnston for this example.

10 In common-law systems, discretion is considered to be broader than in civil-law systems.

11 These indexes are discussed in Chapter 1.3.

12 See the discussion of standards for case disposition in the chapter on case delay.

13 Low executability probably means that court decisions are difficult to enforce, which means the parties to a dispute do not get their dues.

14 On January 1, 2002, 1 Slovak Koruna = 0.02341 Euro; 1 Euro (EUR) = 42.71630 Slovak Koruna (SKK). The exchange rate was calculated by Oanda, http://www.oanda.com/convert/classic?free=1.

15 Georgia is not listed in Johnston's list of syndromes in the Appendix. Based on his methodology, my estimation was that it is most probably a group 4 or group 3 syndrome country. Johnston confirmed my estimation in an email.

16 See the report on that visit in Part 1.
17 Information from a Ministry of Justice official who dealt with the case from the Ministry's side. Notes from the conversation are in my possession.
18 *E/CN.4/2003/65/Add.125, February 2003.*
19 *The Washington Post* quoted Phillips in a story about the Tom DeLay case. It is an illustration of some of the effects of this system of electing judges. Representative Tom DeLay (Republican-Texas), majority leader in the House of Representatives of the United States, had to step down when he was accused of money laundering and conspiracy with illegal election funds, by prosecutor Ronald Early [D]. With the proceeds, the Republicans achieved a majority in the Texas House of Representatives. This majority changed the boundaries of the electoral districts. In the next elections, even more Republicans were elected to the House.
Judge Bob Perkins [D] was not impartial enough, according to DeLay's defense team. He had donated more than $5,000 to Democratic election campaigns. Perkins refused to leave but was taken off the case. Judge B.B. Schraub [R] had to appoint another judge. Prosecutor Earle [D] recused Schraub because he had contributed to the election campaign of governor Rick Perry [R]. Perry was closely associated with DeLay's contested election campaign.
Judge Schraub [R] then left the decision to the president of the Texas Supreme Court, Wallace B. Jefferson [R]. Political activists in Texas then complained about Jefferson's close ties with circles around DeLay [R]. In 2004, Jefferson had been appointed by Perry. He was supported by Texans for a Republican Majority. This group is also a defendant in the DeLay case. Judge Jefferson quietly appointed Pat Priest [D], a retired judge who had donated only $150 each to three Democratic candidates for the Texas House. The defense was expected to ask for a transfer of the case from Austin [D] to another location in Texas [R].
20 Compiled from the *Kathmandu Post* and the *Himalayan Times* of July 2004.
21 http://namenlijst.rechtspraak.nl/Default.aspx
22 As Daniel Kauffmann, one of the authors of the World Governance Indicators, emphasizes in the context of corruption: "Sunshine is the best disinfectant."
23 In order to do Johnston justice: he stresses that his model is not a developmental model in the sense that countries and their institutions necessarily have to transform from a group 4 into a group 3, then group 2 and finally a group 1 country.
24 It is good to keep in mind that, in spite of all efforts to comply with the European Union's acquis communautaire, quite a few EU member countries are not in this group. Belgium, Greece, Italy and Spain were in the elite cartels group (group 2) in 2001, the year of Johnston's measurements. The Czech Republic, Hungary, Poland, and the Slovak Republic, countries which joined the EU in 2004, were in the elite cartels group as well. Bulgaria and Romania joined the EU in 2007. They were in the oligarchs and clans group (group 3) in 2001, and probably still are. Johnston did not classify all EU members, so it is impossible to give a complete breakdown of EU member countries. Appendix 2 has the breakdown as done by Johnston.
25 www.sdnl.nl
26 Human Rights Committee, Eighty-fourth session, July 12-19, 2005, Communication No. 1185/2003.
27 Corte di Cassazione, Sezioni Unite – Sent. N. 500/99.
28 It is quite another matter to get the courts to use them. During my visit to some of the Sri Lanka courts, the World Bank-funded sound system was very much in evidence, but it was turned on only after my request to do so.
29 Singapore, by any standard except economics, is a very small country. That makes it very difficult to replicate the experience there because it will require substantial scaling up. The same holds for very large countries, like the United States, where experi-

ences may have to be scaled down. Moreover, as Johnston also remarks, Singapore's leaders have yet to yield to open and competitive politics.

30 For example: http://www.tinepal.org/ (TI Nepal), http://www.transparency.org/contact_us/organisations/transparency_international_nigeria (TI Nigeria).

31 Information from ZWLA's web site www.zwla.co.zw. ZWLA was off-line following the political crisis in late 2008.

32 Allocating the competence to initiate prosecution to other actors, such as the police, victims, NGOs and the like, should increase the amount of prosecution and reduce the expected gains from corruption.

33 Conversation with Justice G.C. Bharuka in New Delhi, July 2005, notes in my possession.

Part 6 Conclusions

Part 6 concludes this study. It sums up what IT can do to support judicial reform. Chapter 6.1 summarizes the findings of Parts 3, 4 and 5 of this study on the role of IT in judicial reform. Chapter 6.2 explores some directions for new research.

Chapter 6.1 Technology for Justice: How Does Information Technology Affect Delay, Access and Corruption?

The main goal of this study was to generate new knowledge about the ways in which information technology can support judicial reform. The underlying problem this study attempts to help resolve is the lack of understanding of the role of IT in court processes. This understanding is critical for successful reform. Judiciaries, if they are to improve their performance with information technology, need to understand how this technology works in their processes and in their interactions. This study has added some new understanding.

This chapter summarizes the findings. The organizing principle for this chapter is primarily the technology's functionalities: functional, networking and enterprise technologies, and how they relate to judicial reform. This summary of the findings focuses on the roles of those functionalities in resolving the problems users complain about most: delay, access, and corruption. These findings are followed by a discussion highlighting (1) the changes the technologies have already brought to courts and judiciaries in each of those areas, and (2) the developments that can be expected, and some changes this entails for the administration of justice.

Methodology

This study investigated IT impacts on the three most frequent complaints about courts and judiciaries: case delay, lack of access and judicial and court corruption. Hence, it studied three areas of court reform:

- Internal case processing (Part 3)
- Interaction with court users (Part 4)

– Guarding integrity (Part 5).

In order to learn more about the ways in which information technology can support reform in those areas, the following approach was chosen. The main activities in this study were to analyze, for each area:

(1) Knowledge about the problem and possible remedies
(2) The role of information
(3) Roles for information technology in resolving the problem.

The sources used in this study are publicly available. The sources are extremely varied, and their use as illustrations was justified specifically in each case. The material used for the analyses includes comparative indexes, empirical studies, and practical examples and illustrations of the use of IT in practice in courts. These examples did not serve to test a hypothesis or to prove that IT supports judicial reform, and they cannot simply be transposed into a different context. However, they do serve to share experience.

1 Functional technology for timeliness and integrity

Functional technologies, office automation and database technology, are the most pervasive information technologies in courts in Europe and the United States (Chapter 2.1). They have increased timeliness and integrity mainly by increasing accuracy and experimentation capacity.

Office automation is used mostly for document production. It has increased accuracy through the use of standard texts and merges with case registration systems.

Database technology has supported more timely case processing. Used for electronic case registration, it has provided insight into processes, influenced culture and supported developing standards. Courts' ability to know their processes has increased greatly.

Looking back, we can say that most courts have used their IT to support their paper processes.

Timeliness

Office automation has supported document production, a classic activity for courts. Changes in the way those documents are produced were developed gradually, as the possibilities of the text production systems were tried out. Examples are the re-use of frequently used phrases, and repositories of standard texts, which have raised accuracy and consistency. Thus, new processes were developed gradually by the users themselves. Experimenting with word processing is relatively easy, because the processing systems do not prescribe processes very strictly (Chapter 2.1). The increased accuracy reduced processing time.

Case registration systems replaced paper dockets. Their introduction has impacted the timeliness of case processing by opening the way for using the information contained in the systems in new ways.

In my view, the most remarkable impact of these systems was the development of case disposition time standards (Chapter 3.1). The database technology in case registration systems has enabled the generation of knowledge about processes: how they work, and what is needed to figure out how to reduce backlogs and improve processes to speed them up. After remedies are implemented, changes can be tracked in order to ensure they are working. And as a concrete example, tracking case processing with a database in Bangalore, India reduced case backlog by 90 percent. This study, particularly Part 3, uses caseload statistics to analyze court processes. Those statistics are available where courts have started using database technology for their case administration.

Case matrix

Using court statistics, I originally developed the case matrix to capture the role of information in case processing, judicial roles and court caseloads (Chapters 3.2 and 3.3). It underlines the need to distinguish case types. It is a useful tool for different purposes. In this study, it was used for:

- Showing the distribution of caseloads in different categories (Chapters 3.2 and 3.3)
- Identifying potential areas for different kinds of electronic processing and other forms of IT support (Chapter 3.3)
- Displaying party configurations with regard to differing information needs for increasing access to justice (Chapter 4.3).

For the purpose of understanding the role of information in court case processes, the level of predictability of the outcome of certain case types and their party configuration are distinguishing factors. Using the matrix, court cases can be sorted according to the level of predictability and the party configuration of zero-sum (one party wins) and win-win (both parties gain) outcomes. The resulting categories reflect judicial roles as well as case characteristics and processes.

In Figure 7, the percentages in the matrix reflect the group's share in the overall caseload.

For the Dutch civil jurisdiction, the matrix demonstrates how each group merits its own approach.

- In the majority of the cases (groups 1 and 2) processed in the Dutch civil jurisdiction in the first instance, there is no dispute resolution because there are few disputes there. Titles are provided for undefended claims (role 1, title role), and arrangements in family and similar situations are marginally tested (role 2, notarial role). In such

Figure 7 *Matrix of Different Judicial Roles and Caseloads in the Dutch Courts*

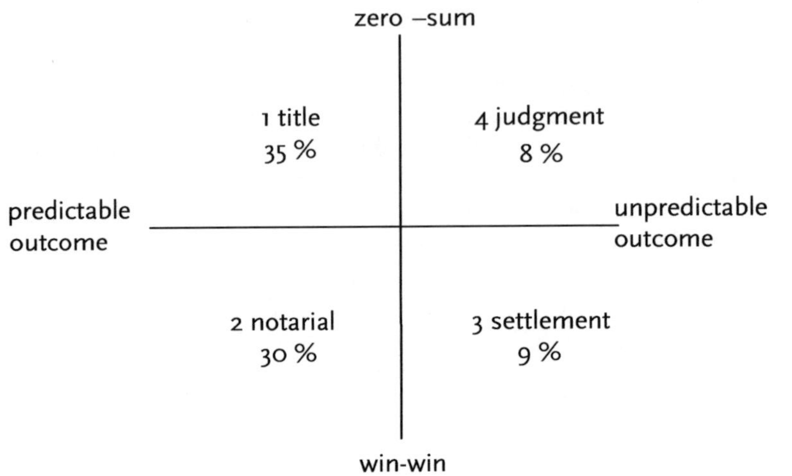

Source: Chapters 3.2 and 3.3.

cases, there is no dispute. Consequently, the information available when the case is first filed is sufficient to finalize the case and produce a decision. Therefore, processing those cases is relatively simple. That makes these groups the first candidates for automating parts of processes. Routines and standards will need to be developed in order to automate sub-processes. The result may be that fewer individual decisions need to be taken in each case. This will make *cases move to the left* in the matrix, potentially reducing processing time.

- Almost half of all the cases are most probably resolved with a settlement (groups 2 and 3). Cases in the notarial and settlement groups are largely resolved by the parties themselves. Providing the parties with information to help settlement will *move cases down* in the matrix, enhancing self-help. By reducing the number of disputed points, the processing time will also be reduced.
- Fewer than 20 percent of all cases (groups 3 and 4) need more information during the court procedure in order to bring a resolution of the dispute closer. This makes the information handling process more complex.
- Only 8 percent, a small fraction of the total caseload, constitutes a dispute that is concluded with a judicial decision (group 4). Judicial dispute resolution, most often mentioned by the different stakeholders, is not the most prevalent court activity from the point of

view of the total caseload. However, it is the role taking up most of the judges' time. The judges' information in this group is primarily for support with managing large amounts of information in individual case files.

Case processing

This study found no previous academic research suggesting that IT in courts has led to more expedient disposition times.[1] The case studies in Chapter 3.3 showed how courts still distribute and process case files mainly in paper form. Networking technologies have led to changes, but not to fundamentally new ways of working. Courts' internal processes and their interactions with the parties have, so far, not changed fundamentally under the influence of IT. Most of the effort of implementing court IT has gone into caseload management through simplification and process control. This observation fits with the general trend in IT use: supporting large-scale control by manipulating large amounts of information.

Communication with the users is still mostly one-sided. Resolution of complex problems and innovative problem solving are not supported by IT to any great extent yet. There is no indication that automating judicial reasoning for the purposes of dispute resolution is a perceived need.

The results of the Netherlands civil justice case study produced some conclusions regarding the impacts of IT support. The first group of conclusions is about direct reduction of case delay. The second group deals with less direct effects on case processing and on reducing corruption. The third group applies to access to justice, with the more abstract role of courts as setters of norms and with engendering public trust.

Reducing case delay

The case processing matrix suggests some opportunities for electronic information processing to reduce case delay (Chapter 3.3).

For all groups, electronic filing of claims, online data entry and electronic case files reduce the amount of activities court staff need to perform when processing cases. Automating routines and e-filing will directly affect processing time.

Automating routines goes together with simplification. Simplification was found to be an effective remedy for case delay. Simplification means reducing the number of individual procedural and substantive decisions that need to be taken in each case. It will move cases to the left in the matrix.

Internet functionality for public information and electronic forms are support for the notarial group. Here, better preparation of party documents can reduce processing time in court.

Public information can help the parties settle more of their dispute, thus reducing the number of issues to be resolved in court and moving cases down in the matrix, which will affect both the notarial and the settlement group cases. Software supporting negotiations can support processing specifically for the settlement group.

Electronic files and software supporting knowledge management are the main tools specifically for case processing in the judgment group. They can help to manage large quantities of information.

Culture and standards to reduce case delay

Culture was found to be an important factor in efforts to reduce processing time. Implementing a case registration system in court, and making information about processes transparent, can also affect court culture with regard to case processing.

Besides tracking whether cases are disposed in a timely manner, case registration systems can serve to affect the expectations and assumptions of actors in the administration of justice process by providing factual information (Chapters 3.1, 3.2 and 3.3). Comparing case processing across courts and even systems can shed new light on those assumptions. The findings indicate that courts in about a third of all countries worldwide dispose ordinary civil cases within the ABA Trial Court Performance Standards time standard, and courts in about two-thirds of all countries dispose those cases within the ECHR jurisprudential standard for case delay in ordinary civil cases. Results like these provide a basis for discussion about what constitutes a reasonable disposition time, and can be a starting point for developing standards.

Judiciaries, as independent institutions, should be able to set standards for themselves. Such self-imposed standards do not interfere with judicial independence. Standards can be developed based on information from various sources: actual practice, like the American Bar Association Trial Court Performance Standards, cross-country comparison and jurisprudence on timely case processing, for example that of the European Court of Human Rights (ECHR) (Chapter 3.1). Standards will help as orientation points for timely case disposal. Where goals for improved disposal times have been set, the systems can help to track whether those goals are being met. Case registration systems' tracking role is essential in judicial reform.

Reducing corruption

Case registration systems improve tools for process control, and thus support ensuring integrity and reducing corruption. Institutional weakness was found to be an important factor in the level of corruption in institutions, including courts (Chapter 5.1). This weakness occurs more often in countries where economic development is low. It manifests itself in insufficient or even absent process control. Effective process control reduces discretion and increases the risk of detection.

Implementing a case registration system can be an opportunity for developing basic bureaucracy, introducing process control process control, where this does not yet exist (Chapter 5.3). Introducing basic office technology can support the basic processes needed to process cases in an orderly, transparent manner.

More transparent and more expedient case processing can impact the level of administrative corruption in courts in the following ways:

- Increasing the risk of detection and thereby reducing incentives for bribe taking for manipulating files and cases (Chapter 5.1)
- Reducing processing and disposition time, the number of steps needed to reach a judicial decision, and setting time standards, thus reducing opportunities as well as incentives for bribery (Chapters 5.1, 5.2 and 3.3).

Here, two of the problem areas in judicial reform are related: long disposition times and procedural complexity create opportunities for bribery. Reducing case delay thus also impacts the level of administrative corruption.

2 Networking technology for access and integrity

Networking technology enables users to communicate with each other electronically. Court staff, including judges, use email, but largely for informal communications only (Chapter 2.1). Internal networking enables smart merges by combining case registration data with document production. These possibilities were mostly developed by "bricoleurs" within the courts.

The advent of the Internet was a major change. It presents courts and judiciaries with a channel for information and communication for external communication purposes. Information service on the Internet provides access to information for litigants and the general public.

Access to legal information is an important factor in resolving problems (Chapter 4.1). It helps people to resolve their difficulties out of court (Chapter 3.2 and 4.2). Correct information about court procedures increases one-shotters' (occasional litigants) chance of a just outcome to their case (Chapter 4.3). It can improve integrity by providing transparency, thereby reducing discretion, in court procedures (Chapter 5.1).

The case load matrix (Chapter 3.2) suggests that the parties, provided with information on trends in judicial decisions, can settle their differences out of court more often, and adequately prepare their cases for court if necessary (Chapters 3.2 and 3.3). This suggestion points to two distinct roles of courts: the role of courts in deciding individual cases and their role as general setters of norms, also known as their shadow function.

Part 4 of the study is an exploration of the potential of the Internet as a channel for communication by courts. The Internet, probably the most widely used source of information in the world, can be used for providing information and for communicating with others. Internet functionality is constantly evolving. Courts and judiciaries are increasingly present on the Internet. The available evidence gives only a first indication of the extent to which the Internet has been adopted by judiciaries and courts.

Justiciable problems and information needs

How people resolve justiciable problems, serious problems with a potentially legal solution, is examined in Chapter 4.2. This problem-solving happens on a continuum, empirical study shows. The majority of problems are resolved by people themselves, sometimes with some advice or assistance. Problems in long-term relationships are relatively difficult to resolve. Hence, they also come to court more often. Problems come to court mostly through advice or assistance agencies.

Resolution success depends on:

- The nature of the problem
- Availability of adequate information, advice and assistance
- Competence in finding and acting on information.

People who come to court only occasionally, or one-shotters, have specific information needs. The case matrix shows where those needs can arise.

In Figure 8, the case matrix shows the party configurations of cases coming to court (Chapter 4.3). The matrix provides some indications of the information needs of the parties who come to court only incidentally (one-shotters), as opposed to repeat players. The matrix suggests:

- In title provision cases, defendants who do not act against a claim may need information on possible defenses.
- In the notarial group, both parties have a need for information on how to arrange a settlement to be submitted to court.
- In the settlement group, there is a need for guidance on settling disputes.
- In the judgment group, information needs can vary considerably.

Figure 8 *Matrix of Party Configurations*

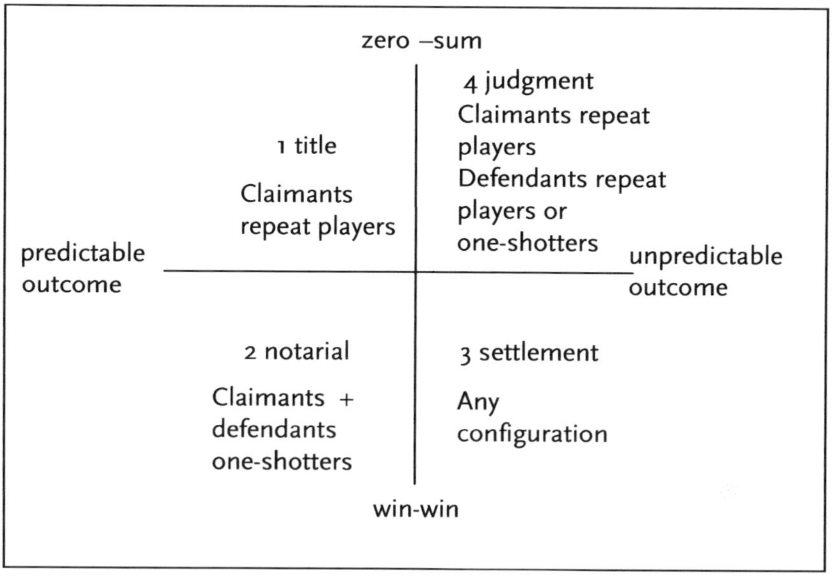

Thus, providing information on a web site can serve to (1) help settlement and keep cases out of court, or (2) help with information on how to bring them into court.

Information for keeping disputes out of court
When people have a serious problem, and they look for information, their first and foremost need is for information on how to solve the problem (Chapter 4.2). The legal information they need is primarily straightforward information about rules and regulations. Next, they look for information about ways to settle and handle disputes. Their main sources are specialized organizations and legal advice providers.

Judiciaries and courts, in their general shadow-of-the-law role, can help keep disputes out of court by providing information about the general approaches judges and courts have for specific types of problems (Chapter 4.3). Settling these disputes is generally done with the support of legal or specialist organizations. Information about those general approaches will need to become publicly available. Increasingly, judicial decision making is supported by policies and decision support systems that reflect policies. Policies and decision support systems, if they are available publicly, can help keep disputes out of court by supporting settlement.

The legal policy dilemma, whether keeping cases out of court or improving court case resolution should be a goal of policy, finds some answers here (Chapters 4.2 and 4.3). Going to court should be a last resort. People generally are more satisfied at having resolved their own problem than they are at having a court resolve it. Hence, helping them to resolve problems out of court is preferable. Devising problem-specific ways to help informal problem solving and diverting them to other dispute resolution mechanisms may keep still more of them out of court. Even when a court decision is compulsory, like divorce, some parts of the dispute can be sorted out by the parties in advance with the necessary guidance.

However, making going to court when necessary less stressful is still a valuable goal in itself. Information on going to court can help reduce people's stress and improve their chances of achieving justice if they have to go to court (Chapter 4.3).

Information for taking disputes to court

Information technology, notably the Internet as a provider of information, can also perform a role in compensating for the information disadvantage for occasional litigants. Information service on the Internet can support courts' role of ensuring fair process. Providing incidental court users with adequate information can help them to achieve better justice.

The justiciable problems that normally come to court tend to be serious and difficult to resolve. Most people who come to court have sought and received some kind of advice beforehand. Access to information increases litigants' chances of a just, fair court decision (Chapter 4.1). For taking their case to court, litigants need information on how to resolve problems, on rights and duties, and on taking a case to court. One-shotters, those who use the courts only occasionally, have a knowledge and information disadvantage compared with those who routinely use the courts. If a dispute needs to come to court, information can reduce the disadvantage one-shotters have in dealing court and with legal issues. In order to better appreciate the Internet's potential as a source of such information, case studies were done on finding and using relevant information.

Finding and using information

The case studies in Chapter 4.3 looked at government and advisory web sites in the United Kingdom and the Netherlands for information on getting a divorce. They tested two aspects: the readability and adequacy of the information. Does the web page tell the reader what to do, and can the reader be confident that the desired result will be achieved? The majority of the web sites did not pass the effectiveness tests on all counts. Some of the information on the sites presented is not adequate because the texts are too difficult for the audience and/or they do not provide sufficiently practical information. As there appears to be a movement toward broadening the scope for self-representation, it is prudent to be prepared for a growing need for direct access to information. Some points of attention:

- Effective information service requires understanding recipients' problems, their information needs and their competences in acting on information (Chapter 4.2). Inability to act on information inhibiting people's participation in court processes may result in problems remaining unresolved. Consequently, people with low levels of competence are likely to need some help in resolving justiciable problems, so there always needs to be backup human help (Chapter 4.3).
- Differences in practice, like compulsory legal representation, affect what information is required. They also affect courts' attitudes to information services. Instead of relying routinely on lawyers and bailiffs, they may need to become more proactive. Information coordination with other information sources, like bailiffs and legal aid organizations, will ensure better consistency of the information provided.
- To be effective, information should be offered on more than one channel by referring to web site information in correspondence with the parties.

There has also been a shift towards generating routines and policies or guidelines for judicial decision making. This type of information can serve as a general guideline for resolving disputes as well. In order to safeguard the quality of the information, it is necessary that it is generated and disseminated by the courts themselves. Collecting knowledge from court decisions and practices for the purpose of developing routines and policies constitutes a major change and a new activity for an organization geared to processing individual cases.

Providing information on the web will also give rise to new requirements for the court governance: central management will be needed to make the information service effective and to help unify some court practices. A centralized information service requires changes in decision rights, making individual courts lose some of their autonomy. This may well constitute a major change for some court systems.

Public trust and transparency
The Internet also provides judiciaries and courts with a means to communicate with the general public. This form of communication sup-

ports both the role of courts as setters of norms as well as the courts' public image.

The level of confidence people have in the legal system affects whether they feel inclined to use the courts (Chapter 4.3). The issue of public trust becomes even more urgent where users complain about corruption in the judiciary (Chapter 5.1).

At this point, the issues of access and corruption are interrelated. By publishing decisions, information about their processes and information people need for coming to court and preparing a case, judiciaries can actively contribute to improving access to justice and reducing corruption. Judiciaries have a certain monopoly on deciding disputes. Controlling corruption involves balancing that monopoly with accountability (Chapter 5.1). Publishing decisions and information about processes, and providing court users with information about bringing cases to court are tools for reducing discretion, and support impartial processing and decision making.

3 Work flow management and two-way communication

The technologies in this group include work flow management and two-way communication. Implementation of these technologies in courts is largely still experimental. Therefore, this section mainly looks toward the future, but with a few examples pointing the way.

Two-way interaction moves beyond one-sided information "push" (e-government, stage 1) and processing downloadable forms on paper (stage 2). It includes advanced stages of Internet interactivity (Chapter 2.1). For digital access to courts, stage 3 involves electronically receiving and processing electronic forms. This stage has not been reached by many courts yet. Beyond this step, there is stage 4, full electronic transactions: case handling, decision and delivery. These two stages logically belong in the group with the work flow management systems needed to process the electronic information received.

Digital court access

Two-way communication comes in different forms. Digital court access, in the sense of two-way communication, e-filing and full electronic case processing, is still rare. Demand for digital court access will increase as there is more demand for self-representation (Chapter 4.3).

Digital access is not necessarily full online dispute resolution. For judiciaries wanting to expand their services for self-representing litigants, it is quite possible to provide simple forms of access without having a sophisticated system for receiving electronic information directly. Digital access can be increased in stages. It can be developed in small steps, following the advice on IT development in Chapter 2.2. The first step is one-sided information service, discussed extensively in Part 4. The second step is to provide downloadable forms that can be sent back to the court in paper form (Chapter 4.3). The third step, not taken by many courts just yet, is to offer two-way interaction consisting of submitting forms electronically. The step to come next would be that of a full transaction: case handling, decision and delivery.

The steps beyond submission of paper forms are no longer just networking technology as defined in Chapter 2.1. They logically belong in the group with work flow management technology because they require internal electronic case handling processes.

What are the enterprise technology functionalities going to bring?

When posing this question, it is good to keep in mind that, over time, online transactions (stage 4) will become the norm. The public will come to expect electronic services from all government organizations. Judiciaries will need to gear their strategies to moving in the direction of stage 4 IT. Internally, the stage 4 IT will, with work flow management, primarily bring improved process control. Processes can be redesigned and standardized much more easily, and reports on events and activities are much more readily available. Potentially, this improves legal consistency. It can also facilitate balancing caseloads and transparency on case disposition.

Looking at these impacts in terms of the court user complaints, what will be their benefit? Possibly, delays will be reduced with improved process control and incoming electronic information. Improved process control may also reduce incentives for corruption. More digital access to courts may well constitute improved access to justice.

However, this does not mean that all cases can be covered exclusively and fully through an electronic exchange of information, in documents or otherwise. Video communication is far from a regular process in most judiciaries, even the more advanced ones. Early intervention, a proven way to reduce complexity in cases, in most cases still implies face-to-face contact.

What do the enterprise technology functionalities require?

Enterprise technologies affect court work processes more profoundly than either functional or network technologies. At the present state of court IT, work flow functionality appears to be a threshold for judiciaries (Chapters 2.1 and 2.2).

Major shifts in the way courts and judiciaries usually work are required if they choose to use this functionality. Full electronic processing requires complete control over the process of receiving and processing information online. Developing full online proceedings, where effort is centered on translating all the complexity of the paper based procedures into the electronic ones, has been "fraught with difficulty and delays. Never-ending piloting and mounting costs seem to characterize this approach" (Chapter 2.1). In Chapter 2.2., there is some experience on ways to avoid this quagmire.

The first requirement is a strategy that lays out the approach, informed by the understanding of how information about court processes and information in individual cases both drive court processes. The overall goal of the strategy should be to safeguard, and where necessary increase, chances of just, fair judicial decisions. It should at least address the following issues:

- How the court organization will be involved, based on the understanding that IT development and implementation is a process that involves the court organization, how information plays a role in it, and IT expertise.
- The development approach to manage the risks of complexity. The approach should advocate incremental development: starting with either a simple process or a piloting approach, and move forward in small steps, re-using experience from the previous steps. It should also cover simplifying existing processes. The case matrix (Chapter 3.2) can be a helpful tool to identify processes and starting points for simplification, for example the title group with predictable outcomes for simplicity and a large enough proportion of the total caseload to justify an investment.
- The required degree of work process standardization and how to determine it. Total work process standardization may be suitable for hierarchical, bureaucratic processes. It may also be suitable for cases with predictable outcomes, like the ones in groups 1 and 2 of the matrix (Chapter 3.3). Ultimately, the judicial court processes in groups 3 and 4 need to be open-ended because the outcomes can go different ways. Hence, total process control may well be undesirable. Different processes may have different needs for process control.
- An acceptable level of effort and resources. The conventional wisdom is that automating 80 percent of a process can be done at 20 percent of the cost. Here, keeping development simple involves using common, proven technology. The strategy should specify what level should be enough.
- How other court systems' experience will be tapped. Courts and court systems that have already introduced more advanced forms of technology have experience to share.
- Organizational requirements. Much of the information technology identified, in order to be successful, involves or requires standardization of court practices or policy formation with regard to judicial decision making. These activities require active, coordinated work

on the part of courts and judiciaries. These changes also need increased coordination and more centralized management over the individual courts, in order to work well. Therefore, the strategy should include any new organizational requirements. Centralization can concentrate expertise, but it will also bring changes in decision rights. Individual courts may experience this development as a loss of autonomy.

4 What has changed?

Looking back, we can say that most courts have used IT to support their paper processes. Using technology for radical innovation in courts is rare. The technological revolution happens mainly incrementally. Both MCOL and Austria's ERV started small, and have expanded their functionality to other processes and other user groups step by step.

This section looks back. Has IT support improved the way courts and judiciaries administer justice by improving timeliness, access and fairness as in consistency and integrity? This question can be answered in the affirmative.

Timeliness. Disposition time for ordinary civil cases in the Dutch courts went from 608 days in 1996 to 420 days in 2007. This change was brought about by all kinds of interventions: small claims courts' competence was raised to include larger claims, there is more early intervention, and targeted backlog reduction. Those interventions were motivated by information from the case registration systems. There has been development toward standards for disposition times, made possible by the data from the case registration systems. When the information from those data is used with the intention to affect culture and practice, better timeliness is ensured. In short: those who want to, can do it.

Access. On the Internet, legal information institutes like Austlii and Bailii, Dutch Rechtspraak.nl and the European Court of Human Rights' HUDOC database make decisions available free of charge. Public jurisprudence databases have impacted the justice discourse considerably. It has made reporting more accurate, it has increased transparency in decisions, and it has enhanced the courts' shadow function. Reporting in the press has become much more accurate now that decisions can be quoted directly from the source. The courts' shadow function, guarding and affirming norms, has expanded as a consequence. Court decisions, when they need to face this public scrutiny, need to become more transparent. An example is the Promis project in the Netherlands. Court decisions had been written mainly for lawyers and the higher courts; they now need to be understandable for a broader audience. Public information service on going to court is increasing. This means more than providing laws and case law. To be acted on, laws and jurisprudence require context and experience. Court information service requires centralized services to ensure consistency of information.

Consistency. Public scrutiny has also engendered increasing criticism of court decisions. The criticism focuses partly on equal justice, or consistent administration of justice. For judges, jurisprudence databases are very important because they can help prevent inconsistent decisions. Word processing functionalities also have possibilities for increasing consistency, such as standard texts and intelligent merges. There is increased use of guidelines, something that is considered to be very important by the courts. I think that under the influence of the availability of so much information, developing guidelines for consistent decisions has become a more accepted activity. It is still too early to tell whether consistency itself has increased.

Integrity. Evidently, public scrutiny is a factor affecting the judiciary's integrity. The Internet as a medium for communicating to the public is used by judiciaries to explain how they protect and promote their own integrity. Reporting on the way complaints were handled, publishing the ethics code, asset declarations and the judges' outside activities can all help to increase public trust. This means that courts will have to live up to their own standards, and public scrutiny will ensure that they do.

Governance. In many European judiciaries, the governance structure has been changed radically in the past ten years where judiciaries were given governance bodies separate from the Ministries of Justice. The task of these new bodies largely is to administer courts more centrally, particularly with regard to budgeting. I believe these changes were also initiated as a consequence of two developments:

- Increased need for centralized structures to manage the IT
- Increased public scrutiny of the judiciary, bringing higher political risks for ministers of justice.

5 How is IT changing the administration of justice?

This section looks forward. It attempts to chart some of the developments that can be expected based on what we now know about IT and judicial reform. It looks at the way developments in IT will change the way information is used in the processes involved in administering justice and how this will change the way justice is administered. This will also indicate some directions for further research.

As observed at the beginning of this study, the discourse about IT tends to be optimistic and not well founded in empirics. Claims that IT will improve things are taken as a certainty, and not as mere claims. The discussion below attempts to look forward without such speculative rhetoric. Therefore, readers who have become accustomed to the usual upbeat tone of the IT debate may be a little disappointed by the limited scope of the discussion.

Standardization

Online transactions will eventually become the norm in government services. An early example of online transactions is the United Kingdom's Money Claim On Line (MCOL, Chapter 3.3). Online transactions, together with public information on court decisions on the Internet, will be a catalyst for more standardized, predictable outcomes. They will move disputes with predictable outcomes away from the courts. This trend is already discernible.

Online transactions require increasing process control. This process control will be developed incrementally. The development process will also be a catalyst for more standardized, predictable outcomes. Increased process control goes together with a tendency towards standardization.

Public availability of information on the Internet will strengthen this tendency toward standardization. It reinforces the demand for consistency. In the Dutch judiciary, tendencies are discernible confirming that judges are ready to meet this demand with guidelines for frequently occurring case situations. This trend toward standardization is inspired by increased transparency and concomitant public scrutiny as well. Consistency and predictability are considered very important. Public debate in judicial decisions is increasingly met with the development of guidelines. There will be more and more guidelines for judicial decisions in specific categories, limiting judicial discretion. Reasoning in decisions increasingly serves to justify deviation from the guidelines.

As the guidelines for certain case categories become clear, disputes will lose their unpredictability. A predictable next step might be that a court decision will be eliminated from the process. This has already happened in many European jurisdictions with regard to traffic offenses. Traffic offenses are sanctioned by the administration and those decisions are reviewed by a court at the request of the sanctioned party. It has also happened in some countries, where the civil administration handles divorces not involving under age children. In this model, courts will only review decisions by the administration or by other decision making bodies. The judicial role in administrative, criminal and civil justice will increasingly be to review other bodies' decisions at the request of an interested party.

Disintermediation

Online transactions may also reduce the role of intermediaries. In some fields, they have already virtually disappeared. This phenomenon is known as disintermediation. This trend is strengthened by changes in the legal field. The legal profession, the Bar, is increasingly losing its monopoly on representing parties in court. Legal aid for court representation is being increasingly restricted.

In conventional thinking, subsidized legal aid and access to justice are easily associated because of the cost aspect of legal advice and assistance. In this view, the impediment to justice is the high cost of legal advice and assistance. In this perspective, increasing access to justice is largely understood as intervening in the market for legal assistance by subsidizing legal aid. As more people turn to the Internet for information on resolving justiciable problems, publicly funded web information services like Citizens' Advice Bureaus or Legal Kiosks may increase access to justice by offering information, advice and assistance free of charge. Such agencies should be part of a government's access to justice strategy. Such services, provided they are effective, will extend access to justice to larger groups of the population. Effectiveness requires a judicious combination of legal and experience information. They will also require human backup in case of need, since there will always still be people who need assistance.

Disintermediation also means courts will have to deal more directly with non-professional court users. Courts providing their own information on their own web sites on how to bring in cases eliminate, to a certain extent, the need for specialized expertise in this respect. Digital court access can streamline interaction with self-representing court users. However, assistance in human form will still be necessary for some types of cases and for people who cannot do without assistance. This means the need for staff providing this type of support in court will increase.

Integrity and independence

Will all this public information harm the independence of courts? Schmidt has argued that information, in the hands of the executive, could be a threat to judicial independence (Schmidt p. 460). The line of reasoning is that the executive, holding the purse strings, can then determine what judges do, and what they should be doing. Consequently, judiciaries and individual judges will be rendered less free to hand down impartial decisions. Transparency, in this view, allows more control over the judiciary. I have found no empirical evidence that this is the case. This study has learned how increased scrutiny offsets the risks of judicial monopoly and increased transparency limits discretion, and thereby prevents opportunities for corruption. Public information about the way the courts are run, by reporting, based on court case statistics, is a way to offset the judicial monopoly by accounting for the way public resources are used. Moreover, a process whereby the budget is awarded by parliament based on plans and reports justified by statistics is more transparent and less of a threat to the judiciary's institutional independence than a process without such a factual basis. Hence, such transparency supports judicial independence.

Knowledge sharing

This study's approach has obscured the view on some very important impacts of IT: those on sharing knowledge and information among professionals such as judges and lawyers. I consider this unfortunate because knowledge sharing in a very broad sense is critical for the quality of administering justice. From the Dutch user surveys, we know court users value judicial expertise highly. In the Netherlands judiciary, the extent to which knowledge is acquired, shared and kept up to date is part of the quality measuring framework. Judiciaries should be knowledge-based professional organizations.

The way networking technologies are used in this knowledge sharing will be a useful field for study. It will help us to understand how IT systems may support developing judicial expertise, from email, to blogging, to developing expert guidance systems.

What is in it for developing countries?

Does this study hold a specific message for developing countries? Yes and no. On the one hand, the IT developments are now the same the world over: office automation and the Internet are global influences. What is also the same is judiciaries' inexperience with implementing IT for their processes. The mechanisms described in this study, how information works to reduce delay (Part 3), increase access (Part 4) and reduce corruption (Part 5), are the same everywhere. On the other hand, differences in levels of development relate to the political context and have consequences for institutional functioning and available resources (Chapter 5.3). They need to be assessed carefully to determine starting points for judicial reform, and how to use IT to support them. However, this advice for context specific programming applies everywhere.

What does it all mean for judiciaries?

Ultimately, the core business of courts everywhere is in deciding matters where no one knows the right outcome in advance. This involves unpredictability and a certain degree of discretion. There is no reason to assume the use of IT will change it. Both tendencies toward simplification will have for an effect that cases that still need to come to court will be more complicated in nature. There will be relatively more cases that are the core of judicial business.

The increase in public information service means judiciaries have an opportunity to exercise their shadow function more actively. It will also bring more public criticism. Increased exposure and transparency in individual court cases may well increase the need for courtroom technology.

In view of all these changes, judiciaries will need to adjust their structures and develop more expertise in order to leverage IT for improving the administration of justice.

Chapter 6.2 New Research

This is the last chapter of the study. It suggests some topics for further research. After the summary of what we know from this study in the previous chapter, this final chapter proposes some areas where more research might deepen and broaden this study's findings.

Some topics had to be excluded from the study's scope for practical reasons. For the same practical reasons, the scope of treatment of each of the three issues, delay, access and corruption, had to be limited as well. Each of them deserves much more study. Other subjects emerged as noteworthy in the course of the study. Knowledge about IT support for judicial reform would benefit from studying the fields of learning from experience with court IT, and the role of information in judicial integrity and in judicial processes. In all instances, empirical study and the development of conceptual frameworks should go together.

For each topic, there is a brief exposé on the problem and how new research can contribute to its resolution.

1 Learning from experience

Judiciaries can learn from each other when it comes to using IT. For some, moving to increased digital access presents problems, both strategic and more practical ones. Learning from other judiciaries and from other organizations' experience will help to build understanding on how IT can improve judiciary performance. This learning would require organizational frameworks for information exchange, such as wikis, web sites, publications, conferences and platforms. In order to facilitate this learning, two subjects urgently need more study: a conceptual framework for court IT, and implementation and experimentation experience.

A meaningful conceptual framework

Learning would also benefit from a conceptual framework for court IT. This framework should serve the purpose of diagnostics and also for comparing of implementation levels and systems.

What information on IT in courts is available? There are collections of country reports by IRSIG (Fabri 2001 and 2003) and there is the CEPEJ database. There are ad hoc reports from other judiciaries on the state of IT. The IRSIG reports offer a lot of interesting information, but comparing the information and putting it into a wider context is difficult. The CEPEJ reports' main weakness is that the IT functionality reported by the COE member countries is not very clear. This makes categorization difficult. The frameworks used so far have not been adequate.

A conceptual framework should support understanding by facilitating categorization that is capable of enabling statements of cause and effect. Research, building on Chapter 2.1 and on the other findings of this study, to build a conceptual framework can reduce this weakness; it will also help to draw lessons from experience as discussed in the next research proposal.

Experimentation and domestication, implementation experience

The experience is that IT applications become fully useful only after considerable experimentation by users. Here is where the real effects of IT on the quality of judicial performance become visible.

This study found that implementation is an underestimated issue. Implementation can be problematic, for lack of understanding how judiciaries and courts actually work or because of underestimating the implementation requirements. Lack of experience can be an underlying cause of both. Empirical and comparative research on implementation could help to fill this information gap, and avoid pitfalls. Mapping the experimentation that courts are doing in their daily practice would be an important source of information for the courts and IT leadership that should inform their IT policies.

The results of such research will help in improving judicial performance with a better understanding of the workings of IT in judicial processes.

2 The roles of information in judicial integrity

Empirical research into corruption in judiciaries is extremely scarce. The findings in this study have produced some insights, but they cover only a small part of what is relevant. From the findings on judicial and court corruption in this study, it seems that a more elaborate conceptual framework could aid more targeted empirical research. This empirical research, in turn, would inform a more accurate conceptual framework, including a repertoire of remedies.

3 The role of information in judicial processes

How information works in judicial processes was one of the themes of this study. Empirical study into those processes is extremely scarce. This study's scope was largely limited to relatively simple civil procedures. The same approach could be applied to the other fields of law in order to identify the needs for IT in those fields. Moreover, more complex civil procedures should be studied to uncover their information needs.

Information processes in criminal law

The topic of information in the criminal justice sector was eliminated from this study because it deserved more attention than I could have given it. It needs much more study. The consensus is that an effective criminal justice information chain improves security in society. The criminal law chain has its own dynamic when it comes to information. Hence, it also has its own IT issues. Information primarily comes to the courts from one source: the prosecution, who get their information from the police. Increasingly, information in police investigations is electronic: surveillance camera and wire tapping recordings, and mobile phone records. In the Dutch file-based civil law system, the courts get descriptions of the content of this information on paper, or in a word processing format. However, developments are moving in the direction of much more immediate fact-finding in hearings under the influence of ECHR jurisprudence. There are issues of quality of information, and of reliable evidence decisions. There is the question of equal access to information for all the parties. Consistent sanctioning is also an issue.

All these problems make IT in this chain an important issue. Experience with developing IT systems for the criminal justice chain is diverse. The Ontario project and the HBS project are examples of early failure (Chapter 2.2). In the Netherlands, the development of a new system for both the prosecution and the judiciary has already taken more than five years. Empirical study of such development experiences is a necessity. Experience with courtroom technologies becomes more relevant. For more consistency in sanctioning, database technology could support generating information on sanctioning trends discussed below.

Information processes in administrative law

Information in the administrative law chain had to be excluded from this study because administrative law is not my field of expertise. It generally has one-shotters as the initiators and repeat players on the responding side. It is a very diverse field. Institutional arrangements differ from one legal system to the next. In contrast to the criminal justice chain, there are multiple repeat players. The repeat players will mostly have internal electronic work processes and files. They will also have policies. There is room for keeping cases out of court here too if the repeat players take court decisions into account in their policies.

Research into these processes can help in the understanding how information technology can help to improve judicial performance.

How to generate trends in judicial decisions

Trends in judicial decision making will become more prominent. The Internet opens up new possibilities for the judiciary's shadow function. In keeping cases out of court, and in preparing for one's case in court, there is a need for information on how judges generally approach issues. Increased demand for judicial consistency also requires information on trends. We see policy formation on the rise in alimony, labor compensation, and criminal sanctioning. For policy formation, too, ideally information on trends is needed. Information on trends is fundamentally different from traditional jurisprudence or case law. It is a quantitative aggregation of the largest possible number of cases of a certain type. How to generate this from all those thousands of decisions is an interesting technological challenge.

Information on trends can help the general public and justice seekers and those advising and assisting them in making choices that are more informed. They can help judiciaries and individual judges form policies, thereby increasing consistency in their decisions.

Information in complex civil justice processes

If judiciaries want to make better use of IT for their core processes in group 4, complex civil cases, more study of those processes is needed. The mass compensation claims in banking cases present themselves as an interesting case for study. The lawyers representing the clients in those cases are using technology to manage the large numbers of cases. A study into how the courts dealing with those cases have come to use information technology to manage the case flow and the information in each case should provide some answers regarding the development of electronic case processing toward full online dispute resolution.

Note

1 The only apparent exception is the article by Buscaglia and Ulen, which in fact only found faster processing time in the decision writing phase when word processing was used.

Samenvatting in het Nederlands

Vraagstelling en methodologie (deel 1)

Deze studie beoogt een bijdrage te leveren aan kennis omtrent de rol van informatietechnologie bij het verbeteren van rechtspraak. Begrip van de rol van informatietechnologie in rechtspraakprocessen is noodzakelijk voor effectieve verbetering met IT. Daartoe wordt onderzocht op welke wijzen IT al heeft bijgedragen aan zulke verbeteringen, en wat op basis daarvan nog te verwachten valt.

Na een inventarisatie van de stand van IT in de rechtspraak en de meest voorkomende problemen met invoering (deel 2) zijn de effecten van informatietechnologie op de drie meest voorkomende klachten over rechtspraak, traagheid, toegang en corruptie, voorwerp van onderzoek: de behandeling van zaken (deel 3), interactie met gebruikers van gerechten (deel 4) en integriteitsbewaking (deel 5). Voor elk van deze onderwerpen wordt de bestaande kennis geinventariseerd, de rol van informatie wordt bestudeerd aan de hand van voorbeelden uit de praktijk, en tenslotte worden conclusies getrokken omtrent de rol van IT bij de oplossing van de klacht. De bronnen, grotendeels openbaar, zijn heel gevarieerd: vergelijkende indices, empirische studies en voorbeelden van IT-gebruik in de praktijk van de gerechten.

Deel 2: Informatietechnologie

Deel 2 onderzocht (1) welke IT in gebruik is in de gerechten en (2) wat de belangrijkste knelpunten zijn bij ontwikkeling en invoering van IT in organisaties die zich met rechtspraak bezighouden.

Hoofstuk 2.1 inventariseerde welke technologie in gebruik is in verschillende landen, en stelt vast wat knelpunten zijn bij de invoering van IT, aan de hand van inventarisatieonderzoeken in West-Europa en de Verenigde Staten.

De meest algemeen ingevoerde technologieën ondersteunen de papieren processen: tekstverwerking en zaaksregistratie ter vervanging van de rolkaarten. Netwerktechnolgie, indien aanwezig, wordt vooral voor interne, informele doelen gebruikt. Externe electronische communicatie is het terrein waar de voorlopers nieuwe toepassingen aan het ontwikkelen zijn. Werkstroombesturing en andere systemen voor organisatiebesturing lijken in die ontwikkeling niet veel aandacht te krijgen. Tien jaar geleden stond bij de systeemontwikkeling de werkstroomtechnologie op de voorgrond, en de studie van CEPEJ laat zien dat deze nog steeds geen gemeengoed is geworden in de meeste gerechten. Technologie voor gebruik in de rechtszaal krijgt in Europa, in tegenstelling tot de Verenigde Staten, weinig aandacht.

De inventarisatie zegt ook iets over ontwikkelaanpak. Pogingen om de complexiteit van gerechtelijke processen volledig te vertalen in IT lijken duur, moeizaam en uiteindelijk zonder succes te zijn. Succesvoller waren incrementele ontwikkeling van één eenvoudige procedure, of van een complexere procedure nadat die eerst was vereenvoudigd. De applicatie wordt vervolgens stap voor stap opengesteld voor andere terreinen, of voor nieuwe gebruikersgroepen.

Organisaties kunnen verschillende, en zelfs tegengestelde behoeften aan IT hebben. Wie vooral behoefte heeft aan een systeem dat zorgt voor verantwoording in de hiërarchie wil een strak proces zonder uitzonderingen. De rechtspraak heeft vooral behoefte aan een systeem dat helpt met experimenteren en met procedures die zich aanpassen aan de aard van het geschil. Voor effectieve implementatie is het noodzakelijk om voor die behoeften, die voortkomen uit de rol van informatie in de processen van de organisatie, te begrijpen, een bijpassende strategie te ontwikkelen en de behoeften van de organisatie te managen.

Hoofdstuk 2.2 onderzocht veel voorkomende problemen bij het ontwikkelen en invoeren van IT. Het materiaal werd gevonden in overzichten van evaluatieonderzoeken van projecten en inventarisaties van veel voorkomende problemen bij ontwikkeling en invoering van IT. De slotsom is dat rechtspraakorganisaties hun denken en hun organisatie mogelijk flink moeten veranderen om de mogelijkheden van IT beter te gebruiken.

- De leiding van de rechtspraak en de IT-functie moeten allebei begrijpen hoe informatie werkt in hun gerechten en wat de implicaties van IT kunnen zijn. Dit vereist training en onderzoek. Veranderingen in de besluitvormingsstructuur kunnen nodig zijn om de vorming van stratege en beleid, en het prioriteren van budgetten op basis daarvan mogelijk te maken.
- Herontwerp van processen, waar nodig, vereist mensen die kennis van rechtspraakprocessen combineren met IT-kennis, zodat IT-ontwikkeling en processen in samenhang kunnen worden verbeterd. Bovendien is IT-staf nodig die de gerechtelijke processen begrijpt.
- Experimenteren met het vertalen van de behoeften van rechtspraak in termen van IT-applicaties moet worden geinstitutionaliseerd. De

resultaten van dit soort experimenten zijn belangrijk voor innovatie. Op deze manier kan de IT-functie leren van de gebruikers. Gerechten kunnen ook leren van de ervaringen van andere rechtssystemen en andere organisaties.

Deel 2 concludeert dat het belangrijkste tekort wordt gevormd door een gebrek aan strategische visie op rechtspraakprocessen, gevormd door kennis en begrip van de rol van informatie in gerechten. De volgende drie delen van de studie hebben tot doel om dat begrip te vergroten. Ze onderzoeken de rol van informatie in de interne processen (deel 3), in externe communicatie (deel 4) en in het bewaken van integriteit (deel 5).

Deel 3: Traagheid

Deel 3 onderzocht IT als middel tegen traagheid, door te kijken naar de interne processen van de rechtspraak. Hoofdstuk 3.1 is een eerste verkenning van de mogelijkheden van IT om doorlooptijden te verkorten. Database technologie voor het registreren en managen van zaken is de eerste mogelijkheid die zich aandient. Deze kan

- Inzicht bieden in de manier waarop zaken gedaan worden
- Helpen bij het ontwikkelen van normen zoals de Trial Court Performance Standards
- Effectiviteit meten van interventies om doorlooptijden te verkorten.

Hoofdstuk 3.2 onderzocht, aan de hand van de civiele rechtspraak in Nederland, het behandelen van zaken als een vorm van informatieverwerking. De rol van de rechter blijkt een bepalende factor te zijn voor de manier waarop informatie wordt verwerkt, en voor de behoefte aan IT die daar bij past.

- *Titelverschaffing* (rol 1) bij onweersproken vorderingen vereist geen extra informatie gedurende het proces, en evenmin samenwerking tussen partijen om een oplossing te bereiken
- De *notariële* rol (rol 2), marginale toetsing van door partijen tot stand gebrachte arrangementen, meestal in familiezaken, vereist doorgaans geen nieuwe informatie gedurende het proces, maar wel samenwerking tussen partijen voor een optimaal resultaat
- De *schikkings*rol (rol 3) heeft zowel nieuwe informatie als samenwerking tussen partijen gedurende het proces nodig
- De rol van de *rechterlijke beslissing* (rol 4) heeft doorgaans wel nieuwe informatie nodig, maar samenwerking tussen partijen is voor het eindresultaat niet vereist.

Statistische analyse van de Nederlandse civiele rechtspraak leert dat de titelverschaffing en de notariële rol, waar eigenlijk nauwelijks geschillen worden beslecht, het grootste deel van de case load van de eerste aanleg zijn. De schikkingsrol en die van de rechterlijke beslissing vormen nauwelijks 20% van de totale case load, terwijl ze wel het rechterswerk bij uitstek zijn.

Hoofdstuk 3.3 groepeert de Nederlandse civiele zaken per rol, bestudeert voor elke groep van zaken de informatieverwerkingsprocessen in de civiele rechtspraak meer in de diepte, en trekt conclusies over de behoefte aan IT om traagheid te bestrijden:

- Voor alle groepen is electronische aanlevering van gegevens een manier om de afhandeling van zaken te bespoedigen omdat dan gegevens niet opnieuw handmatig hoeven te worden ingevoerd. Hoe dat kan gebeuren is mede afhankelijk van procedureregels.
- Voor groep 1, titelverschaffing, is er behoefte aan intern procesmanagement om zaken zoveel mogelijk af te handelen zonder menselijke interventie. Dat vereist het ontwikkelen van routines en beleid om de afhandeling van zaken te standaardiseren en te vereenvoudigen.
- Voor groep 2, de notariële rol, kan bovendien informatie via het Internet, informatie over het tot stand brengen van regelingen en het gebruik van on line formulieren partijen helpen om een goed voorstel aan de rechter voor te leggen. Dit vereist de organisatie en de attitude om informatie te verstrekken.
- Dit laatste geldt ook weer voor groep 3, de schikkingsrol. In deze groep blijkt ook een behoefte aan informatie om geschillen buiten de rechter om te regelen. Functionaliteit voor het ondersteunen van onderhandelen, zoals email of speciale software, kan voor deze groep ook interessant zijn.
- Voor groep 4, de rechterlijke beslissing, is vooral hulp nodig bij het hanteren van complexe informatie. Electronische dossiers zijn daarvoor een mogelijkheid. Hier blijkt ook behoefte aan kennismanagement, en systemen die dat kunnen ondersteunen.

De informatieverstrekking via het internet, vooral van belang voor de groepen 2 en 3, is het onderwerp van deel 4. De processen in groep 4 kunnen zeer complex zijn. Ze verdienen een meer diepgaande studie.

Deel 4: Toegang

Het hoofdonderwerp van deel 4 is, hoe gerechten de toegang tot het recht kunnen verbeteren met vormen van IT. Hoofdstuk 4.1 bespreekt de betekenis van het idee van toegang tot het recht voor rechtspraakhervorming in ruime zin. Het onderzoekt factoren die de toegang tot het recht belemmeren. De conclusie van hoofdstuk 4.1 is dat toegang tot juridische informatie een belangrijk terrein voor nader onderzoek is. In de eerste plaats omdat toegang tot informatie de eerlijkheid in de rechtspleging kan vergroten: door mensen, wanneer ze problemen hebben met een potentieel juridische oplossing, te voorzien van informatie die ze helpt om adequater op te treden. Informatie kan tot op zekere hoogte de achterstand van one-shotters bij het procederen compenseren, en daarmee hun kansen op een eerlijke beslissiing verhogen. In de tweede plaats kan het internet een kanaal voor juridische informatie zijn, maar de meeste rechtspraakorganisaties hebben nog maar weinig ervaring met het verstrekken van zulke informatie aan het publiek.

Hoofdstuk 4.2 onderzocht, welke informatiebehoeften mensen met *"justiciable problems"*, ernstige problemen met een potentieel juridische oplossing, hebben. Die behoeften worden, zo blijkt, vooral bepaald door de aard van het probleem. De mensen losten de meeste van hun problemen zelf op, soms met behulp van informatie van elders, soms met advies of bijstand. Die hulp wordt geboden door verschillende organisaties, maar vooral gespecialiseerde organisaties (voor consumenten, huiseigenaren) en verstrekkers van rechtshulp en alternatieve geschillenbeslechting. De verschillende informatiebehoeften kunnen als volgt worden onderscheiden:

- Informatie om het probleem op te lossen
- Informatie over regels en regelingen
- Hoe kan een probleem worden opgelost
- Rechten en verplichtingen
- Hoe kan/moet een zaak voor de rechter gebracht worden.

Hoofdstuk 4.3 onderzocht de implicaties van die bevindingen voor de rol van gerechten in het verbeteren van de toegang tot het recht met behulp van informatie op het internet en electronische toegang tot de rechter. Aan de hand van onderzoek naar een aantal web sites (bijlage A) met informatie over hoe te handelen bij echtscheiding, worden conclusies getrokken over wat er nodig is om die rol effectief te vervullen. Er lopen twee rode draden door dit thema: geschillen bij de rechter weg houden en de gang naar de rechter te voorkomen, en geschillen voor de rechter brengen.

Informatie om de gang naar de rechter te voorkomen

Partijen in een geschil kunnen, met vuistregels over hoe de rechter oordeelt, hun geschillen makkelijker regelen en ze zo bij de rechter weghouden. Dit is een impliciete veronderstelling bij juridische informatie op het internet. Die informatie kan het regelen van geschillen "in de schaduw van het recht" bevorderen. De meeste van dit soort geschilbeslechting wordt gedaan met de steun van juridische of gespecialiseerde organisaties. Informatie over de manier waarop rechters in het algemeen bepaalde problemen benaderen kan informele oplossing van deze geschillen helpen. Dit vereist dat informatie over zulke benaderingen beschikbaar komt. Voor sommige onderwerpen bestaat er binnen de rechtspraak beleid in de vorm van richtlijnen of orientatiepunten, of zelfs beslissingondersteunende systemen. Om het regelen van geschillen te bevorderen moeten deze richtlijnen en systemen openbaar toegankelijk zijn.

Informatie om geschillen voor de rechter te brengen

Moet een geschil toch voor de rechter komen, dan kan informatie de achterstand van "*one-shotters*", mensen die maar een enkele keer procederen, tot op zekere hoogte compenseren. Toegang tot informatie voor individuele procespartijen zonder procesvertegenwoordiging kan hun kans op een eerlijke beslissing vergroten. Partijen hebben informatie nodig over het brengen van een zaak voor de rechter. Die informatie moet voor de ontvanger begrijpelijk en eenvoudig toegankelijk zijn. Het gebruik van verschillende informatiekanalen naast elkaar, zoals een brief die verwijst naar informatie op een website, kan aan die informatiebehoefte tegemoetkomen. Daarnaast gaan meer interactieve vormen van netwerktechnologie in toenemende mate toegang tot de rechter bieden. Volledig electronisch case management en electronische dossiers zijn daarvoor niet per se nodig. Het verdient aanbeveling de electronische toegang tot de rechter incrementeel te ontwikkelen. Voor een effectieve informatieverschaffing vereisen de hier besproken diensten dat een rechtssysteem een centrale voorziening heeft, en het vereist een proactieve, vraag-gestuurde opstelling.

Vertrouwen in de rechter

Tenslotte blijkt het vertrouwen in de rechtspraak een belangrijke factor te zijn voor toegang tot het recht. De rechtspraak kan op dit terrein actief de toegang tot het recht verbeteren door te zorgen voor juiste informatie over de processen. Het vertrouwen in de rechter wordt een urgenter probleem wanneer gebruikers van gerechten klagen over corruptie. Deel 5 gaat over corruptie, en over de vraag hoe IT kan bijdragen aan het verminderen van corruptie.

Deel 5: Corruptie

Deel 5 onderzocht verminderen van corruptie en verbeteren van onpartijdigheid en integriteit in gerechten met behulp van IT. Hoofdstuk 5.1 inventariseert bestaande theoretische inzichten in corruptie en het bespreekt het specifieke kader voor corruptie in de rechtspraak. Dat omvat gedrag van rechters of ondersteuning dat niet passend is omdat het

– voor eigen gewin – afwijkt van de gedragsregels die voortvloeien uit de internationale conventies inzake rechterlijke onpartijdigheid. Corruptie is primair een inbreuk op de norm van onpartijdigheid. De corruptie kan zich voordoen wanneer rechters:

- Een beslissingsmonopolie,
- Ruime beslissingsbevoegdheid en/of
- Een beperkte verantwoordingsplicht hebben, zodat de kans op ontdekking gering is.

Een kleine pakkans wijst op gebrekkig functioneren van de rechterlijke organisatie. Hoe zwakker de organisatie, hoe groter de kans op corruptie. Deze zwakte houdt verband met het ontwikkelingspeil van een land en de vorm die de corruptie aanneemt (het corruptiesyndroom). Wat een goed startpunt is voor corruptiebestrijding hangt van deze factoren af. Het startpunt moet dus per land of rechtssysteem specifiek bepaald worden.

Hoofstuk 5.2 onderzocht de vormen die corruptie in verschillende rechtssystemen heeft aangenomen aan de hand van voldoende gedocumenteerde voorbeelden. De voorbeelden wijzen uit dat het ontbreken van heldere informatiestromen en gebrekkige interne administratie belangrijke zwakheden zijn die leiden tot tekorten in de verantwoording en een lage pakkans. Clientelisme en politiek ingrijpen in benoemingen en bevorderingen hangen samen met gebrek aan carrieremanagement. Informatie is een belangrijk instrument in de bestrijding van corruptie, zo blijkt uit de conclusies van hoofstuk 5.2:

- Meer transparantie in de interne aministratie verhoogt de pakkans
- Slecht werkende administratie hangt samen met procedurele complexiteit
- Carrieremanagement op basis van kwaliteit veronderstelt toegankelijkheid van kennis en informatie
- Meer transparantie kan de publieke controle vergroten, en dus – uiteindelijk – onpartijdige rechtspraak bevorderen.

Hoofdstuk 5.3 onderzocht hoe IT corruptie in gerechten kan helpen bestrijden. Daarvoor is onontbeerlijk om de oorzaken van corruptie en mogelijke bronnen, oplossingen en remedies goed uit elkaar te houden. Een grondige diagnose voor ieder land op zichzelf is een noodzakelijke basis voor het vinden van aangrijpingspunten voor verbetering. De benadering in corruptiesyndromen is daarvoor een goed kader omdat die inzichtelijk maakt wat in de verschillende syndromen (zie bijlage B) de mogelijkheden, risico's en aangrijpingspunten zijn. De conclusies over syndromen worden geëxtrapoleerd om een indicatie te kunnen geven voor remedies voor corruptie in de rechtspraak.

- Voor landen met syndroom 1, economisch hoog en institutioneel goed ontwikkelde landen, is het voornaamste probleem gebrek aan vertrouwen. Een betere publieke verantwoording kan een remedie zijn, als tegenwicht tegen beslismonopolies en ruime bevoegdheden. Die kan bestaan uit verantwoording van het gebruik van publieke middelen, openbaarheid van de carriere, de nevenfuncties en vermogensbestanddelen van de rechters, en informatievoorziening over rechterlijk beleid inzake zaaksbehandeling en integriteitsbeleid. Het Internet is een kanaal voor openbaarheid in de verantwoording.

- Landen met syndroom 2 kennen gesloten politieke netwerken met enigszins zwakke instituties die onvoldoende onafhankelijk kunnen functioneren. Versterking van institutionele onafhankelijkheid is voor de rechtspraak een remedie die de constitutionele onafhankelijkheid kan schragen. Daarvoor zijn nodig: professionalisering van de rechters gepaard aan de bijbehorende salariëring, en de ontwikkeling van integriteitsbeleid en handhaving daarvan. De professionalisering omvat ook standaarden voor zaaksafhandeling en zaakstoedeling.
- In syndroom 3-landen zijn de instituties, met inbegrip van de gerechten, heel zwak. Dientengevolge is er veel onzekerheid, onveiligheid en onrecht. Als in de gerechten computers worden geintroduceerd kan dat een goed aangrijpingspunt zijn om processen te verbeteren met meer transparantie, zodat de pakkans bij ongelijke behandeling omhoog gaat. Als procedures vereenvoudigd worden is er minder aanleiding voor omkoping. Openbaar toegankelijke informatie over regels en tot rechterlijke uitspraken kan onzekerheid over het geldende recht verminderen. Verbetering van zaaksafhandeling is in het algemeen een goed startpunt voor syndroom 3-landen.
- Het allerzwakst zijn de instituties in landen met syndroom 4. Hier plunderen de machtigen en hun protegés straffeloos de economie van een land. De problemen zijn alomvattend, en geen enkele specifieke oplossing is daartegen opgewassen. Geleidelijke opbouw van de maatschappij is een langdurig proces. Gerechten delen het lot van de andere instituties. Ze zijn dermate zwak dat invoering van IT schier onmogelijk is omdat die niet kan worden onderhouden of zelfs maar werkbaar gemaakt bij gebrek aan geregelde processen. Voor syndroom-4 landen is verbetering van zaaksafhandelingsprocessen geen optie, omdat de instituties in kwestie niet in staat zijn om verandering te absorberen en te bestendigen. Het aangrijpingspunt in dit syndroom is in het algemeen training van de rechters en vergroting van de openbaarheid.

De IT - en de samenhang (deel 6)

Hervormingsprogramma's zouden verbetering van de informatievoorziening als expliciete doelstelling kunnen hebben. Heel in het algemeen betekent dat verbetering van de zaaksafhandeling en vergroten van de toegang tot informatie. Hier komen de drie gebruikerklachten bij elkaar. Betere toegang tot informatie kan ook minder vertraging betekenen, en samen kunnen ze corruptie verminderen.

In de praktijk van de verschillende syndromen kan verbetering van de informatievoorziening verschillende dingen betekenen. Toegang tot informatie vormt een beginpunt voor training en opleiding, bijvoorbeeld in het omgaan met zaken en geschillen en ook in gedragsregels. In sommige situaties, meestal in syndroom 4, is zulke training het enig mogelijke aangrijpingspunt. Eenvoudige *kantoorautomatisering* kan de basisprocessen ondersteunen die nodig zijn voor het ordentelijk, transparant afhandelen van zaken. Dat maakt invoering van kantoorautomatisering een goed startpunt voor syndroom 3-landen. *Zaaksregistratiesystemen* kunnen meer geautomatiseerde, verbeterde zaaksafhandeling ondersteunen. Ze zijn een instrument voor de verkorting van doorlooptijden. Minder processtappen en kortere doorlooptijden betekenen ook minder aanleiding en gelegenheid voor omkoping. Registratiesystemen kunnen, als ze goed ingericht zijn en goed gebruikt worden, ook de pakkans verhogen en zo de stimulansen voor het aannemen van steekpenningen en het manipuleren van dossiers verminderen. Als verantwoordingsinstrument kunnen ze institutionele onafhankelijkheid bevorderen, iets dat vooral van belang is voor landen met syndroom 2. *Netwerktechnologie*, vooral het Internet, kan publiek vertrouwen helpen versterken als een effectief communicatiemiddel tussen de gerechten en hun gebruikers en het publiek in het algemeen. Dit is een voornaam aandachtspunt voor syndroom 1-landen. Het kan de manier waarop onpartijdigheid en onafhankelijkheid zijn ingericht en werken zichtbaar maken. Het Internet heeft de schaduwfunctie van de rechtspraak, het bewaken van de rechtsnormen, versterkt. De grotere zichtbaarheid leidt tot een roep om meer consistentie, en dat leidt weer tot het ontwikkelen van richtijnen en beleid.

De bestuursstructuur van de rechtspraak zal voor dit alles wel veranderd moeten worden, want het besturen, ontwikkelen en beheren van IT-voorzieningen, de toenemende behoefte aan centrale sturing en de sterkere publieke controle stellen de rechterlijke organisatie voor nieuwe problemen.

Bibliography

Anderson, J. 2002. *Corruption in Slovakia: Results of Diagnostic Surveys*. Prepared at the request of the Government of the Slovak Republic by the World Bank and the United States Agency for International Development. Available at www.worldbank.org.

Anderson, James, and Cheryl Gray. 2006. *Anticorruption in Transition 3*, Washington, D.C.: World Bank, 2006.

Andvig, Jens Chr. and Odd-Helge Fjeldstad. 2000. Research on Corruption, a policy oriented survey, commissioned by Norad, December.

ARIZ, Informatiebeleidsplan Rechtspraak 2005. Information Policy Plan for the Administration of Justice in 2005. Adviesraad Informatievoorziening Zittende Magistratuur (Advisory Council for Judicial Information Service). 2000.

Asser, W.D.H., H.A. Groen, J.B.M. Vranken, with I.N. Tzankova. 2003. *Een Nieuwe Balans.* Fundamentele herbezinning Nederlands burgerlijk procesrecht. (A New Balance, Fundamental Reconsideration of Netherlands Civil Procedural Law). Leiden/Tilburg/Den Haag.

—. 2006. Uitgebalanceerd. Eindrapport Fundamentele Herbezinning Nederlands burgerlijk procesrecht (Final Balance. Final report Fundamental Reconsideration of Netherlands civil procedural law). Den Haag: Boom Juridische Uitgevers.

Beenker, Nico. Juristen over faalfactoren van ict-projecten. (Jurists about failure factors in IT projects), Informatie.nl 2004/10 at:
http://www.informatie.nl/artikelen/2004/10/ juristenOverFaalfactorenVanIctp.html

Bharuka, G.C. 2003 *Rejuvenating Judicial System through e-governance and attitudinal change.* Naghpur, India.

Black's Law Dictionary. 2001. St. Paul, Minn.: West Group.

Blankenburg, E.R. 1995. Access to Justice and Alternatives to Courts, Civil Justice Quarterly, volume 14, July, pages 176-189.

Blume, Peter. 1999. Changes in the Sources of Law in Information Society. International review of law computers & technology, volume 13, no. 3, pages 325–335.

Brouwer, J. RE RA. 2002. Project-audit Hoger Beroep Systeem (Project Audit Appeal System). January 30. Report to Ministerial Accounting Office of the Ministry of Justice of the Netherlands. Annex to Parliament Document 26352-58.

Buscaglia, Edgardo and Thomas Ulen. 1997. "A quantitative assessment of the efficiency of the judicial sector in Latin America". *International Review of Law and Economics* 17:275-91.

Cannon, Andrew. 2002. Electronic Prelodgement notices in the civil jurisdiction of the magistrates court, at http://www.aija.org.au/tech3/program/presentations/Prelodgm.doc

Capgemini Global CIO Survey 2008. The Role of the IT function in Business Innovation.

Carothers, Thomas ed. 2006. *Promoting the Rule of Law Abroad.* Washington, DC: Carnegie Endowment for International Peace.

CEPEJ 2006a, European Commission for the Efficiency of Justice, Length of court proceedings in the member states of the Council of Europe based on case law of the European

Court of Human Rights. Strasbourg. on: http://www.coe.int/t/dg1/legalcooperation/cepej/

CEPEJ 2006b, European Commission for the Efficiency of Justice, European Judicial Systems Edition 2006 (2004 data). Strasbourg. http://www.coe.int/t/dghl/cooperation/cepej/evaluation/default_en.asp

CEPEJ 2008, European Commission for the Efficiency of Justice, European Judicial Systems Edition 2008 (2006 data). Strasbourg. http://www.coe.int/t/dghl/cooperation/cepej/evaluation/default_en.asp

Church, Thomas, Jr. Justice Delayed. 1998. *The pace of litigation in urban trial courts.* Williamsburg, Va.: National Center for State Courts.

Cotterrell, Roger. 1992. *The Sociology of Law. An Introduction.* Oxford: Oxford University Press.

Dakolias, Maria, 1999. Court Performance around the World, a comparative perspective, World Bank technical paper no. 430, Washington, D.C.

Dale, Pamela, 2007. Barriers to Justice in Sierra Leone. Justice for the Poor Briefing Notes, September, volume 1, issue 4. World Bank. On: http://siteresources.worldbank.org/INTJUSFORPOOR/Resources/J4PBriefingNoteIssue4.pdf

Davenport, Thomas H. 1993. *Process Innovation, Reengineering Work through Information Technology.* Boston, Mass.: Harvard Business School Press.

Dekker, Pauline, Cora Maas-de Waal and Tom van der Meer. 2004. *Vertrouwen in de rechtspraak* (Trust in the judiciary). Den Haag, Sociaal en Cultureel Planbureau.

Di Vita, Giuseppe. 2006. *Corruption, Exogenous Changes in Incentives and Deterrence.* Working Paper, Fondazione Eni Enrico Mattei. Available at SSRN: http://ssrn.com/abstract=869412

Dijk, Frans van. 2003. see Van Dijk.

Djankov, Simeon, and others, 2003. Courts, *Quarterly Journal of Economics,* May.

Eshuis, R.J.J. en G. Paulides. 2002. *Van Rechtbank naar Kanton.* Evaluatie van de competentiegrensverhoging voor civiele handelszaken in 1999. (From Civil to Local Court, an Evaluation of raising the small claims limit for civil commercial cases in 1999). Den Haag: Boom Juridische Uitgevers.

—. 2005. Versnellingsbeleid in de rechtspraak (Accellerating judicial proceedings). Rechtstreeks, 2005, nr. 2. Den Haag: Raad voor de Rechtspraak.

—. 2007. Het recht in betere tijden (Justice in Better Times, on the effectiveness of measures to accelerate civil proceedings) Den Haag: Boom Juridische uitgevers.

European Union. Benchmarking e-government projects at: www.epractice.eu

Fabri, Marco and Francesco Contini, 2001. Justice and Technology in Europe, How ICT is Changing the Judicial Business. The Hague: Kluwer.

—. 2003. Judicial electronic data interchange in Europe: Applications, policies and trends. Bologna: Lo Scarabeo.

Faundez, Julio. 2006. "Should Rule of Law Projects Take Community Justice Institutions Seriously? Perspectives from Latin America." *The World Bank Legal Review,* Vol. 2: *Law, Equity and Development,* ed. Ana Palacio. World Bank, 113–140.

Federal Judicial Center. 2001. Effective Use of Courtroom Technology. A Judge's Guide to Pretrial and Trial. Washington, D.C.: Federal Judicial Center and National Institute for Trial Advocacy. 2001.

—. 2003. Survey on Courtroom Technology, December 2003. at http://www.fjc.gov/public/pdf.nsf/lookup/CTtech03.pdf/$file/CTtech03.pdf

—. 2006. Roundtable on the Use of Technology to Facilitate Appearances in Bankruptcy Proceedings. Federal Judicial Center August 11-12, 2005, Washington D.C. Judicial Conference Committee on the Administration of the Bankruptcy System, Subcommittee on Automation, Federal Judicial Center.

—. 2007. Roundtable on the Effective Uses of Information Technology for Judges. Federal Judicial Center February 15-17, Washington D.C.

Feld, Lars and Stephan Voigt, 2003. Economic Growth and Judicial Independence: Cross Country Evidence using a new set of indicators. Cesifo working paper no/ 906 April 2003, and European Journal of Political Economy 19: 497-527.

Felsö, Flora, David Hollanders, Jordi van Honk, Miek Laemers, Michiel de Nooij, Wannes Rombouts, De tijd loopt door. 2007. De gevolgen van lange doorlooptijden in de rechtspraak (Time goes on, the consequences of long processing times in courts). Den Haag, WODC.

Freeman, Derek. Ontario's Integrated Justice Project. Presentation at AIJA Technology for Justice conference, Sydney October 21, 2002. At http://www.aija.org.au/tech3/program/presentations/Ontario2002-2.ppt#471

Frissen, Valerie. 2004. De domesticatie van de digitale wereld (The domestication of the digital world). Inaugurele oratie (Inaugural Lecture). Rotterdam: Erasmus Universiteit.

Galanter, Marc. 1974. Why the Haves come out ahead: speculations on the limits of legal change. *Law and Society Review*, Vol. 9, nr. 1, p. 95-160. http://marcgalanter.net/Documents/papers/WhytheHavesComeOutAhead.pdf

—.1983a. The Radiating Effects of Courts, at http://marcgalanter.net/Documents/papers/scannedpdf/RadiatingEffectsofCourts.pdf

—. 1983b. Reading the landscape of disputes, *UCLA Law Review*, October.

Genn, Hazel. 1999 *Paths to Justice. What people do and think about going to law.* Oxford and Portland, Oregon: Hart Publishing.

Goerdt, John A. 1991. *Reexamining the pace of litigation in 39 urban trial courts.* Williamsburg, Va.: National Center for State Courts.

Gottschalk, Peter. 2007. Knowledge Management Information Systems in Law and Enforcement, Idea Group Publishing, Hershey Penn. U.S.A..

Griffiths, John. 1991 De Rechtbank als fietsenfabriek. (The Court as a Bicycle Factory) *Nederlands Juristenblad (Netherlands Legal Weekly)*:129-130.

Hammergren, Linn. 2007 *Envisioning Reform: Improving Judicial Performance in Latin America.* University Park: Pennsylvania State University Press.

Hartendorp, R.C. 2008 Praktisch gesproken. Alledaagse civiele rechtspleging als praktische oordeelsvorming. Practically Spoken. Everyday civil justice as practical judicial decision making.

Hoogen, Ronald van den , see Van den Hoogen.

Hough, Bonnie Rose, Mark O'Brien, Glenn Rawdon, Richard Zorza, 2007. Technology and the Access to Justice Crisis: Analysis, Models and Approaches, presentation at the 10th NCSC Court Technology Conference, October, Tampa, Florida. On http://www.attendancemarketing.com/~attendance/ncsc/ctc10/pdf/E6-49-Presentation-Tech-and-Access-to-Justice-ADO.pdf

International Bar Association 2001. "Sri Lanka: Failing to Protect the Rule of Law and the Independence of the Judiciary". London: International Bar Association. on www.ibanet.org.

—. 2006. Letter from the IBA Human rights Institute to President of Sri Lanka, February 2006. on www.ibanet.org.

Johnston, Michael. 2005. *Syndromes of Corruption: Wealth, Power, and Democracy.* Cambridge: Cambridge University Press.

Parliament of the Netherlands, Letters of the Minister of Justice to the Second Chamber of Parliament, Kamerstuk 26352-52 & 58.

Kaufmann, Daniel. 2005. "Myths and Realities of Governance and Corruption". World Economic Forum. Global Competitiveness Report 2005-2006. Chapter 2.1 by Daniel Kaufmann. (November). Available at SSRN: http://ssrn.com/abstract=829244

—. 2007. Kaufmann, Daniel, Kraay, Aart and Mastruzzi, Massimo, "Governance Matters VI: Governance Indicators for 1996-2006" (July). World Bank Policy Research Working Paper No. 4280 Available at SSRN: http://ssrn.com/abstract=999979

Klein Haarhuis, C. and F.L. Leeuw, 2002. Corruptiebestrijding (Combating Corruption), Bestuurskunde, jaargang 11, nummer 4, juli, pp. 177-186

Klitgaard, Robert.1988. *Controlling Corruption.* Berkeley: University of California Press.

Koo, Gene, 2007. New Skills, New Learning, Legal Education and the Promise of Technology. Harvard Law School Berkman Center for Internet and Society Research Publication No. 2007-4.

Lambsdorff, Johann Graf. 1999. Corruption in Empirical Research - A Review. on http://www.icgg.org/downloads/contribution05_lambsdorff.pdf

Langbroek, Philip, and Marco Fabri. 2007. *The right judge for each case.* Antwerp-Oxford: Intersentia.

McAfee, Andrew, 2006. Mastering the Three Worlds of Information Technology, *Harvard Business Review,* November:141-149.

Macdonald, Ros, and Anne Wallace. Review of the extent of courtroom technology in Australia. *William and Mary Bill of Rights Journal.* Vol. 12, 2003-2004, 649-659.

Mahoney, Barry, and Antoinette Bonacci-Miller. 1992. *Improving civil case flow management in urban trial courts.* Denver: National Center for State Courts , Institute for Court Management.

Meer, H.T. van der, see Van der Meer.

Mein, A.G., S. Verberk en J.W. Vos. 2008. Communiceren met justitiabelen (Communicating with court users). A study into the need of, appreciation of and expectation with regard to information of court users. The Hague. B&A Group.

MCOL Money Claim on Line Statistics 2001-2004. March 2004.

National Center for State Courts, *CourTools,* on
http://www.ncsconline.org/D_Research/CourTools

Nederlands Juristenblad (NJB, Netherlands Legal Weekly) Rechters in Nederland, een enquete (Judges in the Netherlands, a survey) 2001. blz. 1923-1986.

NVVR. Report of the working party of the Netherlands Association of Magistrates on extra judicial costs. 2002. Nederlandse Vereniging voor Rechtspraak. On www.nvvr.org.

Organisation for Economic Co-operation and Development (OECD). 1976. *Measuring Social Well-Being: A Progress Report on the Development of Social Indicators,* Paris: OECD, 1976.

—. 2008. Statistics from StatExtracts. at
http://stats.oecd.org/WBOS/Index.aspx?QueryName=251&QueryType=View&Lang=en

Ontario 1999. 1999 Report of the Ontario Court (General Division). At
http://www.ontariocourts.on.ca/scj/en/archives/ocs/1999.htm

—. 2001. Annual Report. Ontario Ministries of the Attorney General and Public Safety and Security. 2001 Section 3.03 – Integrated Justice Project.
http://www.auditor.on.ca/en/reports_en/en01/303en01.pdf

—. 2003. Annual Report. Ontario Ministries of the Attorney General and Pubic Safety and Security. 2003 Section 4.03 – Integrated Justice Project. at
http://www.auditor.on.ca/en/reports_en/en03/403en03.pdf

Oskamp, Anja. 2008. Technologie en verandering van het recht (Technology and legal change) in: Dommering-bundel: opstellen over informatierecht aangeboden aan prof. Mr. E.J. Dommering (Essays on information law offered to prof. E.J. Dommering). Amsterdam. Cramwinckel.

Ostrom, Brian J., and Roger A. Hanson. 1999. *Efficiency, Timeliness, and Quality: A new perspective from nine state criminal trial courts.* Williamsburg: National Center for State Courts.

Oxford Dictionary of Law. 2003. Oxford: Oxford University Press.

Prisma, Tevreden genoeg. 2008. Klantwaarderingsonderzoeken onder gerechten in de periode 2005-2007. (Satisfied enough..., user satisfaction surveys in Dutch courts 2005-2007). Utrecht: Prisma.

Raad voor de Rechtspraak, Jaarverslagen 2002-2007. Public annual reports of the Dutch Council for the Judiciary, on www.rechtspraak.nl

Radlmaier, Steffen (ed.) 2005. *Het proces van Neurenberg* (The Nuremberg Trial). Amsterdam. W. Hansen en Uitgeverij Cossee BV.

Reiling, Dory. 2003. Rechtspraak in de digitale delta. (Administering justice in the digital delta). Nederlands Juristenblad (Netherlands Legal Weekly) 2003-44, p. 2286-2291.

—. 2006. "Doing justice with information technology." *Information & Communications Technology Law* 15 (2006): 189-200.

—. 2007. with Linn Hammergren, Adrian Di Giovanni. Justice Sector Assessments Handbook, World Bank 2007 on http://www.worldbank.org/lji

Rekenkamer A. Algemene Rekenkamer, 2007. Lessen uit ICT-projecten bij de overheid. Deel A. (General Accounting Chamber, Lessons from government ICT-projects. Part A). Den Haag.
http://www.rekenkamer.nl/9282000/d/p449_rapport_def.pdf

Rekenkamer B. Algemene Rekenkamer, 2008. Lessen uit ICT-projecten bij de overheid. Deel B. (General Accounting Chamber, Lessons from government ICT-projects. Part B). Den Haag.
http://www.rekenkamer.nl/9282000/d/p449_rapport_def.pdf

Rose-Ackerman, Susan. 1999. *Corruption and Government.* Cambridge: Cambridge University Press.

Rottman, David B. 2000. Public perceptions of the state courts: a primer. National Center for State Courts. The Court Manager, Vol. 15, Number 3 p. 1-15.
http://contentdm.ncsconline.org/cgi-bin/showfile.exe?CISOROOT=/ctcomm&CISOPTR=24

—. and Alan J. Tomkins. 1999. Public Trust and Confidence, What public opinion surveys mean to judges. Court Review, Volume 36, Issue 3 – Fall, p. 24-31.
http://contentdm.ncsconline.org/cgi-bin/showfile.exe?CISOROOT=/ctcomm&CISOPTR=97

Schmidt, Aernout, 2007. IT and the judiciary in the Netherlands – A state of affairs. Computer Law & Security Report 23 453-460. Elsevier.

Schuyt, Kees, Kees Groenendijk, Ben Sloot, 1976. *De Weg naar het Recht (The Way to Justice).* Deventer: Kluwer.

Shapiro, Martin. 1986. Courts. *A comparative and political analysis.* Chicago and London: University of Chicago Press.

Sijanski, Grozdana, and Jimmy Barber, The German order of payment procedure (Mahnverfahren), German Law Archive, at
http://www.iuscomp.org/gla/index.html

Steelman, David C., 2000. with John A. Goerdt and James E. McMillan. *Case Flow Management.* National Center for State Courts.

Steelman, David C. and Marco Fabri, Can an Italian Court use the American approach to delay reduction? *Justice System Journal,* volume 29, no. 1 (2008), pp. 1-23

Struiksma, D. and A.W. Jongbloed. 2006. "Bailiffs on the e-Highway". *Information & Communications Technology Law* 15: 201-206.

Susskind, Richard. 1998. *The Future of Law.* Oxford University Press.

Timms, Perry. 2002. Presentations at the 2002 Netherlands Judiciary IT Conference and at the 2003 NCSC Court Technology Conference, CTC8.

Transparency International 2007. Global Corruption Report (GCR) 2007. *Corruption in Judicial Systems,* Cambridge: Cambridge University Press.

—. 2008. Corruption Perception Index 2001-2008 at www.transparency.org/policy_research/surveys_indices/cpi

United Nations Development Program. Human Development Index at www.hdr.undp.org/en/statistics

United Nations Organization on Drugs and Crime (UNODC) 2001. Strengthening Judicial Integrity Against Corruption . Vienna, March.

—. 2006. "Assessment of the Integrity and Capacity of the Justice System in Three Nigerian States." Technical Assessment Report. Vienna http://www.unodc.org/pdf/corruption

Van Dijk, Frans. 2003. Economisch belang van de rechtspraak (Economic importance of the courts). On: http://www.rechtspraak.nl/NR/rdonlyres/3FC8D3D0-BF30-41E8-B8E0-9CA3D49172AF/0/Economischbelangvanderechtspraak.pdf

Van den Hoogen, Ronald. 2007. E-Justice. Beginselen van behoorlijke elektronische rechtspraak. (E-Justice. Principles of proper electronic administration of justice). Den Haag: SDU Uitgevers.

Van der Meer, H.T. and G.J.J. Rensink. 1996. Achter de aanbevelingen. De aanbevelingen van de kring van kantonrechters dd. 8 november. 1996 nader bezien. (Behind the recommendations. A closer look at the recommendations of the local judges association of November 8 1996), Sociaal Maandblad Arbeid (vindplaats nog opzoeken)

Van Velthoven, B.J.C., and M. Ter Voert. 2004. *Geschilbeslechtingsdelta 2003*. Den Haag: Boom.

—. 2005. *The value of the judicial infrastructure for the Dutch economy*. Research memorandum no. 1 volume 1. The Hague: Raad voor de Rechtspraak (Netherlands Council for the Judiciary). At http://www.rechtspraak.nl/NR/rdonlyres/E80FB805-465F-4152-804B-915EFA4F9478/0/vertaling051215.pdf

Velicogna, Marco. CEPEJ. Use of Information and Communication Technologies (ICT) in European Judicial Systems. European Commission for the Efficiency of Justice. CEPEJ Studies no. 7 at http://www.coe.int/t/dg1/legalcooperation/cepej/series/Etudes7TIC_en.pdf

Velicogna, Marco, 2007. Justice Systems and ICT. What can be learned form Europe? *Utrecht Law Review*, Volume 3, Issue 1 (June).

Vera Institute of Justice. 2003. *Measuring Progress toward Safety and Justice: A Global guide to the Design of Performance Indicators across the Justice Sector*. New York, Vera Institute of Justice. On http://www.vera.org/publication_pdf/207_404.pdf

Victoria, Parliament of, Law Reform Committee, Technology and the Law, May 1999, Melbourne, Australia.

Waters, Craig, Tricia Knox and Phillip Pollock, 2007. Web Accessibility for your Court Web Site, presentation at CTC10, October, on http://www.ctc10.org/sites/S69/File/pdf/E32-40-Presentation-Web%20Disability%20Acess.pdf

World Bank n.y.. (Judicial Sector Indicators (JSI), a World Bank Information System at http://www4.worldbank.org/legal/legop_judicial/whatisjsi.html.)

—. 1997. World Development Report, *The State in A Changing World. New York*, N.Y. Oxford University Press.

—. 1999. Bulgaria justice sector assessment.

—. 2002. World Development Report. *Building Institutions for Markets*. New York, NY: Oxford University Press.

—. 2005a. Mauritanie, Rapport sur l'Observation des Normes et Codes, Evaluation des standards du groupe d'action financière sur le blanchiment des capitaux et le financement du terrorisme (not public).

—. 2005b. Nepal, The legal and judicial environment for financial sector development. A review. Washington, D.C.: Finance and Private Sector Development Unit, South Asia Region, World Bank.

—. 2006a. "Doing Business 2007: How to Reform." World Bank/International Finance Corporation.

—. 2006b. Quality of Information and Communication Technology (ICT) Components in Bank Projects. A QAG Assessment. July 18. Washington, D.C.

—. 2007a. "Doing Business 2008: Comparing Regulation in 178 Economies." World Bank/International Finance Corporation.

—. 2007b. World Governance Indicators. On http://info.worldbank.org/governance/wgi2007/

—. 2008a. Doing Business 2009: World Bank/International Finance Corporation.

—. 2008b. Doing Business. An Independent Evaluation. Washington. D.C. The International Bank for Reconstruction and Development. http://siteresources.worldbank.org/EXTDOIBUS/Resources/db_evaluation.pdf

—/International Monetary Fund. 2005. Financial Sector Assessments.

World Factbook, CIA, at https://www.cia.gov/library/publications/the-world-factbook/index.html

Zuckerman, A. 1999. Civil Justice in Crisis. Comparative perspectives of civil procedure. London: Oxford University Press.

Index

Page numbers in **bold** indicate figures, boxes and tables

E

F

G

H

I

J

Appendix A : Web Pages on Divorce

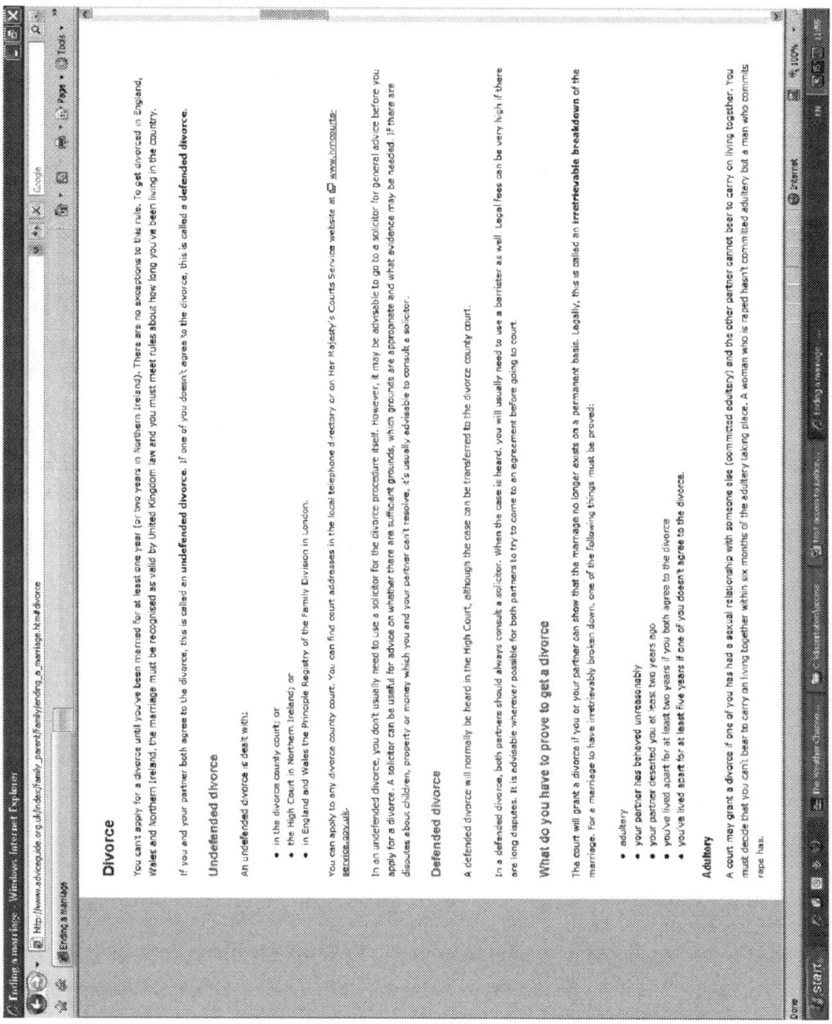

Ending a marriage - Windows Internet Explorer

http://www.adviceguide.org.uk/index/family_parent/family/ending_a_marriage.htm#divorce

Divorce

You can't apply for a divorce until you've been married for at least one year (or two years in Northern Ireland). There are no exceptions to this rule. To get divorced in England, Wales and Northern Ireland, the marriage must be recognised as valid by United Kingdom law and you must meet rules about how long you've been living in the country.

If you and your partner both agree to the divorce, this is called an **undefended divorce**. If one of you doesn't agree to the divorce, this is called a **defended divorce**.

Undefended divorce

An undefended divorce is dealt with:

- in the divorce county court; or
- the High Court in Northern Ireland; or
- in England and Wales the Principle Registry of the Family Division in London.

You can apply to any divorce county court. You can find court addresses in the local telephone directory or on Her Majesty's Courts Service website at www.hmcourts-service.gov.uk.

In an undefended divorce, you don't usually need to use a solicitor for the divorce procedure itself. However, it may be advisable to go to a solicitor for general advice before you apply for a divorce. A solicitor can be useful for advice on whether there are sufficient grounds, which grounds are appropriate and what evidence may be needed. If there are disputes about children, property or money which you and your partner can't resolve, it's usually advisable to consult a solicitor.

Defended divorce

A defended divorce will normally be heard in the High Court, although the case can be transferred to the divorce county court.

In a defended divorce, both partners should always consult a solicitor. When the case is heard, you will usually need to use a barrister as well. Legal fees can be very high if there are long disputes. It is advisable wherever possible for both partners to try to come to an agreement before going to court.

What do you have to prove to get a divorce

The court will grant a divorce if you or your partner can show that the marriage no longer exists on a permanent basis. Legally, this is called an **irretrievable breakdown** of the marriage. For a marriage to have irretrievably broken down, one of the following things must be proved:

- adultery
- your partner has behaved unreasonably
- your partner deserted you at least two years ago
- you've lived apart for at least two years if you both agree to the divorce
- you've lived apart for at least five years if one of you doesn't agree to the divorce.

Adultery

A court may grant a divorce if one of you has had a sexual relationship with someone else (committed adultery) and the other partner cannot bear to carry on living together. You must decide that you can't bear to carry on living together within six months of the adultery taking place. A woman who is raped hasn't committed adultery but a man who commits rape has.

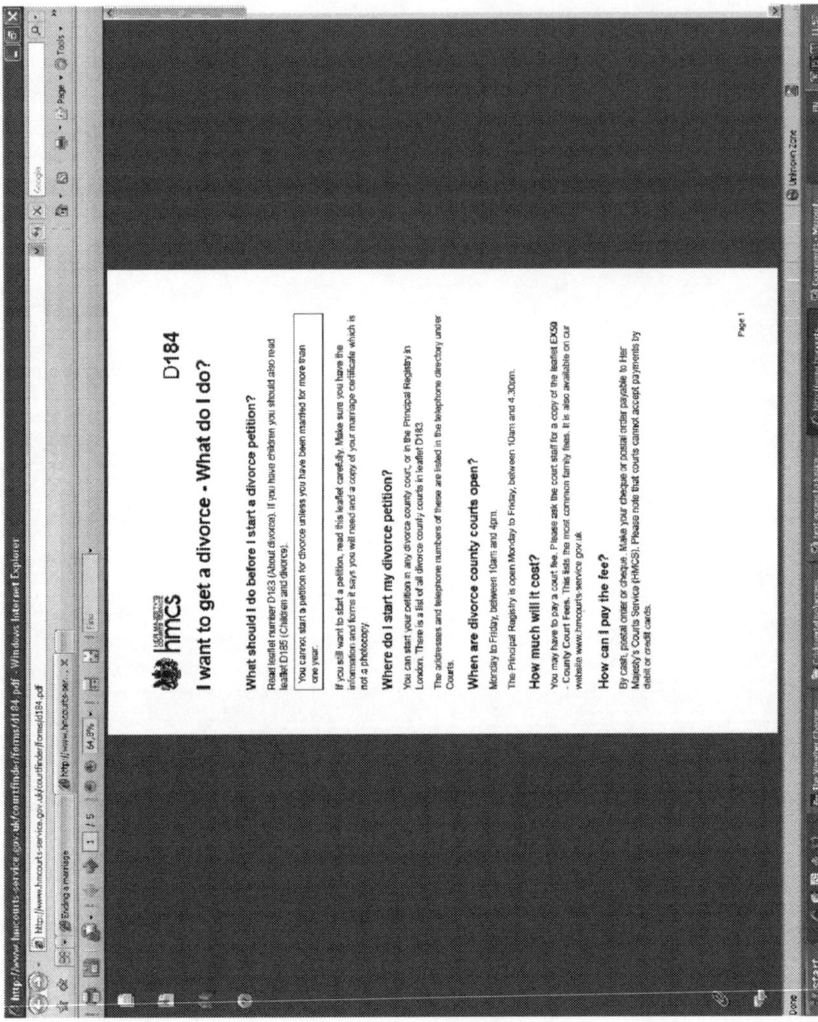
http://www.hmcourts-service.gov.uk/courtfinder/forms/d184.pdf - Windows Internet Explorer
hmcs
D184
I want to get a divorce - What do I do?
What should I do before I start a divorce petition?
Read leaflet number D183 (About divorce). If you have children you should also read leaflet D185 (Children and divorce).
You cannot start a petition for divorce unless you have been married for more than one year.
If you still want to start a petition, read this leaflet carefully. Make sure you have the information and forms it says you will need and a copy of your marriage certificate which is not a photocopy.
Where do I start my divorce petition?
You can start your petition in any divorce county court, or in the Principal Registry in London. There is a list of all divorce county courts in leaflet D183.
The addresses and telephone numbers of these are listed in the telephone directory under Courts.
When are divorce county courts open?
Monday to Friday, between 10am and 4pm.
The Principal Registry is open Monday to Friday, between 10am and 4.30pm.
How much will it cost?
You may have to pay a court fee. Please ask the court staff for a copy of the leaflet EX50 - County Court Fees. This lists the most common family fees. It is also available on our website www.hmcourts-service.gov.uk
How can I pay the fee?
By cash, postal order or cheque. Make your cheque or postal order payable to Her Majesty's Courts Service (HMCS). Please note that courts cannot accept payments by debit or credit cards.
Page 1

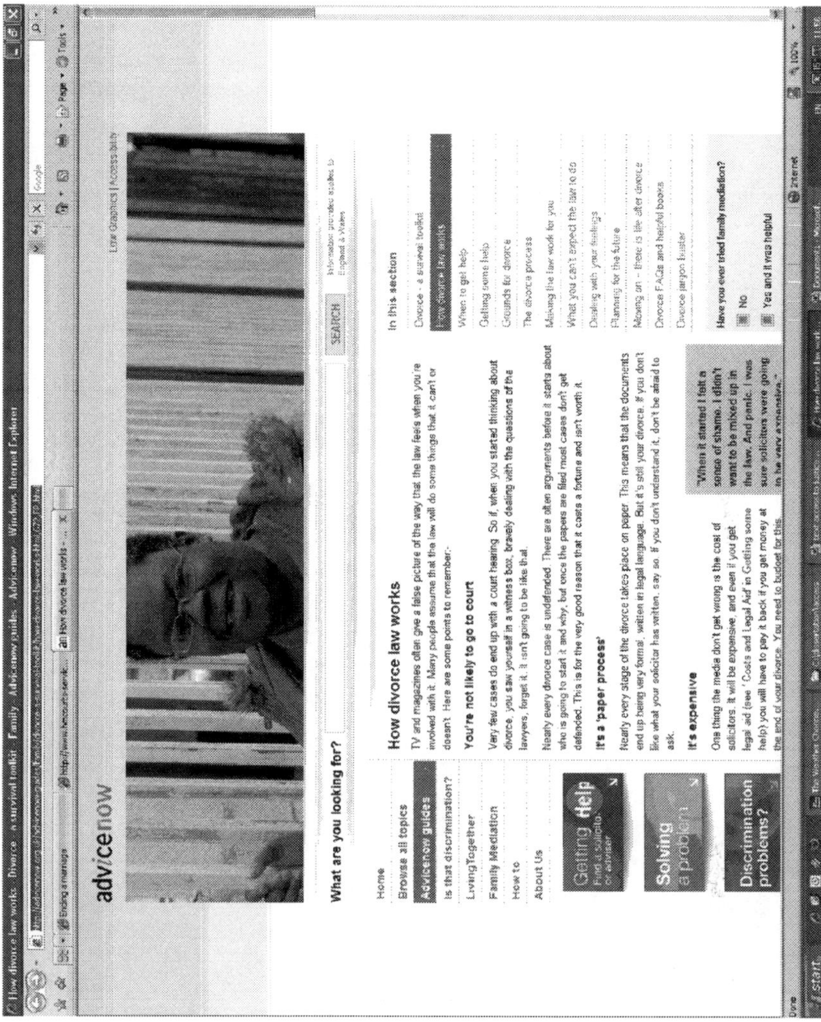

How divorce law works - Divorce - a survival toolkit - Family - Advicenow guides - Advicenow - Windows Internet Explorer

advicenow

Low Graphics | Accessibility

What are you looking for? SEARCH

Information provided applies to England & Wales

Home
Browse all topics
Advicenow guides
Is that discrimination?
LivingTogether
Family Mediation
How to
About Us

Getting Help Find a solicitor or adviser

Solving a problem

Discrimination problems?

How divorce law works

TV and magazines often give a false picture of the way that the law feels when you're involved with it. Many people assume that the law will do some things that it can't or doesn't. Here are some points to remember:-

You're not likely to go to court

Very few cases do end up with a court hearing. So if, when you started thinking about divorce, you saw yourself in a witness box, bravely dealing with the questions of the lawyers, forget it. It isn't going to be like that.

Nearly every divorce case is undefended. There are often arguments before it starts about who is going to start it and why, but once the papers are filed most cases don't get defended. This is for the very good reason that it costs a fortune and isn't worth it.

It's a 'paper process'

Nearly every stage of the divorce takes place on paper. This means that the documents end up being very formal, written in legal language. But it's still your divorce. If you don't like what your solicitor has written, say so. If you don't understand it, don't be afraid to ask.

It's expensive

One thing the media don't get wrong is the cost of solicitors. It will be expensive, and even if you get legal aid (see 'Costs and Legal Aid' in Getting some help) you will have to pay it back if you get money at the end of your divorce. You need to budget for this.

"When it started I felt a sense of shame. I didn't want to be mixed up in the law. And panic. I was sure solicitors were going to be very expensive."

In this section

Divorce - a survival toolkit
How divorce law works
When to get help
Getting some help
Grounds for divorce
The divorce process
Making the law work for you
What you can't expect the law to do
Dealing with your feelings
Planning for the future
Moving on - there is life after divorce
Divorce FAQs and helpful books
Divorce jargon buster

Have you ever tried family mediation?
No
Yes and it was helpful

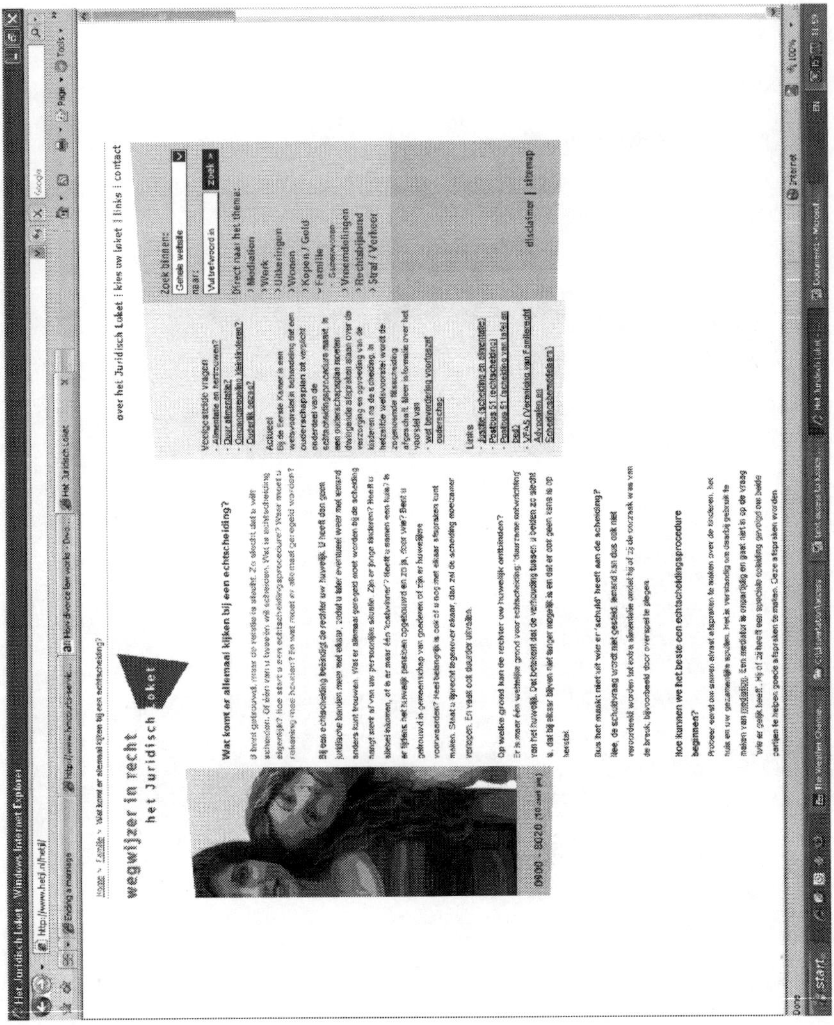
Het Juridisch Loket - Windows Internet Explorer
wegwijzer in recht
het Juridisch Loket
Wat komt er allemaal kijken bij een echtscheiding?
over het Juridisch Loket | kies uw loket | links | contact
Zoek binnen:
Direct naar het thema:
0900 - 8020
disclaimer | sitemap

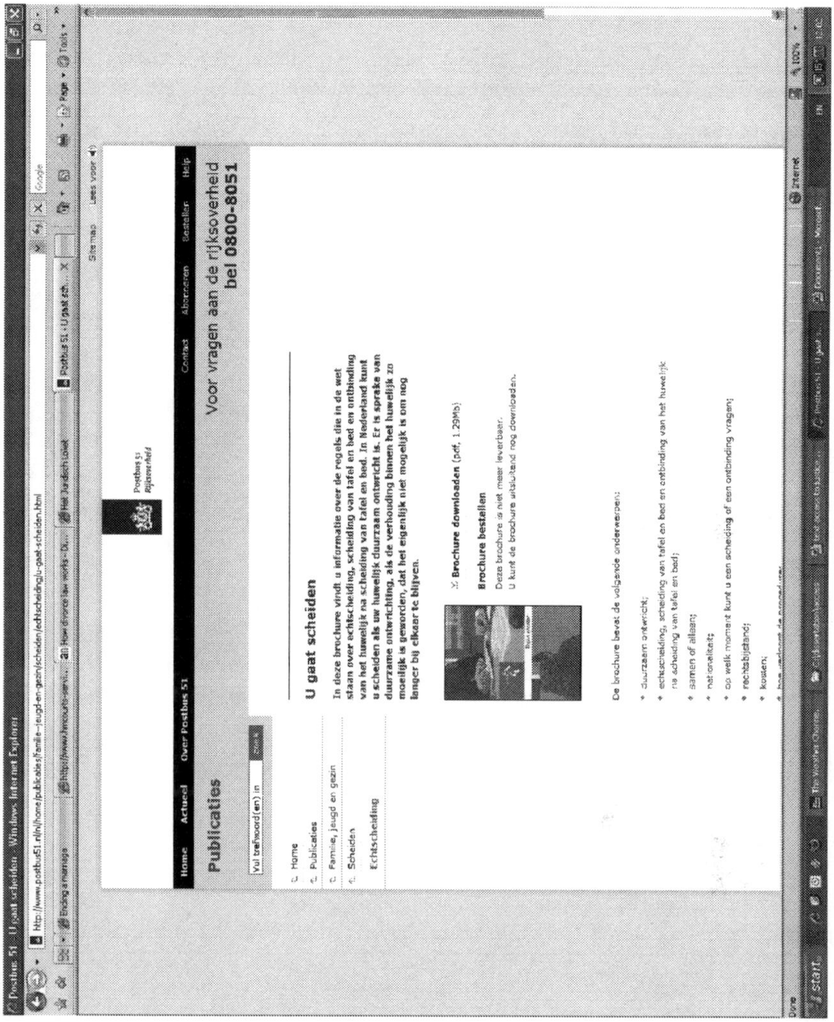

This page was accessed on October 14, 2008. The page tested in September 2008 has been taken off the site.

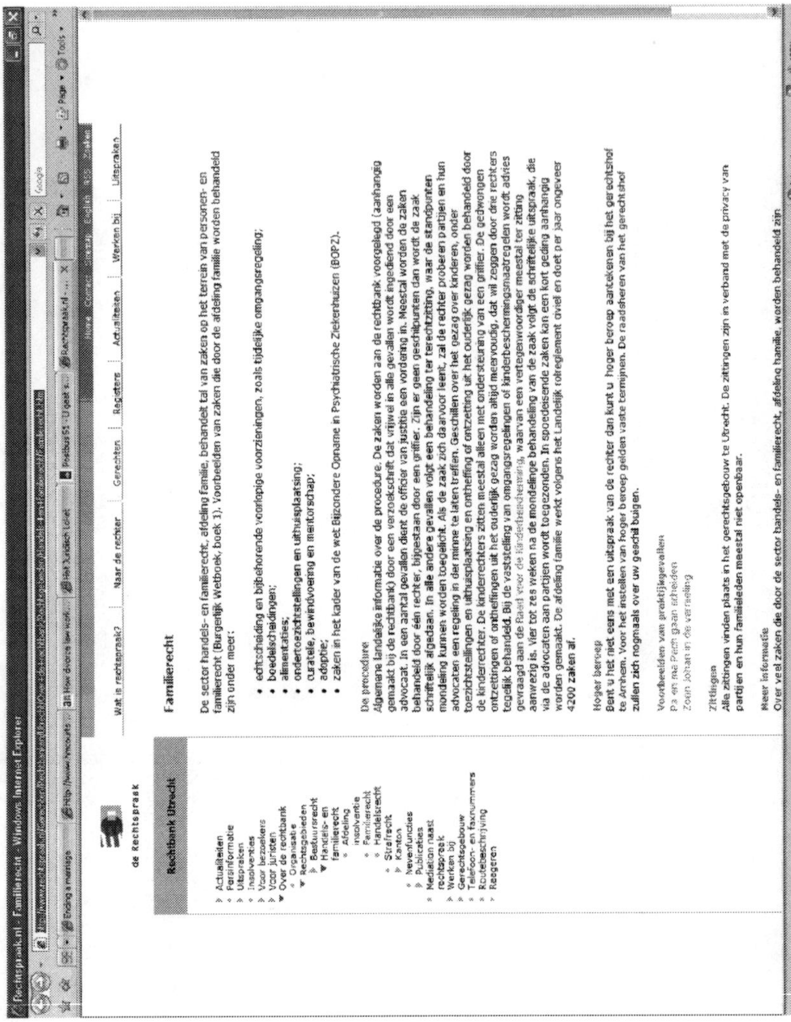
Rechtspraak.nl - Familierecht - Windows Internet Explorer
de Rechtspraak
Rechtbank Utrecht
Familierecht

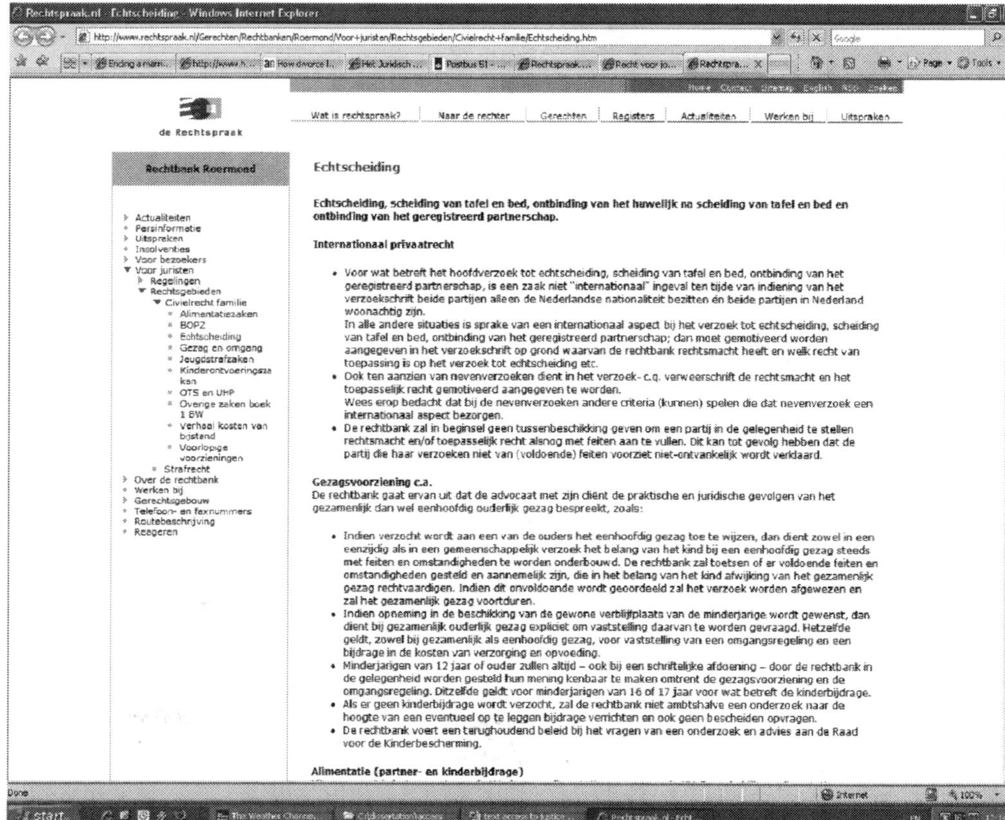

Rechtspraak.nl - Echtscheiding - Windows Internet Explorer

http://www.rechtspraak.nl/Gerechten/Rechtbanken/Roermond/Voor+juristen/Rechtsgebieden/Civielrecht+familie/Echtscheiding.htm

Home | Contact | Sitemap | English | RSS | Zoeken

de Rechtspraak

Wat is rechtspraak? | Naar de rechter | Gerechten | Registers | Actualiteiten | Werken bij | Uitspraken

Rechtbank Roermond

- Actualiteiten
- Persinformatie
- Uitspraken
- Insolventies
- Voor bezoekers
- Voor juristen
  - Regelingen
  - Rechtsgebieden
    - Civielrecht familie
      - Alimentatiezaken
      - BOPZ
      - Echtscheiding
      - Gezag en omgang
      - Jeugdstrafzaken
      - Kinderontvoeringszaken
      - OTS en UHP
      - Overige zaken boek 1 BW
      - Verhaal kosten van bijstand
      - Voorlopige voorzieningen
    - Strafrecht
- Over de rechtbank
- Werken bij
- Gerechtsgebouw
- Telefoon- en faxnummers
- Routebeschrijving
- Reageren

Echtscheiding

Echtscheiding, scheiding van tafel en bed, ontbinding van het huwelijk na scheiding van tafel en bed en ontbinding van het geregistreerd partnerschap.

Internationaal privaatrecht

- Voor wat betreft het hoofdverzoek tot echtscheiding, scheiding van tafel en bed, ontbinding van het geregistreerd partnerschap, is een zaak niet "internationaal" ingeval ten tijde van indiening van het verzoekschrift beide partijen alleen de Nederlandse nationaliteit bezitten én beide partijen in Nederland woonachtig zijn.
  In alle andere situaties is sprake van een internationaal aspect bij het verzoek tot echtscheiding, scheiding van tafel en bed, ontbinding van het geregistreerd partnerschap; dan moet gemotiveerd worden aangegeven in het verzoekschrift op grond waarvan de rechtbank rechtsmacht heeft en welk recht van toepassing is op het verzoek tot echtscheiding etc.
- Ook ten aanzien van nevenverzoeken dient in het verzoek- c.q. verweerschrift de rechtsmacht en het toepasselijk recht gemotiveerd aangegeven te worden.
  Wees erop bedacht dat bij de nevenverzoeken andere criteria (kunnen) spelen die dat nevenverzoek een internationaal aspect bezorgen.
- De rechtbank zal in beginsel geen tussenbeschikking geven om een partij in de gelegenheid te stellen rechtsmacht en/of toepasselijk recht alsnog met feiten aan te vullen. Dit kan tot gevolg hebben dat de partij die haar verzoeken niet van (voldoende) feiten voorziet niet-ontvankelijk wordt verklaard.

Gezagsvoorziening c.a.
De rechtbank gaat ervan uit dat de advocaat met zijn cliënt de praktische en juridische gevolgen van het gezamenlijk dan wel eenhoofdig ouderlijk gezag bespreekt, zoals:

- Indien verzocht wordt aan een van de ouders het eenhoofdig gezag toe te wijzen, dan dient zowel in een eenzijdig als in een gemeenschappelijk verzoek het belang van het kind bij een eenhoofdig gezag steeds met feiten en omstandigheden te worden onderbouwd. De rechtbank zal toetsen of er voldoende feiten en omstandigheden gesteld en aannemelijk zijn, die in het belang van het kind afwijking van het gezamenlijk gezag rechtvaardigen. Indien dit onvoldoende wordt geoordeeld zal het verzoek worden afgewezen en zal het gezamenlijk gezag voortduren.
- Indien opneming in de beschikking van de gewone verblijfplaats van de minderjarige wordt gewenst, dan dient bij gezamenlijk ouderlijk gezag expliciet om vaststelling daarvan te worden gevraagd. Hetzelfde geldt, zowel bij gezamenlijk als eenhoofdig gezag, voor vaststelling van een omgangsregeling en een bijdrage in de kosten van verzorging en opvoeding.
- Minderjarigen van 12 jaar of ouder zullen altijd – ook bij een schriftelijke afdoening – door de rechtbank in de gelegenheid worden gesteld hun mening kenbaar te maken omtrent de gezagsvoorziening en de omgangsregeling. Ditzelfde geldt voor minderjarigen van 16 of 17 jaar voor wat betreft de kinderbijdrage.
- Als er geen kinderbijdrage wordt verzocht, zal de rechtbank niet ambtshalve een onderzoek naar de hoogte van een eventueel op te leggen bijdrage verrichten en ook geen bescheiden opvragen.
- De rechtbank voert een terughoudend beleid bij het vragen van een onderzoek en advies aan de Raad voor de Kinderbescherming.

Alimentatie (partner- en kinderbijdrage)

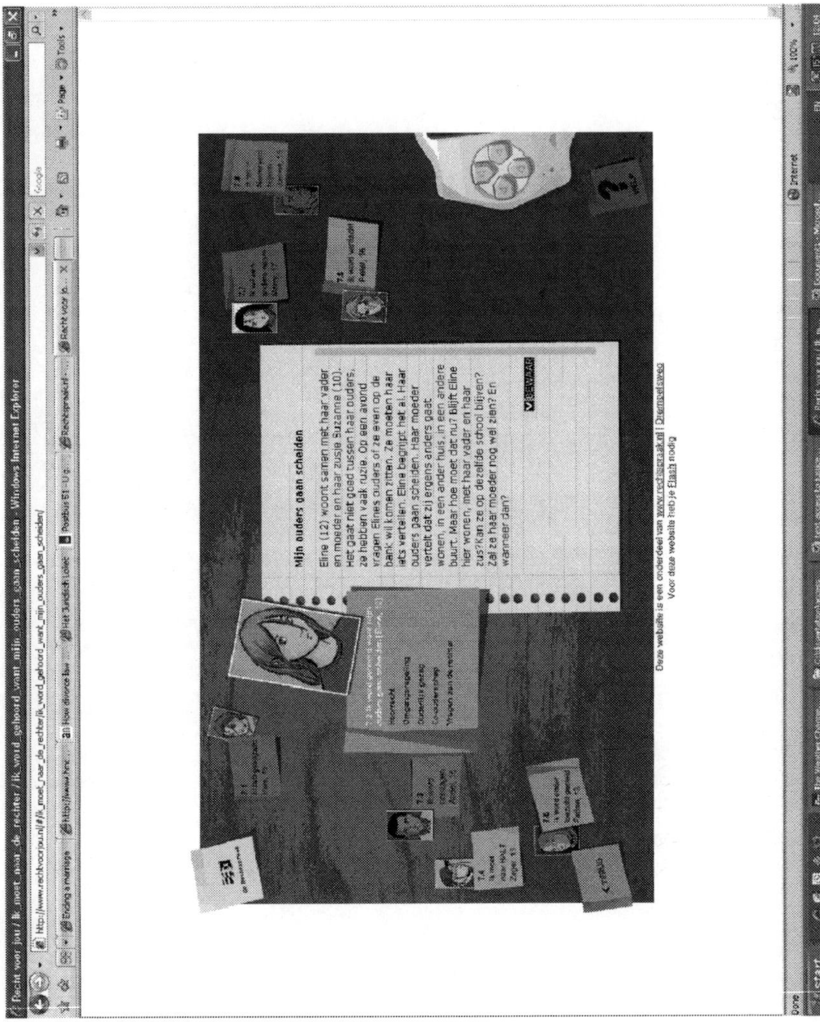
Mijn ouders gaan scheiden
Eline (12) woont samen met haar vader en moeder en haar zusje Suzanne (10). Het gaat niet goed tussen haar ouders, ze hebben vaak ruzie. Op een avond vragen Elines ouders of ze even op de bank wil komen zitten. Ze moeten haar iets vertellen. Eline begrijpt het al. Haar ouders gaan scheiden. Haar moeder vertelt dat zij ergens anders gaat wonen, in een ander huis, in een andere buurt. Maar hoe moet dat nu? Blijft Eline hier wonen, met haar vader en haar zus? Kan ze op dezelfde school blijven? Zal ze haar moeder nog wel zien? En wanneer dan?
BEWAAR
Deze website is een onderdeel van www.rechtspraak.nl | Drempelsweg
Voor deze website heb je Flash nodig

Appendix B: Syndromes of Corruption

Reprinted by permission of the author

Countries in each cluster and distances from statistical cluster centers

Group 1: *Influence Markets (N = 18)*

Country	Abbrev.	Distance
Australia	AUL	7.28073
Austria	AUS	3.60012
Canada	CAN	2.78126
Costa Rica	COS	3.83813
Denmark	DEN	3.64826
Finland	FIN	8.24365
France	FRN	9.23645
Germany	GER	2.31558
Ireland	IRE	8.29991
Japan	JPN	2.91684
Netherlands	NTH	3.86855
New Zealand	NEW	0.91241
Norway	NOR	7.65654
Sweden	SWD	8.76099
Switzerland	SWZ	13.65410
UK	UK	1.28457
Uruguay	URU	9.89902
USA	USA	3.86244

Group 2: *Elite Cartels (N = 21)*

Country	Abbrev.	Distance
Argentina	ARG	5.71114
Belgium	BEL	9.06837
Bolivia	BOL	8.02854
Botswana	BOT	3.64404
Brazil	BRA	5.53851
Chile	CHL	2.34284
Czech Rep.	CZR	2.48849
Greece	GRC	9.00947
Hungary	HUN	5.74995
Israel	ISR	6.87926
Italy	ITA	2.97926
Korea South	ROK	3.21965
Namibia	NAM	4.57171
Panama	PAN	5.72047
Paraguay	PAR	4.64561
Poland	POL	3.74996
Portugal	POR	2.63078
Slovak Rep.	SLO	2.30728
South Africa	SAF	5.51737
Spain	SPN	7.38652
Zambia	ZAM	10.62383

Group 3: *Oligarchs and Clans (N = 30)*

Country	Abbrev.	Distance
Albania	ALB	8.67352
Bangladesh	BNG	9.40557
Benin	BEN	1.63571
Bulgaria	BUL	3.69379
Colombia	COL	4.81347
Ecuador	ECU	3.99340
El Salvador	SAL	2.30953
Ghana	GHA	6.99291
Guatemala	GUA	3.62980
Honduras	HON	2.98866
India	IND	3.72422
Jamaica	JAM	9.03862
Madagascar	MDG	6.78694
Malaysia	MAL	7.20240
Mali	MLI	2.47827
Mexico	MEX	7.09493
Nepal	NPL	3.08030
Nicaragua	NIC	2.86318
Niger	NER	9.06853
Pakistan	PAK	14.73081
Peru	PER	11.62208
Philippines	PHI	4.14257
Romania	ROM	4.25395
Russia	RUS	12.68638
Senegal	SEN	7.89667
Sri Lanka	SLK	9.48985
Thailand	THI	7.53286
Trinidad & Tobago	TRT	8.89195
Turkey	TUR	3.23513
Venezuela	VEN	8.28116

Group 4: *Official Moguls (N = 29)*

Country	Abbrev.	Distance
Algeria	ALG	5.86685
Cameroon	CAO	2.81497
Central Africa	CAF	10.59637
Chad	CHD	2.94259
China	CHN	6.12066
Congo, Rep. of	CRP	11.17139
Egypt	EGY	5.57582
Gabon	GAB	5.50351
Guinea-Bissau	GNB	7.92945
Haiti	HTI	2.54349
Indonesia	INS	9.59441
Iran	IRN	11.65739
Ivory Coast	IVO	7.19949
Jordan	JOR	13.76616
Kenya	KEN	2.10563
Kuwait	KWT	5.55828
Malawi	MAW	13.84777
Morocco	MOR	7.78743
Myanmar	MMR	11.53267
Nigeria	NIG	10.03197
Oman	OMN	8.63007
Rwanda	RWA	2.93964
Syria	SYR	12.32687
Tanzania	TAZ	5.66171
Togo	TGO	3.96091
Tunisia	TUN	2.36309
Uganda	UGA	13.63157
United Arab Emirates	UAE	7.43969
Zimbabwe	ZIM	8.38316